FIGHTING MONKS AND BURNING MOUNTAINS:

MISADVENTURES ON A BUDDHIST PILGRIMAGE

PAUL BARACH

AUTHOR'S NOTE

*To write this book, I relied upon my personal journal, pho-
tographs, and my own recollections. I consulted with several
people who appear in the book to provide background or further insight. Some individual's names have been changed. I
occasionally omitted people and events, but only when that
omission had no impact on either the veracity or the sub-
stance of the story.*

Thanks for reading. I hope you enjoy it.

Published in the United States of
America by Sky Dagger Press

Cover and Book design by Damonza.com

ISBN 978-0-9909304-0-2 (pbk.)

ISBN 978-0-9909304-1-9 (ebook)

Registered through Bowker Identifier Services

Contact through

www.paulbarachcomic.com

paul.barach@gmail.com

Twitter @PaulBarach

For Matt Swanson and Cori Sparks,

Without you, neither this book nor I would be here.

I'd be somewhere over that way.

TABLE OF CONTENTS

Section Three

Ehime: The Land of Enlightenment

Section Four

Kagawa: The Land of Nirvana

GLOSSARY OF TERMS

gaijin – foreigner

Hannya Shingyo – a 278-character sutra considered the heart of the Buddha's teaching on emptiness

henro – a Shikoku pilgrim

honzon – each temple's central deity

nansho – dangerous or hard-to-reach temple

Nio – heavenly kings whose statues guard each temple entrance

Nio-mon – the main temple entrance

onsen – Japanese spa

osamefuda – a rectangular paper name slip offered at temples or to helpful individuals in return for gifts or assistance.

ossetai – gifts or other assistance given to pilgrims by locals

tsuyado – free pilgrim lodging provided by a temple or citizen

zenkonyado – free pilgrim lodging house

Every day some new fact comes to light—some new obstacle which threatens the gravest obstruction. I suppose this is the reason which makes the game so well worth playing.

—Robert Falcon Scott
(Died exploring the South Pole)

Adventure is the result of poor planning.

—Roald Amundsen
(Did not die exploring the South Pole)

PROLOGUE
I BLAME NINJAS

AS THE BRIGHTEST stars pierce the twilight sky above Japan, the priest lands a right cross into my solar plexus. I slide back to regain my distance and we square off, the dirt in this mountain temple's courtyard now a tight circle of smeared footprints. His lead foot plants, telegraphing a roundhouse kick. I slide in to blunt the momentum.

It's a feint.

Now I'm in range.

A sharp hook impacts beneath my armpit. There's a wet smack and the number of stars I see multiplies.

So far, it's still one of the least painful things I've experienced this month while walking the ancient pilgrimage trail circling Shikoku Island. I'm here because, at age twenty-eight, I felt lost in my life. So I decided to travel to a land I didn't know, with a language I didn't speak, to search for some direction.

Also, I blame ninjas.

My obsession with Japan began at age four, when I learned that in a distant land across the ocean lived black-clad master assassins capable of karate-chopping through tree trunks and beheading enemies with throwing stars. Later, when I accepted that "ninja" wasn't a viable career path, my obsession softened into a broader interest in martial arts, Zen Buddhism, and anime that extended all the way into college. In my junior year I enrolled in Japanese Religion and Culture, hoping we'd cover these three topics, and spend at least one class on smoke-bomb-wielding mercenaries. I'd soon be disappointed, just as I was when Intro to Jewish Mysticism did not teach how to conjure a mud golem. Most of the class was a blur, but one day I remember clearly.

The professor was covering the millennium-old Shikoku Pilgrimage trail. Still traveled on foot by a tiny percentage of the devout and masochistic, the route runs across mountains, beside the ocean, and through the farmlands, villages, and cities of an isolated land. A television replaced the professor, a documentary whirred on the VHS, and I glanced from the window at the crackling screen.

Dressed in a conical straw hat and white vest, the narrator meditated beneath waterfalls and prayed inside Buddhist temples. He strolled past waving rice fields, staff clicking against the concrete. Suddenly I saw myself there in his place, striding beside yellow stalks with my staff in hand and standing beneath the cascade in serene contemplation. Then it was gone. The professor resumed droning on and I turned to stare out the window again. White blossoms fell in the quad of my small college in southern Minnesota that I couldn't wait to leave.

In the years after graduating, as my friends and siblings began their careers, I worked temporary jobs and traveled. My parents admonished me to "grow up" and choose a career, preferably one rhyming with "octor" or "awyer." The children of striving immigrants, they'd kept a close watch on me ever since a family vacation to the La Brea Tar Pits ended with toddler Paul falling in, probably in an attempt to ride a half-submerged mammoth. Not much changed as I got older. Lacking whatever gene allowed my siblings to sit still, I spent most of my youth wandering off toward something shiny and falling into trouble along the way.

I eventually gave up on telling my parents that I was searching for something deeper. Even I heard how immature and vague it sounded. Still, I knew I was supposed to be somewhere else and it ate at me. So I kept looking. Meanwhile, my friends became professionals and my married brother began his career in New York. By the time my sister entered law school, I'd left to teach English in South Korea.

When I returned home to Seattle at age twenty-seven, I still felt lost. And old. So when my father invited me over for yet another pointed chat about how I needed to be an adult and settle down, I finally gave in. I had to pick a career. It was the responsible thing to do. Despite my spotty résumé, a large Northwest software company offered me a temporary contract, and the boss made it clear there was room to become a permanent employee. A coveted Blue Badge!

Though my embellished employment history said opposite, I'd never liked office work. Monotonous hours of sitting and entering numbers into spreadsheets always made me ill. However, I had no other marketable skills, and this was an adequate job with room for advancement, which paid decently and offered health care. The dream of every American. So I resigned myself to walking down institutionally bland hallways of dropped ceilings and fluorescent lights, typing in data, and leaving sick in the evening.

As the days melted into months, a nagging feeling grew. If this was going to be my future—waking up sighing to a series of one "okay" day after another—then I wanted one final journey. Something so epic, physically challenging, and personal it would close one chapter of my life and begin the next. Then the memory of that day in college returned. And I saw myself striding past the vast rice fields of an island where there once lived an order of black-clad master assassins.

I didn't know what to expect that first day I arrived on Shikoku and began walking this ancient path. A month into the pilgrimage, as I block late and the temple priest lands another blow into my ribs, I still don't. But after thirty-three of the most grueling days of my life, I'm still here, ready to endure whatever else the priest or Shikoku throws my way until I find my path.

Damn ninjas.

SECTION ONE

TOKUSHIMA: THE LAND OF AWAKENING FAITH

1
I WAS NOT
EXPECTING BOAR

YOU WOULD THINK boars are awesome because they're made of bacon, but their mouths are filled with knives. Naturally territorial and aggressive, they're extra frightening when your only weapons are a Swiss Army knife buried somewhere in your forty-pound pack, and a lightweight walking staff you're too exhausted to wield.

It's mid-August 2010, and my first day on the Shikoku Pilgrimage is coming to a close on this pine-shaded mountain trail. After ten hours and thirteen miles spent hiking through Japan's record-breaking summer heat, each lumbering footstep is a welcome surprise. This mother boar, not so much. Her downy piglets cower behind her as we size each other up.

She's about three feet tall at the shoulder, an amber-gray, bristling mass of tusks, fat, and muscle, charged with a biological imperative to protect her offspring with violent, slashing fury. I'm six feet and one hundred and ninety pounds of bald Ashkenazi Jew, strong on paper from years of karate training but barely capable of fighting gravity at this point. The boar grunts, squares her shoulders, and lowers her tusks, threatening to charge. I emit a couple of sharp, terrified vowels in no order and freeze.

A boar attack is the last thing I'm expecting today, but the list of what I am prepared for here is dangerously short. I knew that when I arrived on Shikoku Island this morning. But I began walking anyway, hoping to change my life.

Twelve boar-less hours earlier.

I wake to the sound of bells, an orange slice of sunlight cutting across my face through the drawn curtains of the overnight bus. Behind the rows of dozing university students and businessmen snuggled beneath black suit jackets on this cheap ten-hour ride from Tokyo to Tokushima City, my first fellow *henro* stands in the aisle.

A slender woman somewhere in that frozen Japanese age range between twenty-seven and fifty-five, she grasps the tattered walking staff of a pilgrimage veteran. The frayed fabric grip at the top is sun-worn from previous summers, the bottom a brush of splinters from repeated impacts on the trail. The bells tied below the grip jingle as she taps it on the bus floor in anticipation. Our eyes meet and we share a smile. Of the estimated 500,000 people who undertake the pilgrimage every year by bus, bike, or car, she and I are two of the few hundred still choosing to walk the entire 750-mile *henro* trail.

Nestled south of Honshu and east of Kyushu across the narrow Seto Sea, Shikoku Island's pilgrimage route begins at Temple 1 (T1) in the northeast province of Tokushima. From there, the *henro* trail runs clockwise around the island's bulbous outer rim before returning to T1. Using sidewalks and highway shoulders for about ninety percent of the distance, this veteran *henro* and I will cross wide valleys and climb steep mountainsides, pass through major cities and small farming villages, and parallel the crashing Pacific Ocean and gentle Seto Sea. At each of the eighty-eight temples along the route, we'll pray beside other *henro* asking for redemption from past mistakes or wisdom in avoiding future ones, giving thanks for business success or a loved one's recovery, or simply sightseeing in a rural countryside so historically isolated that a bridge to the mainland didn't exist until the 1980s.

I don't know what this veteran *henro* is seeking as she adjusts her backpack straps and dons her conical sedge hat. For me, it's adventure and answers. I hope to find both through Shikoku's four prefectures of Tokushima, Kochi, Ehime, and Kagawa, as each corresponds to one level of spiritual progress: Awakening Faith, Ascetic Training, Enlightenment, and Nirvana. Unlike her, I have little idea what lies ahead. But upon returning to T1 after seven hundred and fifty miles, I expect a different person will be standing in my footprints: someone finally ready to settle down and move on with his life.

However, it's also an ancient pilgrimage in an exotic land, so my imagination's running wild. Maybe my years of meditation will lead to enlightenment while I traverse the long fields. Maybe I'll test my half-decade of karate training by fighting a monk on a mountaintop like in the kung fu movies. Maybe a wizened old man will emerge from the woods and hand me a sword. I don't expect any of this to happen, but hope's free.

The overnight bus sits thrumming in its terminal as the businessmen and students gather their belongings and adjust their suits. I haul my weighty backpack onto my shoulders and nod, silently wishing my first fellow *henro* luck. She nods back, probably wishing this bald *gaijin* would stop staring at her. With a hydraulic hiss, the doors open and the air-conditioned comfort disappears into the humid sunlight and chatter of the Tokushima Transit Center. While I gain my bearings, she disappears into the crowd milling around on the snaking concrete.

At the nearby train station, I escape the scorching rays and step onto a blue-and-white passenger car bound for Dobutsune, the closest station to T1. Outside the window are some of the hundreds of mountains running east to west across Shikoku, creating a land of towering peaks, wide valleys, and rich alluvial plains where fruit, wheat, and rice harvests flourish. The car jolts forward and my heart jumps with it.

In less than an hour, I'll begin a journey I've waited and saved a year for.

And as the parabolic landscape rolls past the window, I realize that despite all the pilgrimage websites and books skimmed in the spare moments at my desk, I still have little idea of what to expect besides a lot of walking and not much talking. It's finally sinking in why the following conversation had been repeated with nearly every person I told about the pilgrimage in the past year:

> *Person:* I didn't know you spoke Japanese.
>
> *Me:* I don't.
>
> *Person:* Nothing?
>
> *Me:* Well, I can express disbelief a monster is attacking the city and that I'll roundhouse-kick it in the thigh. I can also say "water" and "thank you."
>
> *Person:* You don't think that'll be a problem?
>
> *Me:* No, I'm sure I'll get by. It's Japan, not Liberia.
>
> *Person:* (*Tight-lipped smile and nod*)
>
> *Me:* (*Oblivious to their reasonable concern*)

I figured I'd learn everything I needed to while on Shikoku, just as I had as a student in Spain, a backpacker in Europe, a teacher in South Korea, and all the smaller travels I'd undertaken in between. I'd made it through each safely; why should this be any different? Sure, all those trips had some kind of structure, were in cities, and had other Westerners around. And true, I'd never been on one solo multiday hike, let alone traversed long distances by myself for months in the rural countryside of a foreign country without any means of communication. And yes, occasionally I get crippling anxiety attacks while traveling.

But I'm sure I'll be fine. The challenges are part of the journey.

Why focus on the thousands of reasons this is a bad idea?

Outside the passenger-car window, the blurred landscape of Tokushima slows and sharpens as the train's wheels screech to a halt. Through the PA system comes a flurry of announcements not about monster attacks, and I pick out the name of my stop. Lugging my backpack onto my shoulders, I buckle the gray fanny pack that contains my map book around my waist. Prepared or not, I'm about to embark on an epic journey in a foreign land. It's either a grin or a grimace, but the edges of my mouth are straining toward my ears.

Two *henro* sleep off their completed pilgrimage on the slatted benches beside Dobutsune's ticket office, their sedge hats resting atop their packs and their staffs leaned reverently beside their heads. At the moment I'm a solitary, bald foreigner in my sunglasses, basketball shorts, and totally awesome gray fanny pack. However, upon acquiring an identical pilgrim vest, hat, and staff at T1, I'll be a *henro,* traveling beside Kukai, the famous eighth-century monk and founder of Shingon Buddhism.

Born on Shikoku in 774 to a noble family, Kukai dropped out of college and spent years wandering the island as an ascetic monk, performing miraculous intercessions, overseeing engineering projects, and establishing temples. Posthumously given the name *Kobo Daishi*, or "Great Dharma Teacher," his presence permeates Shikoku in landmarks, legends, and the *henro's* apparel. The kanji on the back of a *henro's* white vest announces that they travel beside him, their conical sedge hat bears his name in Sanskrit to lead them, and their staff embodies Kukai traveling beside them. Because of this, the staff is to be wiped reverently before it enters any room and is placed in the corner beside the pilgrim's head when it is time to sleep.

I crack open my pristine map book, a palm-size paperback containing the only information I have about the entire pilgrimage. A slight breeze carries through the narrow streets of high brick walls leading to T1. As I sweat my way toward my first temple, I recite the three main oaths a *henro* makes before walking:

1. Believe that Kukai will save all living beings, and will always be by the pilgrim's side.
2. Do not complain when things go wrong on the pilgrimage. Consider such experiences to be part of ascetic training.
3. All things can be saved in the present world. Continually strive for enlightenment.

To these rules I add my own, to further invest myself in this last big trip of my life:

1. No music—limit your distractions.
2. No running—focus on your surroundings.
3. No booze—stay sharp, drunky.
4. Daily journal entries—record as much as you can.
5. Daily meditation—every morning and while walking.
6. Visit every temple—collect every stamp, recite every prayer.
7. Enjoy your time—don't panic.

I look up from my map book to find that, ten minutes into my pilgrimage, I'm already lost. A passing driver offers a direction correction with a helpful honk and a finger pointing out the window. I backtrack to the first of the eighty-eight temples, **Ryozenji: Vulture's Peak Temple (T1)**.

Beneath the gateway's sloped roof stand carved statues of red-skinned monsters with the muscular build of DC Comics villains. These are the *Nio*, heavenly kings whose fearsome visages guard the temple against demons and thieves. Flanking the main entrance in twin alcoves, they form the liminal barrier known as the *Nio-mon*. I begin the ritual, bowing at the *Nio-mon* to ward off evil spirits and show reverence. Now properly humbled and de-ghosted, I enter the complex. Various offices and outbuildings flank the main and *Daishi* halls, which dominate the courtyard. I check the temple protocol listed in my map book for the next step in the twenty-minute ritual of bows, bell ringing, hand washing, prayer chanting, and stamp collecting. As robotic as it feels, I'm committed to performing the entire thing at each temple, and thanks to my years attending synagogue, I'm used to repetitive rituals and arcane prayers. At the free-standing belfry, I swing the log clapper into the iron bell to announce my presence to the gods, wash my hands and mouth out with water from a tin dipper at the ritual basin, and head to the gift shop.

A couple of purchases later, I emerge transformed from backpacker to *henro*, completing the illusion that I belong in this thronging courtyard. Clad in a pristine white vest and sedge hat, my right hand grips my walking staff while the other holds a stack of the white paper name slips called *osamefuda*. Eager to begin, I scrawl my signature down the side of the rectangular strip and slip the *osamefuda* into a slotted tin box at the main hall, then drop an offering of coins into a second box. I bow three times to the *honzon*, the temple's central deity enshrined within the hall, and thumb over to the list of seven phonetic Buddhist prayers in my map book. This should be the easy part, but the heat and the unfamiliar vowels quickly rob me of oxygen. Midway through chanting *Hannya Shingyo*, the Heart Sutra, a weight grows in my chest and I sink to the ground, gasping out the rest of the prayers from there while passing *henro* cast perturbed glances. Rising quickly to salvage my pride, I cross the busy courtyard and repeat the same prayers to a statue of Kukai at the *Daishi* hall, falling to my knees again. I should be concerned, because this has never happened in synagogue, but that temple has air conditioning.

With the prayers complete, the next step is getting the temple's name recorded in my stamp book. A sort of spiritual passport, the stamp book holds eighty-eight blank pages that will eventually be filled with a calligraphy of each temple's name and three red stamps at a cost of ¥300[1] each. The first page is christened unceremoniously by a rounded, wrinkled woman who grunts as she flips open my book, already sick of them just hours after sunrise. Dunking a horsehair brush in ink, she slides a haphazard series of vertical loops and angles across the page, slams three red-ink stamps down and extends an open palm for the yen. With a final bow at the *Nio-mon* while facing the shrines, the ritual is complete.

One temple down, eighty-seven more to go.

Cars and buses roar past me along the road, but once inside **Gokurakuji: Pureland Temple (T2)**, it could be centuries earlier. I stand on a hill behind the main hall, where furry bat-size moths flit around gathering nectar and cicadas cling to branches, singing their buzz-saw anthems to late summer. In the empty courtyard below, men and women in colorful silk robes scrape their bamboo rakes across the gravel, clearing the detritus below the thousand-year-old cedar tree planted by Kukai. Tied around the massive, lumpy trunk is a special plaited rope with three zigzag strips of white paper hanging down.

---

1 A little over three U.S. dollars.

Known as a *shinemawa*, it's an ancient symbol indicating that spirits reside within. This courtyard is what I'd been hoping to see when I came to Shikoku—the "traditional," romanticized Japan that mostly exists in fiction. However, some pockets still remain on this isolated island. It's worth falling to my knees again while I complete the ritual of bow, bell, wash, pray, pray, stamps, bow, and leave for a second time.

My walk to T3 is accompanied by the pleasant melody of my walking staff's metronome click as it resounds off a stone tunnel's walls, and the distant tolling of railroad bells in the silence of a graveyard. There's a harmony to the swish of my shoes through the tall grasses, the clatter of crickets scattering before me while scarecrows in demon masks haunt the nearby fields. This pilgrimage may be a lot of walking and not much talking before I return to work, but these ephemeral moments hint at something extraordinary hiding beneath. Somehow I think it'll be more.

By noon, the roasting air befits the dragons filling the courtyard of **Konsenji: Golden Spring Temple (T3)**. One dragon snakes around the washbasin, water hissing from its open mouth into the pool, while the other has wrapped itself around a sword backed by a wall of flames. Near the entrance sits the Benkei Stone, a big, lumpy rock that the famous warrior-priest Benkei picked up and then set back down in the twelfth century.

Unbeknownst to me at the time, and of slightly greater note than lifting heavy things, Benkei was a legendarily powerful ogre of a man, and fiercely loyal to the gifted general Yoshitsune, the only man to defeat him in combat. In the aftermath of the general's victory against the ruling Taira clan, Yoshitsune's older brother, Yoritomo, declared his sibling a traitor and sent an army to apprehend him. Rather than giving Yoritomo the satisfaction of capture, Yoshitsune committed ritual suicide in his castle while the loyal Benkei defended the drawbridge from the army with his *naginata* polearm blade. After the warrior-priest single-handedly massacred three hundred soldiers with his *naginata*, the generals learned their lesson about fighting behemoth death machines by hand and launched a storm of arrows into him. Unfazed, Benkei continued brandishing his weapon, keeping the soldiers at bay until they realized he was no longer moving beneath the arrows feathering his armor. Though dead, Benkei had provided his friend and master the time for an honorable death.

That none of this is mentioned on a plaque beside the stone is sheer negligence by the Shikoku Tourism Board.

By early evening I've performed the ritual of bow, bell, wash, pray, pray, stamps, bow, and leave at **Dainichiji: The Temple of the Great Sun (T4)** and **Jizoji: The Temple of the Earth-Bearer (T5)**, still dropping to my knees midway through the sutras. In a haze, I search for some place to collapse one final time for the night, preferably near the highway and not in the center of it. There's a covered rest hut by T6, but as I leave T5, there's an inexplicable, magnetic draw uphill toward a temple off the main route called Taisanji: Big Mountain Temple. According to legend, the general Yoshitsune prayed for victory in the Genpei war against the Taira clan there, and should have also thrown in a request to defeat his brother.

With the sun setting, there's no reason to be hiking this steep path through apple orchards. But I continue up, then further up, and ridiculously more up. I've been dripping sweat all day, but as the switchbacks keep multiplying through the forest, it begins flooding out. I scan for a flat area to set up my tent, briefly considering a hillside graveyard, but the draw continues until a crest of red daylight glows through the branches.

I break free of the woods with an amount of functioning brain cells in the low prime numbers and steady myself on a fence bordering a small pasture. The few dozen cattle and I stare dumbly at each other. Neither of us expecting the other on the top of a mountain, we're both thinking the same thing: *mu.*[2]

I'm debating whether the cows will avoid a limp body in the grass when the farmer waves from her doorstep, gesturing down the road to make clear that I'm close to the temple. Ecstatic at this news, I press forward along the pine-shaded dirt pathway as my limbs fill with wet cement. A posted sign says 500m. Thank gods.

Rounding a blind corner, I startle a boar crossing the road with her piglets.

She's really, really angry about it.

Her fire-yellow eyes bore into mine as she squares up,

---

2 Nothing

grunts, and lowers her tusks. I use the last of my voice to yell in terror, raise my hands, and agree that *Yes, I am too close to your piglets.* She lunges and I backpedal out of sight around the corner.

I lean quaking against a tree as the grunting continues behind me. I pray someone will show up on this empty path, preferably a wizened old man with a samurai sword, but the farmer has returned to her home and I haven't seen anyone else since the orchard. My stomach sinks. All I can think of is a hunting clip I saw years ago, in which a boar drove its tusk up the hunter's forearm, the bulge of flesh splitting as the tooth tunneled through. I unclasp my pack and wait for the grunting to get louder, sucking in oxygen for one final, futile sprint.

Nothing.

I peek around the corner. The boar is nowhere to be seen, but that doesn't mean she's gone. Prepared to drop my pack at the first snort, I make a shambling break for the temple, my heart racing at each blind curve.

Fearsome *Nio* guard the two hundred and fifty stone steps leading to the courtyard. In the failing light, a golden shroud of mist conceals the peak. I climb entranced past stoic red cedars and upstart bamboo toward what looks like Samurai Heaven, where loyal retainers go after killing a couple hundred soldiers so their master can disembowel himself undisturbed. The world is silent but for the last twittering of birds. I'd believe the boar killed me and I'm ascending to the next world, if my body wasn't telling me I'm still slogging through this one. With my calves impersonating sewing machines, I fall halfway up the steps and can't go on.

Then I remember the pack isn't part of my body and drop it.

Released from the weight, I rush to the top with the last of my energy, wrap the belfry's rope around my fist, yank down the cord, and announce my presence to the gods with an echoing clang. Then I stumble to a bench as my calves writhe. Night falls in the empty courtyard and I realize that I still don't know where I'm sleeping. When I catch what remains of my breath, I trudge back to retrieve my pack from the steps and consider lying down there.

I've slept on staircases before.

Doing it sober will be a new experience.

Instead, a monk in dark brown robes discovers me setting up my tent in the billowing dust behind the *Nio*, which I'm hoping also deter boar. He motions up the steps, inviting me to sleep at the temple. Mud-streaked, shaking, and non-verbal, I make it clear that I'm as mobile as my luggage. Returning with a van, he arranges my bag, staff, and body onto the bench seats, then delivers all three to the residential quarters. He points to the cushions stacked in the corner. I nod dumbly and arrange them on the tatami mat floor. When he returns with a dinner of grapes, sliced apples, and tea, I croak out a *"thank you"* and devour my first real meal in ten hours.

Curled up on the cushions, I shut my eyes and end my first day on Shikoku in comfort, safe from boars and the mosquitoes whining outside the window screen. Despite my lack of preparation, I've been welcomed to the Land of Awakening Faith with food and shelter. Every night may end this well.

They don't, and there are worse things than boar coming my way.

I should have prepared better.

2

ICHIRO SUZUKI AND OTHER GODS

I'VE JUST FINISHED meditating at Big Mountain Temple when the monk brings me a breakfast of fresh fruit, miso soup, and rice balls. A grateful bow, an *osamefuda*, and I dig into the invigorating meal. In my brief experience on Shikoku, this happens every day. After stretching, I set out on the forested descent back to the pilgrimage trail.

A twig snaps underfoot.

I freeze, listening for angry grunts.

Silence. So it'll remain a good morning.

Though my second day has just begun, somehow it already feels like I've been here for years. My body disagrees. Still weak from the heat and mileage yesterday, I'll spend today unrushed, enjoying the pilgrimage's unique culture.

Forest becomes foothills becomes fields, where a farmer waves me down from his rice harvester. I cross the rows of bristly yellow nubs sticking up amongst the collapsed stalks, which crackle underfoot. The farmer dismounts the rumbling machine, essentially a giant hair trimmer on tank treads, and offers me a small bottle of liquid vitamins from his shirt pocket.

"*Ossetai*," he smiles.

It's my first of many *ossetai*, gifts or assistance given by locals as an offering to the *Daishi* traveling beside me. As is tradition, I hand him an *osamefuda* in return and receive the bottle with both hands in gratitude.

As he puzzles over my signature, I discreetly check the label. Liquid vitamins are common in Asia and I drank them all the time while teaching in South Korea. My favorite had an elk as its mascot. Years later, I would learn it was liquefied antlers. The elk was the ingredients list. This label is mammal-free, so I twist the aluminum cap and drink the apple-juice-sweet liquid. However, this morning the real gift I need is a toilet.

Fast.

While the farmer watches in curiosity, I search through my useless phrase book for "toilet," unsuccessfully and increasingly frantic. I find out how to check my luggage at the train station and tell the server I'm vegetarian, but "toilet" remains hidden frustratingly far from my vocabulary. Giving up, I resort to pantomime. After five minutes of squatting and making a flushing noise while the farmer frowns in concentration, I realize this also isn't working.

I scan through the book again. There it is: "*toire*," which I pronounce "toy-r," the way English grammar rules dictate. This makes the farmer more confused, so he calls his son over. Now both of them frown in concentration as I squat, flush, and repeat "*toire*" for another couple minutes before the son's brow shoots up.

"Toilet."

He points to the garage.

"*Arigato*," I reply and awkwardly jog in the direction of his outstretched arm.

Communication is a recurring problem here. The only real conversation I have with anyone is about where I am from, and I'm only understood because of one man: Ichiro Suzuki.

In 2010, Ichiro is a fan favorite on the Seattle Mariners, our right fielder and at times the only reason to watch disappointing season after disappointing season. He's even more famous in Japan. According to his agent, "When you mail Ichiro something from the States, you only have to use that name on the address and he gets it [in Japan]. He's that big." Back in Korea, even they knew his name, said as an invective as they watched him break the 3-3 tie in the final game of the 2009 World Baseball Classic with a two-run single. I withheld my celebration at the time, since the restaurant I was in would have poisoned my food. But I did rub it into my morose students the next day.

This summer, he's on every baseball fan's mind here in Japan and back in Seattle. Holding the single-season record for hits with 262 in 2004, he's on track to make history again by completing his tenth consecutive 200-hit season. His fame and my inability to pronounce the name of my home city leads to the following exchange, which repeats for the entire pilgrimage:

> **Japanese Person:** Where are you from?
> **Me:** Seattle.
> **JP:** Cee-ah-tu-ru?
> **Me:** (*slower*) Seattle.
> **JP:** Cee-ah-tu-ru?
> **Me:** (*pantomime swinging bat*) Ichiro.
> **JP:** Ah! Ichiro Suzuki! Cee-ah-tu-ru Ma-ri-nah!
> **Me:** *Hai.* (Yes.)
> **JP:** (*nods*)
> (*Awkward silence*)
> **Me:** Bye.
> **JP:** Bye-bye.

It's not much, and it's ninety percent of all conversations I'll have here.

After leaving the farmer, it's another half hour through the fields. Wives in blouses and bonnets nod to me as they wade through the paddies, pulling up green shoots and laying them in wet clumps on the concrete. Their husbands, similarly sun-protected, wave from their roaring machines. The air is filled with the sputtering whoosh of chaff spraying from pipes attached to the threshers' grain bins.

Finally I'm back on a road, but not the *henro* trail. Checking my map again, I ask directions to T6 from an old woman in a motorized wheelchair who either has that Michael Jackson skin disease or is in witness protection from the yakuza. Beneath a wide sunhat, sunglasses, and a surgical mask, her hunched form is wrapped in a flowered blouse, pants, and a blanket. Instead of directions, she raises her gloved hand and motions that I follow, so we set off on the long road to T6 past swaying stalks of head-high grass. Motorists beep and swerve around us on the one-lane road as she putters along with me in tow, the state's witness and her court-appointed bodyguard. Heading farther off my map book's page, I lose faith in her route and break right.

Thus begins a long, tiring detour path in the early morning heat, strangers pointing me down a series of streets that finally bring me to T6 along a back alley. Four blocks away from the temple, I watch the wheelchair lady putter across the road into the entrance. I gotta learn to trust the elderly.

My feet already aching, I bow at the *Nio-mon* and enter **Anrakuji: The Temple of Everlasting Joy (T6)**, then plop onto a bench outside the stamp office to tape up my new blisters. Peeling open the sweat-curled pages of my map book at the main hall, I recite the seven prayers listed in my book, announcing I've come to praise the Buddha, praising the Buddha, then chanting *Hannya Shingyo.* Next I recite the mantra to the enshrined *honzon*, pray to remove misfortune, praise Kukai, and pray my good deeds spread to the world. My chest grows heavier with each sutra, and I finish them from the ground again. This doesn't bother me as much as how empty these prayers feel at every temple, even if I knew the English translation. Being raised Reform Jewish and practicing Zen meditation, which focuses on present awareness, means the number of deities worshiped in my own life have ranged from one to the current zero. In contrast, here on the pilgrimage, a pantheon surrounds me.

At this temple, I'm reciting the mantra to the *honzon* Yakushi Nyorai, one of the many enlightened beings I'll bow to on this journey. Like patron saints or archangels, each *honzon* is prayed to for intercession or help with a specific cause. While Catholics pray to Saint Luke before surgery, Saint Joseph before flying, or Saint Hubbins for quality footwear, Buddhists pray to deities like Kannon for wisdom or Yakushi for health. Crossing the courtyard, I bow at the *Daishi* hall and recite the seven prayers to Kukai, yet another member of Shikoku's holy pantheon.

Known to history as a gifted calligrapher, scholar, and engineer, Kukai is also a figure of legend: a wandering holy man who could control rebirth, an earth bender who created wells with his staff and tamed rivers, and a wizard whose incantations cast out demons and incarcerated dragons. Within the set list of prayers is one specifically for Kukai, and every day I chant the belief that he is my salvation. Another hollow claim.

After getting my stamps, I search the courtyard for a famous tree that has grown around an archer's bow before learning that my guidebook is out of date and that the tree has died. Disappointed, I move on to T7.

I'd like for the ritual to gain meaning for me, but in the meantime I'm enjoying the stark contrast from the religions back home, where people bow to a scroll or a martyred carpenter. Every day here, I bow to fearsome, sword-wielding heavenly kings before entering a courtyard filled with gods and demons on this island where Hindu, Buddhist, and the indigenous Shinto folk traditions merge.

The small courtyard of **Jurakuji: The Temple of Ten Joys (T7)** is filled with stone statues of Jizo, the guardian of travelers, children, and the underworld realms. Depicted as a bald monk with a halo, Jizo carries a staff to force open the gates of hell and a jewel to light the darkness. Besides a magic staff, these Jizo statues hold toy pinwheels, offerings from parents grateful for his divine intervention in healing their ailing child. Worshippers have also tied red bibs around the statues' necks. Both the pinwheels and the bibs are holdovers from Japanese folklore, red being the color for fertility, healing, and demon quelling. Throughout the pilgrimage, both Shinto and Buddhist gods are clothed in red bibs or red knit hats.

More imposing than the bowling pin-size Jizo is the fifteen-foot statue of the fearsome demigod Fudo Myoo.

Surrounded by a halo of flame, the Fudo's deep-set eyes glare out from a wide demonic face, one fang upturned in his stern frown. To enforce perfect mental discipline in all beings, he's armed with a sword to cut through delusion and a lasso to rein in focus. I like these the best, because it's a demon with fire and a blade. Like chocolate peanut butter ice cream, three things I love separately, together at last. The smaller Fudo statues spread through the courtyard with pinwheels stuck in their hands are less intimidating.

Upon exiting, I bow again to the carved *Nio*, which differ from temple to temple in the form, the paint, and the maintenance or decay of the wood. While reciting the sutras may feel hollow, bowing to the statues has quickly become my favorite part of the pilgrimage. Divine monsters with weapons deserve a respectful prostration.

As I approach **Kumadaniji: Bear Valley Temple (T8)**, the bus *henro's* transport pulls into the parking lot. A gaggle of elderly in pure white vests disembark, their pristine walking sticks tapping the slick asphalt. Their guides exit last, hauling duffel bags full of stamp books and scrolls to be signed, assembly-line style, at the stamp office. I avoid the group as they pray at the main and *Daishi* halls, searching the grounds for an ancient tree shaped like a dragon before learning that this, too, has died.

Bus *henro* make up the majority of pilgrims here on Shikoku. Each year, hundreds of thousands purchase one of the competing bus-tour packages. Costing ¥200,000[3] for a two-week tour of Shikoku, the package includes three meals, lodging, stamps, and a priest to lead them in prayer and expound on pilgrimage lore. Two days in, I have little respect for these vacationers ferried around in air-conditioned comfort as I trudge beneath my heavy pack, sweat darkening my splintered staff. As a walking *henro*, I'm putting in the real work.

Step by blistering step, I'm earning this journey.

Still, heading toward T9 across the roads that bisect the wide rice plots, I'm envious of the air-conditioning part as the spiking heat bounces back from the concrete. I glance at the paddies' irrigation canals and see that the muddy water is boiling, the opaque surface filled with tiny bursting explosions. For a moment, I'm convinced Japan is falling into the sun. On further inspection, I discover hundreds of tiny fish in a thrashing feeding frenzy, fattening themselves up for the cranes gently falling from the sky.

In this muggy summer, gelatinous skins of algae bloom across the ponds surrounding the pathway. Each has a sign warning children against cooling off with a dip. Instead of anything official, posted on the chain-link fences are pictures hand-painted by kindergarteners. They depict the bloodthirsty demons called Kappa pulling children into the water to drown, one dragging a small boy all the way into hell. While it does look like baby-eating

---

3 Around twenty three hundred U.S. dollars

monsters live below these scummy pools, who's swimming in this muck?

For the rest of the day I'll be surrounded by Kappa, the most famous of the Japanese folklore demons known as *Youkai*. Resembling frogs with beaks and tortoise shells, Kappa have infiltrated pop culture to the point that Hello Kitty has one in her circle of friends, despite their favorite food being the blood of small children they've drowned.

Also cucumbers.

Inhabiting any body of water, Kappa are also powerful on land as long as liquid remains in the shallow depression atop their skulls. To defeat one, you must bow to them. Obsessively polite, they'll return the gesture, spilling their head water and weakening them.

The sheer idea-density packed into each *Youkai* is one of my favorite parts of Japanese culture. When teaching in Korea, I learned of a couple of their traditional demons, such as the Tokkaebi, a one-horned ogre with a club that loves gold, and the Cockatrice, a fire-breathing chicken/lizard hybrid whose mere glance can kill.

These don't compare to the sheer random amalgamation of traits contained in Japanese paranormal characters like the Konaki-Jiji, an infant spirit that cries until it is picked up, then increases its weight until it crushes you. Or the Ashiarai Yashiki, a giant disembodied foot that busts through the ceiling and demands that the terrified homeowner wash it. Or the Tanuki, a raccoon dog with gigantic dangling testicles that can stretch into any shape, such as a tent, club, or protective shield. Or the Shirime, which greets travelers late at night by bending over to reveal an eyeball in its asshole, then runs off (giggling, I assume). My favorite, however, is the Kudan, a human-faced calf that predicts a calamity and then dies, because there's only one way I imagine this encounter happening.

Me: (*walking through forest*) Holy shit! Man-face baby cow!
Kudan: EARTHQUAKE!!!!! (*dies*)
Me: Noooooooooooooo!!!!!!

The day begins to close as I pray to Sakyamuni Buddha at **Horinji: Dharma Wheel Temple (T9)**, the only reclining image of the Buddha in the eighty-eight temples. Carved by Kukai, as are many of the *honzon*, it's known to cure illness of foot and waist, as do many of the *honzon*. I'll understand why only as my total mileage rises.

From a hilltop pagoda overlooking the valley below and the mountains beyond, I take in the day's journey, relaxed, unhurried, and enjoying my new environment. Then the elderly stamp lady tells me T10, over a mile away, will be closing in twenty minutes. Past that temple there is an *onsen*, a Japanese spa, offering free lodging. After mentioning the three hundred and thirty steps to the *honzon* shrine, she insists on drawing me a map, interpreting my look of pained disbelief as confusion of direction. Now in a rush, I politely thank her for the map, then for slowly leading me out the temple's exit, then again for making sure I know which direction is left by pointing left several times.

As I race past the calm rural landscape, blisters grow beneath the thick calluses on the balls of my feet. It'll be worth it when I'm relaxing afterward in the hot baths. Powering up the three hundred and thirty steps, I burst through the gate of **Kirihataji: Weaving Cloth Temple (T10)**.

Even rushing, it still takes about fifteen to twenty minutes to complete the entire temple ritual before my book is stamped and I'm sitting beside a family, enjoying the sunset from a circular stone bench in the courtyard. After a few pleasantries, they help me locate the *onsen* on my map and find the phone number. I dial the courtyard pay phone. The person who picks up at the *onsen* doesn't speak English. For some reason, I hadn't considered this a possibility. The sun is setting, my energy's flagging, and I again have no place to sleep.

I race through the fields at dusk, scanning for a place to set up my tent, but it's just road and rice. Birds fly in whiplashing clouds through the reddening sky as the world below transforms into muted violet shades. With great clarity, I remember every break I took to appreciate the culture of this pilgrimage. Because of all those times spent contemplating a temple or statue, looking at Kappa, or talking about Ichiro, I'm now speeding along a narrow road searching for a place where my tent won't be run over at dawn by a car or thresher. There is a flip side to taking everything slow and not having a plan. My hopes for another temple to magically appear, a monk waiting in the doorway with cushions and dinner, are growing dimmer along with the path.

My headlamp blinking, I charge through darkness and the carbon stench of the rice chaff smoldering in piles along the road. Bicyclists with no lights or helmets pedal past on the road, guessing by my safety precautions that I'm American. For a culture so afraid of direct sunlight, they don't seem to fear the dark at all. Any visibility is a relief as I cross an unlit narrow bridge, stepping to the extreme edge to avoid the cars roaring past. On the opposite bank, a sign with happy, pink Kappa pixies warns children that they'll drown in this river and be dragged to hell by monsters.

I crest the grassy bank and behold a distant Ferris wheel towering over an abandoned amusement park. It seems like a good place to sleep, but I can't walk that far.

Also, it looks pretty haunted.

A gray-haired couple on their evening stroll approaches, motioning that they'll lead me to T11. Unlike this morning, I'm ready to trust the elderly. I follow them until I collapse into a roadside bus stop, my legs spasming. They indicate there is farther to go. I politely make it clear that going farther will require a length of rope and some vigorous dragging. They shrug, accept my *osamefuda*, and return home.

I do my best to wrap insect netting around my hat brim, but mosquitoes whine in my ears as I cram my body into the narrow wood bench. The noxious repellent I slathered on my arms burns into my nostrils. So far, in my experience on Shikoku, a good night's sleep happens half the time, but rushing at the end of the day is a guarantee. Maybe there won't always be a monk waiting for me, but at least some friendly strangers helped me find a place to sleep tonight. The island will provide for me.

Tomorrow I learn that I really, really should have prepared better.

3
BURNING MOUNTAINS

THE OMINOUS SONG I wake to should warn me of the day ahead, but it's quickly forgotten as violent cramps twist from my soles to my palms. Almost worse, the mosquito repellent bottle in my pack burst last night. The acrid odor now saturating my bag, clothes, and bracelets will remain for weeks, reminding me of today. Unpacking my limbs from the narrow bench, I'm hoping that the twitching will stop if I groan at the correct pitch. On the other hand, daylight and distance make the abandoned amusement park look no less haunted. I stand by my choice.

Groggy from the amount of sleep one would expect while crammed into a hard bench beside a busy highway, I set off down the highway. There's no breakfast to be found along the two-mile descent through paddies, orchards, and ramshackle farmhouses, which is fine. By the time

I've reached the tree-shrouded valley floor of **Fujiidera: Wisteria Temple (T11)**, the rising temperature has suppressed both my appetite and my will to live.

As the last twisting wisps of mist disappear from the courtyard with the morning chill, I mumble through the sutras on wobbly legs. It's the first time I've remained upright, and not without effort. Damp shirt pasted to my chest, I glance around for a soda machine to buy a Pocari Sweat sports drink. No such luck. Bland, zero-calorie water it is.

Construction scaffolding encircles the residential complex, where I fill my Nalgene-brand water bottles from an outdoor spigot. In the shade of rustling blue tarps, I guzzle and refill until a half-gallon sloshes in my empty gut. After wiping my palms dry, I crack open the map book that I still can't read. From T11, the thirteen-kilometer route of red dots meanders down the page to T12 across blobby mountains, with elevations ranging from greenish-tan to less greenish-tan to tannish-green. Seems easy enough. Pondering whether this hike will take two or three hours, I don't notice the priest standing over me.

"*Atsui, desu neh* (Hot, ain't it)?" he asks, using the ubiquitous summer greeting.

"*Hai, atsui* (Yes, hot)," I reply to the only non-Ichiro conversation I'll have in these first muggy weeks.

We nod through the awkward silence and I return to the map book. The priest remains.

"Do you need help?" he asks, using the "*Please leave now, gaijin*" tone.

Taking the hint, I stow the map book.

The dirt steps wind into the woods past stone Buddha shrines dug into the crumbly mountainside, their sloped roofs dusted with moss. Had I read further into the map book, I'd know that the T12 is the first *nansho*, the "dangerous place" temples. This would explain the offerings from previous *henro* piled at the Buddha's feet, asking for protection on the arduous journey ahead. After snapping a final picture of T11, I hike into the forest. The stream gurgling through the valley floor grows fainter and fainter. Meanwhile, the islands of Japan bow further toward the sun.

Thirteen centuries ago, Kukai climbed through a roaring inferno to **Shosanji: Burning Mountain Temple (T12)**, where he battled the dragon that'd set the slopes alight. Following in his footsteps in 2010, I have a hard time believing that story. There's no way this mountain could get any hotter. By the time the steep path levels off into a clearing, I've already sweated out my first beer from high school.

Chest heaving, I drop onto a bench across from a red shrine and ask whichever god is inside for strength. I've never done well with non-historically significant heat, but over the past two days I've drained both 32-ounce water bottles on an hourly basis and still haven't peed while the sun was up. I didn't make it far in Boy Scouts, but I remember that being a bad thing.

A couple yards away the trail disappears behind a bamboo grove, where another series of switchbacks awaits. I glance over the map book again with no idea where I am on the page. It's too early in the pilgrimage to gauge how far I've actually walked versus how far it feels like I've walked versus how far I'm praying I've walked. All I know is that it's been over an hour since I left T11 and I'm already as drained as I was hiking to Big Mountain Temple that first night. So I must be halfway done. I finish off my first water bottle.

A wizened, gray-haired *henro* passes the bench.

"*Atsui, desu ne?*" he nods, which is an understatement. Clearly we've angered the sun.

"*Hai, atsui,*" I gasp back as he vanishes into the bamboo without breaking stride or a sweat. And with that, the gauntlet is thrown down. I may be tired, but I'm not about to let a senior citizen beat me to the top. Having yet to learn that no amount of fitness matches the Japanese hiking prowess, regardless of age or packs-per-day habit, I charge off the bench. A Jizo stands at the foot of the path, his palm full of coins offered by precautious *henro*. Racing past his outstretched hand, I attack the slope.

I soon overtake the old man, but it's a struggle to stay ahead. Breathing in shallow gasps, my staff drills into the ground hard enough to leave oil wells in its wake. By the time the trail levels off again, each heartbeat is ramming against my ribcage in a desperate attempt to escape and a rapidly depleting reservoir patters to the ground beneath me. Half of my second Nalgene vanishes in one gulp.

The trail is empty for a while, gently undulating along the ridgeline through a dense wall of pines. I'm starting to worry. It's been hours since I left T11, my last water bottle is nearly gone, and I have no idea how far it is to the temple. The wood posts along the path are no help, displaying arrows and distance figures seemingly at random. One says 3 km, but after a long hike up, then down, the next reads 4.6 km. The hikers and *henro* along the path are even more inscrutable. When asked the distance to T12, everyone replies with "five, six kilometers," no matter how far I've gone, always followed by a reassuring "*chotto* (short)." Unable to ask follow-up questions, I nod and keep going, certain that the posts will run out of numbers at some point. I know I'm not lost, thanks to tablets hanging from the branches, the kanji for *henro* written in red paint. Eventually, the path descends along a stone stairway. A small temple comes into view and I let out a whoop. They were right; it was "*chotto.*" I polish off my second Nalgene.

Setting my backpack on the courtyard bench, I drop my coins and *osamefuda* into the slotted box, then pray at an outdoor *Daishi* shrine. I hoist myself onto the veranda circling the main hall. The sliding doors reveal an atrium containing a simple shrine to the *honzon*, where I complete the ritual. After an unsuccessful search of the empty, silent grounds for the stamp office, I shrug and give up. It'll be a blank page, which irks me. But I don't need ink, I need water.

Sitting on the veranda, I tip the last drips from the bottles into my mouth. If no one is around, I'll pull a very respectful Goldilocks. Shoes off, I bow and enter, calling out with no answer. The calendar hanging from the yellowing wallpaper is out of date, but there are slippers beside the staircase and the shrine is swept and maintained. The monks must have gone elsewhere to escape this oppressive heat.

In the kitchen I twist the squeaking faucet handle. With a shudder and a groan, water pours into my first bottle. Through the dirt-caked window is a shallow cave, which must be where Kukai confined the dragon. I place my second Nalgene under the sputtering stream and tip the first to my lips. Just as I taste something musty, the thrumming faucet vomits rust-brown liquid into the bottle. Spewing my mouthful into the sink, I can feel protozoa crawling past my tongue toward my intestines. I keep spitting as I dump the Nalgenes down the drain.

I pass the damp shadow of my lower half soaking into the veranda and return to my backpack to stare blankly at the map again. It can't be much farther to the town below T12.

A *henro* tablet dangles above the bench.

Oh no.

I turn to my right with a bright red flash of panic. Another tablet twists in the breeze above a dirt trail sloping into the forest. 3.1 km, says the distance marker.

You can make three kilometers, no problem, I lie to myself as sweat gushes off my cheeks. *It'll be easy, especially without all this extra liquid weighing you down.*

Since I was a chubby 13-year-old who decided to turn off the TV and start jogging, I've been an athlete, lettering in four sports, bicycling century rides, and running the

Seattle Marathon. So I'm confused when my legs buckle and the blurry ground rushes to my face. This has never happened on any hike, ride, run, or game. I've thrown up on the field and played through. Rolling to my knees, I wipe the smear of mud off my forehead, snatch the hat wobbling beside me, and rise to my feet.

As I collapse again halfway up the switchback, panic alarms begin to strobe. When my eyes refocus, it's finally clear how dangerously unprepared I am for this journey. However, I'm even less prepared to explain to everyone back home why I quit three days in, so I'll continue despite the growing dehydration and my newly malfunctioning legs. Eyes shut, I draw deep inside to the will that years of karate training has instilled: the thousands of push-ups and sit-ups, the hours of drills, the intense rush of tournaments, sprinting barefoot across the snow-covered dunes to fight in the East Sea during the Korean winter. Rising against the pressing weight of my backpack, I pound my staff into the soil.

I will not stop again.

Fifty steps later I'm back in the dirt, curled on my side and glaring jealously at the millipedes' extra legs as they crawl past. A passing hiker places the last of his plastic water bottle in my hand. Chugging gratefully, I watch in disbelief as he speeds up the trail.

The sixth time I crumple into the dirt, the panic alarms are flashing extra bright. When my stomach stops looking for something to throw up I raise my head again. Sunlight filters through the oak and maple branches. I'm near the peak. Thank gods.

With long rests and short hikes I force myself up the switchbacks until I sprawl across the foot of a stone staircase. The benevolent iron visage of Kukai peers down at me. Behind him I hear a soda machine thrumming.

I made it.

In celebration, I gulp the last of the gifted water bottle, which sieves through me to puddle onto the steps. This has been a serious contender for the "Worst Day of My Life" award, but it's over.

I catch my breath and charge to the top. Past the Kukai statue is an empty clearing. No temple, no water faucet, no soda machine. Somewhere between dismay and disbelief lies the noise I make. A middle-aged *henro* rests on a bench, fanning the dewy perspiration from her plump cheeks. She must have passed by me unnoticed on one of my frequent trips to the ground. In broken Japanese I ask where there's water. She shrugs. I ask for a sip of her water. She smiles apologetically and shakes her head. I ask where T12 is. She points farther down the path.

I turn to the statue and yell, "You lied to me, *Daishi*," getting partway through "lied" before my vision goes to static and I fall at his feet. The panic alarms are joined by a klaxon blaring through my skull. For the first time since a childhood prank ended with me getting chased down by a truck, I'm sure I'm going to die.

Since I can't pantomime "emergency medical evacuation" to the *henro* on the bench, I collect myself and think.

The obvious solution is ditching my large backpack for the small daypack crammed in the bottom, which would carry only my essentials. After struggling under the weight for two and a half days, the urge to leave it behind leads to rationalizations like *Do you really need the tent, sleeping bag, and all the clothes? After all, isn't a sleeping bag just a tent without scaffolding? And aren't pants just a thinner sleeping bag with legs? And who really needs pants, when you think about it?*

Sadly, the only thing keeping my belongings from tumbling down the mountainside is how much I paid for them. I look back at the *henro*, who smiles and points away from the clearing again.

"Shozanji. Five, six kilometer," she reassures me. "*Chotto.*"

With a whimper I push off the ground and stand at the edge of the clearing. A cool breeze of no comfort flutters the leaves. It's clear what lies ahead on this path slithering through the forest. With no end in sight I'll collapse in the dirt, rise, bargain with my legs for fifty more steps, then fall again with air igniting my lungs and burning through my limbs. Each time will hurt more than the last until I either reach T12, get rescued incapacitated, or die somewhere between these distance markers and assurances of "*chotto.*"

And in that moment, I accept it.

Until one of those three outcomes happens, I'll live in the awful now, resigned to the weakness, fear, and pain of the upslopes while appreciating the less grueling descents. And with one step into the forest, then another, my pack thudding down on bruised and blistered soles, I continue on toward Burning Mountain Temple.

Of course, this newfound resolve doesn't stop me from praying to find T12 or water at the next peak, around the next bend, or when I walk far, far down into a ravine. At the bottom I discover a pasture with three horses I may have hallucinated and a dry trough with no spigot. Groaning, I drop onto the concrete. Ants scatter from the biblical torrent cascading off my chin, repenting their sins with tiny waving antennae. I wonder if I have it in me to make another climb, and if it's possible to drink sweat from my shorts. After a long rest, I decide *yes, I can* and *no, I shouldn't*, marshal whatever is left inside me, and trudge up another unforgiving slope.

When the trees open for a majestic vista, all I see is a ring of green peaks blocking any hope of escape. I stop asking for water and begin begging from the dirt as hikers pass by in their sweat-wicking technical shirts and tiny backpacks, out for a rousing stroll up a mountain. Some give me what they have left. Others politely decline. I can't blame them as I curl on my side, trying to convince myself you can't die of dehydration in six hours and never really buying it.

Back on my feet I breathe through ragged coughs, electricity crackling through my skin. With each shaky step up the path I promise myself there will be a soda machine at the temple. Or, if I don't make it, in heaven, if they haven't been watching me too closely. In a vision as clear as a commercial, a blue-striped can of Pocari Sweat sports drink tumbles from the soda machine. The tab compresses with a metallic tear and pop; mist escapes in a spiraling burst. I raise the can to my lips, the refrigerated liquid cooling me for the first time today. It will be the greatest moment of my life.

Atop another plateau, the overhanging branches part to reveal blue sky and another empty clearing. With no energy left for hope or disappointment, I lie back on the trailside bench. Across from me a distance marker claims 1 km.

Liar sign.

My sedge hat shielding my face, I dream of cold aluminum cans and wake only to beg hikers for water. A jogger in a green technical shirt shakes his empty bottle, then points down the path.

"Shozanji."

I ask how far.

"One kilometer. *Chotto.*" He motions for me to follow.

Liar jogger.

He's insistent, so I lug my pack onto my shoulders and stagger behind him. The dirt trail soon becomes pebbly, weaving between Buddhas meditating in their lotus thrones and a granite railing bordering the mountainside's sheer drop. I refuse to believe the jogger until we've passed through the *Nio-mon* and stand beneath eight gargantuan cedar columns rising from the courtyard's bleach-white gravel. Up a small staircase stands **Shozanji: Burning Mountain Temple (T12)**. And, more important to my survival, a soda machine. The refrigerator motor hums an angels' chorus. My pack drops to the ground. I lunge up the stairs, remove my dripping wallet from my pocket, and push the sweat-soaked bill into the machine.

It whirs for a moment and returns the bill.

I insert it again.

Rejected.

"Nooooooo!"

My fists slam against the machine as the panic lights burst. I'm scanning through the pebbles at my feet for something large enough to smash the front panel when a meek woman approaches to offer the crazy man a dry bill. I gasp out sounds resembling thanks and the slot swallows the money. With no ceremony, three Pocari Sweat evaporate in my throat. Attached to the stamp office is a cozy restaurant, where I slump onto a bench, my head resting motionless on the wood picnic table. A waitress with red-dyed hair appears over me.

"*Atsui, desu ne?*"

"*Hai, atsui,*" oozes out.

I point in the menu's direction until she understands "food." She returns from the kitchen with a paper fan and places it on the table, whispering "*Ossetai.*" Without the energy to waft it, the fan remains beside my head while I wait for my first meal in twenty hours. An energized group of hikers beside me chatters cheerfully, their small packs filled with whatever they need between here and their car.

"Where are you from?" one of them asks.

"Ichiro," I mumble, weakly swinging my chopsticks.

Nodding, she rejoins her group's conversation. The

moment the waitress sets the noodles and salty soy broth on the table, it vanishes into my gut.

It's getting dark, and I still have to reach the town below. The courtyard bell announces my presence with an almost audible ping, and I preemptively fall to my knees before reciting the sutras to the *honzon*. I bow again at the *Nio-mon,* mostly in reverence to the soda machine, and depart.

The mountain pathway becomes roadway, then driveways. I take shelter at a shuttered elementary school at the edge of town, where a stopped clock hangs from a wall of chipped paint and shattered windows. An ominous silence permeates the abandoned playfield. Shadows gather in the pocked dirt, torn up by students long since gone. Unlike the amusement park, this place is definitely haunted, but walking any farther is laughable.

Setting up my tent beside the remains of desks and toys crusted with dirt and spiderwebs, I beg any spirits still hanging around to let me rest in peace. I'm scared enough already. To leave this valley girdled by steep mountains, I see the same painful struggle awaiting me at sunrise. Quitting is not an option, but I don't know if I'll survive another day like today. It's not as if it's unheard of here. In *henro* tradition, the staff doubles as a gravestone and the white vests are considered funeral shrouds, reminding pilgrims that death can come at any time.

Less comforting, as my head hits the pillow, I remember the song playing in my head when I woke this morning.

The Eels's "Going to Your Funeral."

4
FEAR AND LYING IN INTERNET CAFÉS

I'M SHAKING WHEN I wake up, and it's not cold out. As butter-yellow sunlight melts down the surrounding peaks, I lie in my tent with cramps contorting my twitching limbs. In three days I've walked thirty-seven miles. Further distances remain questionable. I've always had bad anxiety, which I think is because of brain tumors, but it's at its worst when there's something real to focus on. My gut twists at the thought of another climb, but I see no other way out of this valley.

On the bright side, no ghosts last night.

After packing up and leaving the elementary school, I'm invited in for breakfast at a cozy shop set up in a carport. The elderly owners seat me at their kitchen table/ front counter facing the village's bus station and place a cup of watery coffee in my hand. I choose my breakfast from the three shelves of instant noodles, sweet red-bean buns, and potato chips. As the water for my ramen boils on the electric stove, my knotted stomach whimpers at its impending task. A bus arrives across the street, and curious passengers filter in. With the roadside attraction of a white *henro*, there's a steady ring of the cash register as I force calories into my system, repeat "Ichiro," and swing the chopsticks.

A bow, an *osamefuda*, and I'm off. Dragonflies dance above the stalks of the bright, moist fields that butt up against the pine-dark foothills. I take a hard, resigned look at the peaks leading out of this valley, then a short, longing look at the rumbling bus, wondering how far it could take me from here. Shaking off the thought, I hoist my pack onto my stiff shoulders.

You'll probably survive today too, I reassure myself, hiking into another muggy forest of cedar and bamboo.

For the next hour my heart leaps into my throat at every blind corner, fearing it will reveal another incline, another impossible day like Burning Mountain that will break me. When the path exits onto a concrete ribbon winding across the slope, it only gets worse. Mountains echo into the horizon, roofs tucked into their foliage like ticks on a shaggy dog. Every time I glance at the panorama, the pain, fear, and doubt from yesterday are as palpable as if I'm still collapsed into the dirt. Finally I have to stop inside a rest hut, where I cradle my head in my palms.

An ivy-covered gate beside the highway swings open and a Japanese Mother Hubbard shuffles out toward the hut. With a warm smile she whispers, "*Ossetai*" and hands me an ice-cold grape soda as if she's been waiting there for me all day. Bowing, I accept it with both hands. I pop the top, and my concerns disappear as the sweet, chilled bubbles sizzle on my tongue. Then it drains into the gnarl that is my gut as I look down the road, imagining what lies around the next bend.

It's a difficult thing, to be in the moment.

I get up to snap some photos and immediately regret leaving my pack on the bench. Instead of the usual punishing steps, I'm floating forward on a gust of wind, angels whispering sweet nothings into my soles. I resolve to keep the pack's gravity on my aching shoulders at all times, since at that moment I'm ready to roll it off the cliff and not look back. Who really needs a tent, sleeping bag, and extra clothes, when you think about it?

Most of my day parallels the longest river in Shikoku: the Yoshino. From its source close to Mount Ishizuchi, the Yoshino flows west to east across the northern boundaries of Kochi and Tokushima prefectures, reaching the sea at Tokushima City. Beside the river, the hours blur on sloped, then flat concrete as I wait for the other shoe to drop. I stop infrequently, backtracking because I forgot my staff at a shop, or pausing to rebandage my feet. Below hotels perched on cliffs, vacationers bob on inner tubes in the Yoshino's currents as it cuts through the valley. In the late afternoon I break in a public restroom and take yet another bathroom-sink sponge bath to remove the layers of dirt and grime. When it gets dark, I set up my tent in the gravel parking lot of a one-room office beside the road.

When it gets light, I set off for another day of sweating, worrying, and not pissing.

The morning is spent wandering through the Japan I hoped to find in this rural landscape: ancient temples, ancient ruins, and traditional houses. On my way to **Dainichiji: The Temple of the Great Sun (T13)**, I pass by a sprawling home with a stone base, cedar walls, and a sloped roof that bars ghosts from entering, since they can only travel in straight lines. Adding extra protection to the home are the ceramic fish posted on the eaves, which are supposed to repel fire. I detour up a hill to visit an old mountain fort, now a rectangular base of crumbling stones with a commanding view of the land below. Like historical sites in the rest of the country, these relics are nestled within the concrete sprawl of modernity, with its electricity, phone lines, and farm machinery. Given my desire to see the past, I'm surprisingly excited to find one of the more recent examples of Japanese culture, a *Dekotora*.

An abbreviation of "Decoration Truck," *Dekotora* are semi-trucks that look like a glam-rock Optimus Prime. In the 1970s, while Americans were airbrushing Led Zeppelin album covers onto the sides of their vans, Japanese truck owners began tricking out their rides with thousands of yen worth of lights, chrome, and airbrushed art, then more of the same. On the back of this Isuzu flatbed, elemental dragons thrash through raging firestorms and lightning-wracked typhoons, and chrome running boards embossed with flower petals stretch from the rear to the front bumper. The rest of the frame is covered with enough lights to signal Spielberg's *Close Encounters of the Third Kind* spaceship, halogens stacked four high and thirteen across on the luggage rack alone. It's an unexpected break in routine before returning to the temples, which I pass in quick succession, preparing for the next one to be at the top of a mountain.

At **Jorakuji: The Temple of Everlasting Peace (T14)**, the motherly stamp lady must see the exhaustion in my eyes. After handing me a white towel to drape around my neck, ubiquitous in this summer heat, she presses ¥500 into my palm.

"Buy some juice," she coos at me.

Kokubunji: The Official State Temple (T15) used to be Tokushima's prestigious imperial temple, but is at present known for having sustained massive termite damage. An elegant woman in a purple silk robe signs my book with effortless technique. Time slows as the brush performs a graceful dance, unfurling a gleaming black ribbon across the page. I consider purchasing an Ususama Myoo amulet in the gift shop, which one posts against the toilet wall to exterminate dirty karma and scare away termites. However, if the fearsome Ususama Myoo can't protect a holy temple, I'm not going to trust it for my secular toilet.

After performing the ritual of bow, bell, wash, pray, pray, stamp, bow, leave at **Kannonji: The Temple of Kannon (T16)**, I visit the eponymous well of **Idoji: Well**

Temple (T17). According to legend, seeing your face in the water guarantees good luck. If you can't, you'll meet with an accident in a few years. I make sure to see my reflection, needing as much help as I can get here.

I finally reach a city in the late afternoon, and after five days on the walk decide to indulge in an Internet café. Unlike American or European ones with a bank of computers and hard-backed chairs, cafés here boast spacious, padded cubicles and twelve-hour rental packages, plenty of time to navigate your avatar through lands of goblins and mages in plush comfort. They also offer free ice cream, coffee, and cola to power you through your mission. Twenty dollars for ice cream, English, and sleeping on cushions is a bargain. I sign the guestbook, pass the wall-length shelves of manga comic books and magazines, and shut my cubicle door for the night. Since I'm not rushing to finish my journal before passing out and I have the world's knowledge at my fingertips, I sit down and finally do some research on the pilgrimage, starting with T12.

It's reassuring to learn my struggles on the way to Burning Mountain Temple aren't unique. Historically it's where most *henro* give up, and where the supposed first *henro*, Emon Saburo, died. A wealthy, cruel man from Ehime province, Emon refused to give alms when Kukai came begging at his door. When Kukai returned the next day, Emon treated him the same, hurling insults at the ascetic. Kukai returned the day after to the same abuse, and the day after, and so on until the eighth day, when an enraged Emon smashed Kukai's begging bowl. After this, the holy man left for good. The next day, Emon's eldest son died. The day after, his second oldest fell ill, and so on until all eight of his sons were dead. Seeking repentance, Emon distributed all of his possessions to his peasants, donned a sedge hat, carved himself a walking staff, and set out to find Kukai. After circling the island twenty-two times in four years with no result, he reversed course and met Kukai on the path to Burning Mountain. Near death, Emon collapsed at the holy man's feet, where the iron statue in the clearing now stands. With his last breath, Emon begged forgiveness, asking to be reborn as the lord of Ehime so he could treat its peasants with fairness and mercy. Because of Emon's hard work on the *henro* trail, Kukai forgave him his sins. The *Daishi* wrote a message on a small stone, placed it in Emon's left hand, and the *henro* died at peace.

In less reassuring pilgrimage news, I discover to my horror that T12 was only the first of nine *nansho* temples in my future, including two in a row near the end of Tokushima. The hike to T12 was the most agonizing experience of my life, and it's not even the steepest or the tallest *nansho* I'll face, or the only *henro-korogashi4* section. Desperate to lighten my pack, I dump out my belongings and search frantically through the pile of clothes, toiletries, and camping gear spread in front of me. In the end, I leave behind two paperback books that I've already read.

---

4 Literally, "where pilgrims tumble."

I'm stuck with this several-bowling-balls' worth of weight that drags me down with every step.

When I sign in to my email, I'm inundated with excited messages from friends and family back home. All ask the same question:

How's the pilgrimage going? Are you having fun?

My fingers hover over the keys as I consider typing the honest reply: after a year of talking nonstop about this pilgrimage, I'm ready to quit five days in because I'm terrified of another day like Burning Mountain. In between all the hikes, hills, and stairs, it's been an ordeal of constant foot pain, dehydration cramps, empty prayers, and hours of silence broken only by telling strangers that I'm from Seattle or agreeing that it's very hot. I'm beginning to think coming here was a mistake.

In the end, my stubborn pride won't allow me to admit any of this. I write a mass email lying about what a great time I'm having, then fall asleep to vivid MSG nightmares from my dinner of instant ramen.

Because I signed in to the café at 4 p.m., unwilling to wait any longer for ice cream and English, I leave before the sun rises. The gamer in the next cubicle is still up, twelve hours further into his mission than last night. As I lace up my shoes downstairs, two more gamers enter.

Slightly depressed, I retrace my steps through the city back to the path, crossing bridges decorated with images of Awa dancers. I've just missed the Awa Odori festival, which takes place between August 12 and 15 in Tokushima. It's the largest dance festival in Japan, attracting over 1.3 million tourists each year. Groups of choreographed performers and musicians cavort through the streets, chanting and singing in traditional costumes, including hats that look like they stuck their head into an orange slice. I'd have liked to see something more cultural in Tokushima than *Dekotora* and *World of Warcraft*.

Passing through the quiet streets in the dawn light, I try to appreciate the red columns and black arc of torii gates, still shadows against the golden sky. However, it's hard to ignore how many more torii I've seen because I keep getting lost. Even without the map book, the *henro* trail can be navigated by following stickers glued to signposts. Most common are the red arrows that point pilgrims down the correct streets, or blue ovals with round cartoon *henro* happily sharing the trail with you. Also guiding the *henro* are chest-high wooden posts with white arrows, and century-old stone bollards with the number of the next temple. And yet, trying my best to stay on course, I'm failing miserably. Even a meditation break to clear my mind does nothing. The rest of the day is a haze of anxiety, trying to get back to the path leading me to the *nansho* temples ahead.

After getting more disoriented in the twists and turns of a bamboo grove, I finally arrive at T19. Then I check my map again and reverse course to T18. Accepting "lost" as today's status quo, I'm glad that at least I'm backtracking through the shaded groves instead of atop searing concrete. Another wrong turn leads me to a clearing on the edge of a hill. Far beyond the geometric squares of yellow, brown, and green, and the distant rooftops clustered near the shore, the blue curve of the Pacific bulges up against the horizon. Tokushima ends where the ocean begins, and in a day of accidental detours, it's a relief to still be heading in the vaguely right direction.

Onzanji: Gratitude Mountain Temple (T18) is dedicated to pregnant women. While reciting the sutras, I ask the *honzon* to protect my friend Carrie and her baby on the way. She lost the first one to complications and had requested a special prayer in an email last night, so I give her all the support I can. And with that, these incomprehensible sutras gain a purpose besides commitment to the ritual. At each temple going forward, I will hold two people I care about in my mind and ask the *honzon* for their health and happiness. My depression lifts a little and I go off the path again, on purpose this time, to a samurai statue on a grassy hill nearby.

Frozen on his rearing horse, the samurai yells his battle cry while holding his bow triumphantly aloft, twin feathers sticking out of his ostentatious helmet. Sitting in the shade beside a nearby shrine, I watch a tipsy kendo master offer some of his sake to the gods. On wobbling feet, he performs some quick slashes with his hands, then bows and nearly topples over into the shrine. I smile for the first time today and realize that, for a brief moment, I wasn't thinking about what lies ahead.

T19 is the first of the *sekisho,* the barrier temples that block those with impure hearts from entering via tactics straight out of a horror movie. According to legend, an egret guards the bridge to **Tatsueji: The Temple of Arising a Bay (T19)**, who will peck out the eyes of the unworthy. Once inside, another monument to this haunted temple stands in the courtyard: a glass case containing a bell rope with black hairs stuck in the fibers. This is the scalp of Okyo, a nineteenth-century geisha who murdered her husband before eloping with her lover on a honeymoon circuit around Shikoku. When they reached T19's *honzon* to pray, Okyo's hair stood straight on her head, becoming entangled in the dangling bell rope. Lifted into the air, she struggled until her hair and part of her scalp tore loose. The young couple then repented their crimes and became pious Buddhists.

I've always loved stories like these, and am glad that odd religious artifacts aren't confined to the Christian faith. As a student in Spain, I learned that holy relics didn't end with burial shrouds, grails, or skulls. At one point in Europe, eighteen towns and churches claimed to possess Jesus's foreskin before it was lost to history. Upon hearing this, I joked that the search for the foreskin should be the plot of the next Indiana Jones movie. After seeing *Kingdom of the Crystal Skull* on my flight to Japan, I still hold to this.

At T19's stamp office, the monk half-heartedly drags the brush across page nineteen, annoyed at the interruption of his smoke break. When I request a map to the nearby *zenkonyado*, free housing for walking *henro*, the monk hands it over brusquely before waving me off and returning to his manga and cigarette.

Praying to reach the house soon, to rest up for what I have to endure tomorrow, I lumber down the road. Time blurs and repeats itself. The same three fields rotate past: green shoots of rice, waving yellow stalks, and tan bristles on the dry ground. The humid air is filled with the non-stop rumble of farm equipment and the roar of engines. The same pedestrian approaches, I point to the *zenkonyado* map, and he points down the road. I nod and continue until he reappears ahead of me. I ask the same question again and again, and he keeps pointing until I'm outside the *zenkonyado* beside a factory.

I drop my bags beneath the kitchen table in a one-room house with a tatami mat floor. Beside the sliding glass door that doesn't lock hangs a wanted poster with the grim faces of criminals that *henro* should not allow inside. Cushions are stacked against the wall beside a globe with pins for foreign pilgrims. Australia is riddled with thumbtacks and Europe is a close second. I stab my lone pin into Seattle and slump into a chair, ready to fall asleep. The smell of my musty clothing rises from my bag and slaps my nostrils.

With a groan I bend forward and pull out the laundry bag. With a similar noise I stand and carry it to an outdoor bathroom beside the factory. The white-tiled walls, concrete floor, toilet, and sink are spotlessly clean, and there's a hose attached to the faucet. I lock the door, strip, and mumble contentedly as lukewarm water pours over me. It's my first non-sponge bath in a week. After scrubbing hard everywhere, I plug the sink and dump in soap for my shirts and shorts.

Dingy water wrings through my clothes as I stare out the window at the darkening path leading to the *nansho* temples. Tomorrow, I'll again lie crumpled in the dirt with ragged breaths burning my throat and crackling pain in my skin. And for what? Why should I put myself through that again, when all I've learned so far is that I can't read maps and that boars are terrifying in person? I'm talking myself down from thumbing a ride back to Tokushima City when from deep inside I hear *Be here now.*

Suddenly I find myself standing over the sink, doing my laundry. In this new silence I become aware of how rackety the past three days have been, how little of each day I noticed while preparing for things to get worse later. The mountains ahead may be more than I can physically endure, but I am not yet climbing them. In that thought, I am at peace. I wring out my clothes, drain the water, and wipe down the sink before returning to the *zenkonyado.*

The clarity doesn't last long.

After cutting and wrapping more blisters, I lay my sleeping bag on top of the cushions and crawl inside, too tired to care about the wanted poster or the non-locking door. Why worry about the murderers coming later when my feet are killing me now? My mind wanders down the road where two *nansho* temples await, my only consolation being that I now know why I'm saying the prayers if I reach the top. The panic is rising when I hear it again.

Be here now.

Outside the window a lizard crawls across the metal screen and snaps its jaws shut on a large moth, now just wings flapping slower and slower against a scaly snout.

It's a difficult thing, to be in the moment.

But I'm learning.

5
GOOD ENOUGH, PART 1

BY DAWN BOTH the sun and I have risen, prepared to climb through the morning and descend in the evening. However, the sun only has one arc to make today.

I have three.

Eighteen hundred and two thousand feet above sea level sit T20 and T21, *nansho* temples with another mountain between them. I'm starting early because there's a *zenkonyado* near T22 that closes at sundown. After my first *nansho* experience with T12, I'm factoring in extra time for resting/collapsing/sobbing in defeat. On the plus side, these are the last mountain temples in Tokushima, and a reward lies far beyond them at the end of the province: a side temple offering a free *onsen*. Besides the *nansho* temples, reaching it is the only thing on my mind. After all the aimless trudging and occasional panic, I need a win.

In my fantasies I reach the Pacific in Kochi after two grueling days. My footprints lead across the sand into the cold, salty waves that soothe my battered soles. Afterwards, my body lolls in a steaming tub in triumph as the knots in my back and shoulders dissolve.

But the *onsen* lies forty miles away.

The *nansho* temples, closer.

Wincing as even newer blisters press against the insoles, I slide open the glass door and step onto the winding highway. No matter how terrified I am of the climbs ahead, there's nowhere to go but up.

Engines roar past for a long hour before I turn off the concrete into the woods. The silence is striking, a peaceful interlude of cicadas, the tick-tock of my staff, and the gushing rush of water under a bridge before the path rises sharply into the forest. With a sigh and a vague prayer to any of the gods now surrounding me, I head into the foliage. Soon I'm hiking through orchards on the foothills, where I startle a venomous mamushi snake sunning itself beside a drainage ditch. I yelp and it falls into the water. The mamushi reemerges. Brown scales glistening, it glares as I hurry past.

It's early enough that the temperature's only mildly hellish, and I'm grateful I'm not yet bargaining with my legs for fifty steps. Bamboo around one blind turn gives way to cedar around the next, and on the thin dirt roads I give way to barreling trucks, the drivers as confident with their steering as they are reckless with their cargo. Halfway up, a burly black fly starts buzzing around my head. The marble-size nuisance stays with me until the top.

I reach T20 with ragged breaths made of gulps and coughs, bow to the two wooden cranes inside the *Niomon*, and enter **Kakurinji: Crane Forest Temple (T20)**. According to legend, while Kukai studied here a two-inch image of Jizo appeared in an old cedar tree guarded by a pair of cranes, the symbols of long life and good fortune. Even more unusual, since the *Daishi* saw god visions on the regular, is that T20 is one of the only temples in Tokushima that hasn't been burned in war for over a millennium. Given the effort to get to the courtyard, I'm going to guess every general has said, "Fuck it, there are sea-level temples we can torch."

After working so hard to reach T20, it's a short visit. I descend a dirt stairway, the backpack's weight shuddering through my knees into my feet with every step. In disbelief, I find myself looking forward to the taxing upslopes, which I soon reach after passing through a crumbling rock wall and a dirt backyard. The homeowner nods through the window to one of her few hundred trespassers every year. Back in the woods, the fat black fly returns and I give up waving him off. He becomes a tiny *henro*, buzzing his prayers beside me. I'm happy for any company.

The second *nansho* hike isn't any better than the first, and it's only gotten hotter. My sweat must be the only liquid to hit the ground in months, since the region is dry enough to require two forest-fire warning signs. On my way up, a frowning brown bear trapped inside a red circle and slash holds a cigarette in his chubby paw. On my way down, a forest fire sheds a single tear as a group of children and old people armed with water pails yell at it. Hours later I haven't found any smoking bears to admonish, but as bamboo and ferns again give way to cedar boughs shading the lush pathway, I've reached T21.

Just off the main entrance, a granite outcropping overlooks a mountain chain far below. Climbing a rickety ladder to the top of a boulder, I sit beside a knee-high shrine, watching the shadows of clouds glide across the green ripples. While I'm hiking the switchbacks, the dense foliage creates one unbroken moment of exertion. Inside this humid world of wood and earth, my only focus becomes staying upright as my staff punctures the slopes in the hopes of deflating them. Viewpoints like this outcropping are one of the few reminders that I'm actually heading somewhere. Once I've stopped panting, I make a donation to the shrine and pray to get back down the ladder safely.

Bus *henro* disembark from the cable car at the main hall of **Tairyuji: Great Dragon Temple (T21)**. A mossy dragon slithers across the hall's carved entryway, commemorating the one seen here by Japan's first emperor while he fought to unify the country.

In the courtyard a mother opens a cooler and sets out a small picnic lunch for her adolescent son and daughter. She sees me, double-takes, drops the food, and digs through her purse for a camera. With my consent she pushes her reluctant daughter into frame beside me. The son kneels in front and we all smile and flash the peace sign. In return for the photo I gratefully accept a Pocari Sweat from her cooler. It's guzzled in a few glorious seconds.

Near the *Daishi* hall, bows of white paper are tied onto the low branch of a pine tree, which has grown back into the trunk in a near-perfect circle. Called *omikuji*, these paper fortunes are purchased at temples throughout the pilgrimage for a ¥5 donation. The custom for bad fortunes is to fold up the strip of paper and tie it to a pine tree. Since the word for "pine tree" (*matsu*) and the verb "to wait" (*matsu*) are similar, the bad luck waits by the tree instead of staying with the person, because fate is easily fooled by puns.

A *henro* couple near the exit confirm my directions to T22. Thankfully, it's all downhill. Through a clearing I can see a lighthouse far below, perched at the edge of where the earth drops off. Beyond it, forested islands float in the Pacific.

A surge of emotion catches in my throat.

The climbs I've feared for days are past and I'm still standing, albeit slightly desiccated atop Tasered legs. Tomorrow's trek is all on flat ground, and that night I'll be soaking in a hot tub beside the ocean, victorious over Shikoku's first province. I'm calculating distances, estimating when I'll reach the *zenkonyado* tonight, when I'll reach the *onsen* tomorrow, and I hear it again: *Be here now.*

A slow inhalation is all it takes to notice the pleasant breeze and forgiving patches of shade. I kick the large rocks underfoot down the mountainside, clearing the path for the *henro* behind me, and begin walking meditation to stay closer to the moment. My concentration breaks frequently to dodge trucks trundling down the narrow bends until I emerge from the forest back onto flat ground.

I'm recovering at a roadside rest hut when Hiroki joins me on the bench. We'd seen each other at T21, but hadn't spoken since he was too embarrassed by his limited English and I was too wiped to swing an imaginary bat. Offering him my water, I beat him to the punch.

"*Atsui, desu ne?*"

"*Hai, atsui,*" he laughs.

It's roasting, but Hiroki is taking no chances with sunlight. Besides khaki trousers, he wears black spandex sleeves that stretch from his fingertips to the hem of his T-shirt. I'm astounded by this, and by his twelve-ounce water bottle purchased from a *conbini*[5]. Even with basketball shorts and a T-shirt, I'm leaking about twelve ounces a minute, and would be wearing a loincloth if it was still culturally acceptable. Hiroki, on the other hand, is surprised I'm not more covered up. He's also puzzled why I'm camping out every night, which seems uncomfortable. Hiroki spends his nights at *ryokans,* small hotels for *henro,* which explains his gray daypack containing two changes of clothes. Curious, we exchange each other's packs, testing the weight. He groans as he hoists mine to his shoulders, and I enviously lift his with two fingers. Nodding at

5 Convenience store

each other's excellent taste in fanny packs, we decide to join up for the day.

Hiroki's journey is the same as many of the elderly *henro* here, but started decades earlier. Having recently retired from his job in electronics, he now walks the pilgrimage to decide his next path. Our conversation turns to music, but doesn't get very far. He loves Guns N' Roses, which he knows through playing *Rock Band*, and despite his many questions I can only tell him so much about Slash, Axl, and *Chinese Democracy*. He soon exhausts his English, and since no monsters are attacking, my Japanese is useless. Just as our conversation is faltering, a loud screech from a nearby orchard stops us in our tracks.

I wheel toward the sound, tightening my grip on the staff.

An alpha macaque leaps down from the stone retaining wall onto the road, growling as he stalks toward us. He resembles a baby yeti, with his pink face and puffy silver coat. His dark, furious eyes bore into me. The females gather behind him, some cradling infants to their breasts.

The alpha rears on bowed legs and bares his teeth in a demonic laughing grin. Growling, he marks his territory. An amber stream steams across the concrete. Another, louder screech and I choke up on my staff, prepared to swing at his head like Ichiro if he charges and stab him with whatever shard I'm left holding. Our eyes meet, locking each other into this standoff until Hiroki puts his hand on my shoulder and motions that I should not fight the monkey with a stick. The alpha hurls simian slurs at our backs as we walk away.

The adrenaline subsides once we've entered a bamboo grove. It's a peaceful place. The dense foliage absorbs outside sounds so completely that the world becomes the creak of stalks rubbing together and the slow swoosh of fluttering leaves, the susurrus as eternal as waves on a beach. Slowing our pace, Hiroki and I walk in meditative silence until I realize the black-fly *henro* has stopped buzzing around me. There's a tickling on my shoulder, and I slap hard. Three fingers come back covered in blood. The fly falls to the ground dazed, but shakes it off in time to dodge my stomping foot and escape. Given the heft of him, I'd need a hammer to finish the job. Hiroki wipes off the rest of the blood from my shoulder with my bandana, and I wonder how many more animals I'll grow to hate this week.

The forest empties back onto the flat asphalt and open sky of farmland leading to **Byodoji: The Temple of Equality (T22)**. The temple is so named as the *honzon* Bhaisajya-guru Tathagata saves all from disease, regardless of age, sex, rank, or race, unlike all those other Buddhas known for their discrimination and prejudice. We bow at the gate, where the pudgy *Nios*' expressions reflect less terrifying rage than impotent betrayal that someone's eaten the last Ho Ho. Once inside, Hiroki and I groan at the *honzon* shrine perched at the end of a long stairway, as they always are at the end of a hard day's walk. We part to say our same prayers for different reasons: him to find his next path in life, me for the health of those along my own. Outside the temple we purchase each other a soda as *osse-tai* and depart, him to his *ryokan*, me to the *zenkonyado*.

Withdrawing the free-lodging printout from my fanny pack, I'm directed across a red bridge to a local hardware/gardening store, but not told who to speak to. I wander aisles containing every type of seed and floral straw hat known to man, like a spy searching for my contact. The woman at the front desk clears her throat.

"*Atsui, desu ne?*" she asks

"*Hai, atsui,*" I reply and give the code word: "*Zenkonyado?*"

She nods to her seven-year-old, who puts down his pricing gun. I'm led to a one-room house where I'm handed a paper bag and pointed to the weeds poking out of the walkway. After dumping the full bag in the compost, I've earned my stay. I slide open the doors.

This one is posh compared to the previous *zenkonyado*, with a functioning lock and no list of murderers. Also, there's a freezer with Popsicles, of which I eat more than I should while checking the map for tomorrow's walk. Twenty-seven miles away is my *onsen*, twice the distance I just traversed. It's the length of the Seattle Marathon, which I've only done once, on a brisk fall day, and I wasn't carrying forty extra pounds on my back. However, I know I'll make it. I've survived the *nansho* temples, and this is all horizontal. After a week's worth of sponge baths in bathroom sinks, I'll finally feel clean again.

I'm wrapping the cover of my map book in duct tape

to keep it from dissolving further in my sweat when the door slides open. The *henro* couple who gave me directions to T22 enter, carrying grocery bags. In their late twenties and cheery, they kneel across from each other at the short dinner table and place a variety of bento sushi containers in between them. Breaking their chopsticks apart, they dig in.

My stomach growling, I head to the grocery store and buy dinner, breakfast, and more Popsicles, feeling guilty that these *henro* have none. I restock the freezer and hand them each an icy dessert.

Like me, they began their journey from the Asakusa neighborhood of Tokyo, where they work in advertising. Newlyweds, they're hiking the Tokushima section for their honeymoon and will return home after reaching T23 tomorrow. Completing the pilgrimage a section at a time is a common practice due to the constraints on many *henro*'s lives. Known as *ikkoku-mari henro*, it's considered equal to completing the trail all at once. Without the benefit of an overnight bus to bring me back to Shikoku from my home across the ocean, I am a *toshiuchi henro*, in it for the long haul.

The husband is a Shotokan karate black belt and we discuss our different branches, the benefits and challenges of soft- versus hard-style karate. He misses the constant practice, patting a belly gone soft from hours at a desk. Though impressed by my dedication, they laugh at my plans to reach the ocean by sunset tomorrow.

Maybe a Shotokan student can't do it, I think with

arrogance earned from a martial arts regimen that involved doing sit-ups while getting hit in the stomach with an iron bar, *but Kyokushin students are stronger.*

Once the sun sets, the day of two *nansho* temples catches up to us quickly and we're soon snoring.

The *henro* couple departs before dawn. I meditate and stretch in silence. After a potassium-rich breakfast of halibut and bananas to stem the muscle cramps still plaguing me, I set off on the longest distance I've ever hiked. Ivy swallows every shape along the morning's pathway as the hours pass along Highway 55, which extends through most of Kochi province. I catch up to the couple, who pump their fists and cheer, "*Ganbatte* (do your best)!" They overtake me when I pause outside a rustic Shinto temple built on the lumpy forest ground. "*Ganbatte!*" I cheer, putting on my knee braces. When I catch up again, she snaps a picture of the crazy *gaijin henro* who thinks he can walk twenty-seven miles in a day and we exchange contact information. The picture never comes and their business card melts in my damp fanny pack. Somewhere behind me they reach T23 and return home to their married life in Tokyo, planning their next trip to Kochi for their anniversary.

As the couple recedes into the distance a dull ache of loneliness hits for the first time. I have no one to share this with. None of my friends were dumb enough to leave their careers, so I'm left to capture the strange details of each day with my camera and journal. The oddity of a restaurant sign with a joyful squid offering up a disembodied child's head. The terror of walking through ten highway tunnels with only a thin painted line separating me from the trucks roaring past, exiting with a blackened left arm from hugging the walls. The confusion of why I keep hearing gunshots in the distance and an air-raid siren midday, as I check the sky for bombers or Eva Unit deployment. The excitement of seeing those first ocean-born cumulonimbus clouds stumbling over the green mountains. I take my pictures, record it in my journal, and it all feels slightly hollow.

Yakuoji: The Temple of the Medicine King (T23) is where I really need a witness as I experience a "Mr. Sparkle" moment. On a cigarette machine outside T23, the bodybuilder spokesman is my doppelganger. It's a beefier, alternate-reality version, where my love of smoking equals my love of anabolic steroids, but it's the same hazel eyes and chrome dome, with my caveman brow and jaw. If there weren't an *onsen* in my future, I'd stand by the sign flexing to see if anyone notices.

As usual, a steep staircase leads to the *honzon* shrine of T23, where two Yakushi statues sit back to back. According to legend, Kukai carved the first *honzon* in 815, which flew away to the distant Mount Tamazushi when the temple burned in 1188. When T23 was rebuilt, a new *honzon* was carved. During the dedication the old Yakushi flew back from the mountain, I assume out of jealousy. Model ships are scattered throughout the temple grounds, representing the sailors saved by Yakushi's intervention.

Climbing further stairs to the balcony of a red pagoda, I take in the view from the last temple in Tokushima. Homes are clumped up to the edge of the wide, curving tributary emptying into Hiwasa Bay, where waves crash against a sea stack with a 'fro of vegetation. Beyond spreads the Pacific, opaque as mercury. I hear *Be here now* and think *Way ahead of you*.

Tokushima is complete, and my prize waits beside the ocean. I return to the city sidewalks, where spiny acorns are scattered across the concrete like burr pods, waiting for a giant's pant cuff to carry them far away. Back on the open highway, the ocean's presence becomes more frequent. It comes into view between mountains, and the scent of rotting seaweed wafts in the air.

By late afternoon I've walked twenty miles and have to rest on the lip of a shallow canal. Herons bat at each other with outstretched wings, staking their claims to the fish returning to the sea. With the temperature peaking, my brain has fuzzed to the point that left and right turns require double-checking my hands. A van pulls up beside me and the driver offers a ride. I politely decline, committed to walking the entire distance. Thinking I've misheard, since no sane person would be out in this heat, the driver opens the door. A wave of cold air gushes out. He repeats, "*Ossetai.*"

When I decline again, his resigned shrug says it all: *Your funeral.*

I return to the road. Sun blisters bubble on my calves, and there's soft sobbing from inside my shoes, but when my feet are in the ocean and my limbs are in the *onsen*, it'll be worth it.

Hours later I reach the side temple beside the road and let out a celebratory whoop. Today, after walking a marathon, I won. Desperate to drop my pack before heading to the shore, I knock on the door and wait.

No answer.

Maybe I'm at the wrong entrance, or the wrong building. Following a garden path, I pass through rows of crops, then a forest, then trespass through some fields, then return directly back to the front door.

I knock again.

No answer.

I knock harder.

This isn't fair. I've been waiting for this *onsen* for two days. I woke extra early and walked a dozen hours to get here. I planned this all out. Why is no one letting me in? I check the time. It's after 6 p.m. The temple must have closed. No *onsen*, and again, no place to sleep. The crushing disappointment is tempered only by my exhaustion. After a few more knocks, I call out again. And again, no answer.

I give up.

Below the highway I set up my tent in a dry, plowed field within the scent of the ocean, as well as the nearby garbage dump. Everything aches and I missed the *onsen*, but I still deserve something for the effort. Passing the concrete barrier to the sand, I dip a finger in the Pacific where Kochi province begins and proclaim, "Good enough."

Inside my tent, I lie in my sleeping bag. Jagged dirt clumps dig into my back through the fabric. Then it begins to rain. Birds sing happily. I groan. In less than six tries I get the rain fly set up, shove the entire pack into the one-person tent to keep dry, and contort my body across it to fit.

Nine days ago I arrived on Shikoku, certain that I was physically and mentally prepared for this journey. By T12, that confidence was gone. Every day since has been a reminder that I'm weaker and less capable than I thought, causing my hopes for this pilgrimage to lower from "Change your life" to "Anger fewer animals."

Still, I made it this far on an ancient path in a foreign land where I saw myself all those years ago. Splayed over my backpack in my cramped tent next to a garbage dump, with sharp clods poking into my back and blisters growing on my feet, I close my eyes and listen to the birds sing.

SECTION TWO

KOCHI: THE LAND OF
ASCETIC TRAINING

6
THE CAVE AT CAPE MUROTO

Ten days earlier.

AN HOUR BEFORE the overnight bus departs for Shikoku, I'm kneeling at a short lacquered table in Tokyo's oldest tempura restaurant. Across from me are my friends Miwa and Tomo, fellow karate students who've moved back to their native Japan. Since I arrived at Narita airport, bearing our dojo's T-shirts and butchering the phrase *"Please accept these humble gifts,"* we've been racing through the futuristic megalopolis. All day I've been trailing behind as they arranged my bus ticket to Shikoku and completed their own last-minute chores before departing to Hawaii for their wedding. Finally, there's a moment to relax and share a meal before our separate journeys. Moon-faced and petite, Miwa does most of the talking as her fiancé, Tomo, who in both height and physical density resembles a polite oak tree, nods along. With a bottle of sake between us, Miwa asks the big question.

"Why are you going to be a Shikoku *henro*?"

"Because it sounds amazing," I grin.

Of the numerous reasons, ranging from life direction to sword acquisition, it's the easiest to translate. Miwa nods, hoping for a deeper reason to relay to her friends and coworkers, who are astounded that an American has even heard of such a faraway place. The pilgrimage isn't covered in school curricula, and it's said that most Japanese people have visited Paris before setting foot on Shikoku. None of Miwa's friends have even met a *henro*, since everyone but the retired are too busy to take off the two to three months required for such a demanding endeavor. The reigning consensus amongst her friends is respect for my dedication to this physical and spiritual journey, and also that I am insane. Living up to the stereotype of the crazy, it all seems completely reasonable to me.

"Be careful." Miwa cautions. "It is very hot this year." What she means is that the summer temperatures are at their highest since recordkeeping began in 1898.

"I'll be fine." I reassure her. "It's hot in Seattle, too."

Miwa nods, her lips tight.

I nod back, oblivious to her reasonable concern.

With dollhouse-size sake cups we toast to our separate adventures. Tomorrow, Miwa and Tomo will join their families and friends on the beach to celebrate their union. In an hour, I'll be leaving to walk alone in the countryside.

The rice wine warms my fingertips, then my stomach. It's the last booze I'll drink for two months.

"Will you achieve enlightenment?" Miwa teases.

"Sure." I laugh. "Anything is possible."

It's not the first time someone has asked. I have no idea what enlightenment looks like, but I do expect some type of spiritual epiphany after so much walking meditation. Giggling, Miwa bows in reverence to the holy man on a journey. Tomo chuckles and bows as well. I bless them with my beaded bracelet before cracking up. My bus will be arriving soon, and we agree to meet up again when I return to Tokyo so I can tell them about the trip.

By then they will be married. I have no idea who I will be.

The neon-lit neighborhood of Asakusa blinks above me as I navigate the concrete canyons alongside some of its thirteen million inhabitants. Animated characters caper across skyscrapers, and robot women in maid outfits beckon from balconies. Even this feels more like home than where I'm heading: a vast, depopulated expanse of forest, field, and sea. Near the bus stop I pick up an amulet from the ground, its patterned cloth folded around a Buddha stamped in gold leaf. Assuming that someone needs its protection more, I put it back and catch the overnight bus to Tokushima Transit Center, filled with hope for what lies ahead.

Ten days later.

On my first morning in Kochi, "The Land of Ascetic

Training," I meditate on a bench downwind of the garbage dump. I'm groggy and pissed off from a night spent with my cramped legs tangled over the pack, and my back aches from the sharp dirt clods. I'm straining to focus all the way through one inhalation when my off-balance pack beside me slumps off the bench to the ground. Without thought I leap from my meditation, grab my pack's fabric in a fist, and start punching, yelling at it for being so lightly packed and still so heavy, for slowing me down, for making this so hard. A couple minutes later I stop beating the inanimate object I'm swearing at and return to my meditation, thinking of Kochi's other name: "The Devil's Country."

The wildest section of the pilgrimage, in the old days pilgrims faced regular checkpoints and travelers without proper papers were lucky if the locals turned them back with a beating and not a branding. In this place of storm-wracked tides and rough forest paths, the landscape and people were considered so tough and frightening that for centuries a large pile of human shit sat at the province's exit, where travelers demonstrated their opinion of Kochi.

The locals have since softened towards *henro*. The landscape has not.

Considerably harder than the other three, Kochi is the longest province in Shikoku, comprising a third of the distance but only a fifth of the temples. Traveling alongside the Pacific for long, abandoned stretches, I'll swoop down the first peninsula to Cape Muroto, where historically Kukai gained enlightenment, and complete Kochi after the second peninsula, Cape Ashizuri, where historically *henro* kill themselves.

With all that to look forward to, I might as well get started.

I can't even look in the *onsen*'s direction as I trudge past. Even after waking up so early yesterday and walking a marathon, all I proved is that my best effort so far isn't enough here. It burns knowing it may never be. In worse shape than my ego are my feet, which paid the bigger price yesterday and deserve a reward. A narrow dirt path leads to the shore. There I'll revive my morale and my arches.

Red crabs scatter to defensive positions along the trailside, waving their tiny claws in menace. A few steps into the Pacific and I'm renewed. The cool tide recedes, drawing my tension out with it. Then the next wave washes tiny pebbles between my sandals and my tenderized feet. Each jagged facet now distinct underfoot, I return to the path, apologizing with each step on the long stretch of highway that separates me from breakfast.

An old man bicycles toward me on the main street of a seaside town. Steering with one hand, he holds the other vertical to the center of his chest. I return his respectful bow. It's the first of many hospitable gestures in Kochi, where the locals are either overcompensating for their reputation or pitying what a *henro* endures here. When I purchase breakfast in a small shop purveying groceries and sponges for washing tractors, the owner seats me beneath a shaded awning and returns with a cup of watery coffee.

My legs swing freely as I watch thumb-size blue jellyfish pulsate in a clear plastic jug next to me. A bow, an *osame-fuda*, and I'm off with an improved disposition.

The rising sun silhouettes fishermen perched on coolers beneath a bridge, waiting for a tug on their line to reanimate. It boils the ocean into white pillars, the heads turning charcoal gray as they unfurl against the troposphere. In the atmospheric gales, the columns collapse toward the shore, breaking open upon Kochi's sharp peaks. The first curtain of rain falls just as I exit a highway tunnel. Ducking back inside, I dig through my bag for the poncho buried somewhere at the bottom. Once unwrapped from the packaging, it takes some trial and error and elbow hyperextension to get the rear of it up and over my pack. Finally, I exit the tunnel.

The rain stops immediately.

A few hours later it begins again. I break for lunch in a seaside café staffed and patronized by surfers, the air filled with laid-back vowels. The weather hasn't improved by the time I've paid for my meal. Beneath the café's awning I flail my arms backward to get the poncho over the top of my pack. With the assistance of two surfers I finally step out from the overhang protected.

The downpour ceases.

A magic, rain-expelling poncho. Not a bad deal for $5.99.

The storm clouds remain ahead of me for the rest of the day. Walking meditation remains more difficult than I expected, my concentration broken constantly by the exhaustion and heat. By midafternoon I'm applying sunblock for the third time on a bench at a small public beach. Bright surfboards bob like kites in the waves, strings hooked to their riders' ankles as they search for that one curling whitecap to bring them back to shore. My exposed limbs UV-proofed, I toss a few yen into the upturned hat of a guitarist channeling Jimmy Buffett and head off. A mile down the road, following the same weather principles as when you've waxed your car, the sunblock melts off beneath a cloudburst. $5.99 worth of poncho buys no more magic. The drops only get fatter as I rush for shelter.

I slip inside an open-air garage that doubles as a restaurant. Three freshly waxed boards hang from the wall next to an iron grill hooked up to the attached home. A grandmother in a maroon plaid dress emerges from the hallway. I motion apologetically outside and am guided to a lawn chair at a flimsy plastic table. As I watch the puddles grow, she returns with a plate of rice balls and grapes, refuses my money, and disappears back into the house. Soon the shower dissipates. I hoist my pack, then set it back down.

I haven't thanked her.

Guilty, I wander through the hallway and knock on doors, startling children watching TV, surfers waxing their boards on a back patio, and a grandfather reading in his study. I'm asking for what I hope is "*grandmother/ old woman*," but given that I can't pronounce "Seattle" in three tries, it could be anything. This slowly dawns on me, as well as the fact that no family wants a towering bald stranger soaking their wood floors and bursting through doorways to mumble gibberish at them. It's time to cut my losses and leave. Cheeks flushed, I head back to the garage, where the grandmother catches up with me.

A bow, an *osamefuda*, and I flee into the growing darkness.

Farther along the highway is Toyo Town, where my map shows a few rest huts that I have no chance of reaching after my detours from downpours and adventure in home-invasion. Heavy drops begin spattering through the overhanging branches. With no rest huts nearby, I'm preparing for a miserable night of field-testing the tent's rain fly when I pass an unmarked temple off the main path. A monk sits below the eaves, washing a scruffy dog. Bowing respectfully at the gate, I ask "*Tsuyado?*" with a tone somewhere between hopeful query and outright begging. The exhaustion of thirteen miles today is piling on top of the twenty-seven miles from yesterday and a night spent sleeping on rough earth. The monk nods and rises, welcoming me into a courtyard so inundated that a crab feeds in between the stones. The dog pads along with splashing footfalls as the monk leads me to a small hut in the corner.

Once inside I do a respectful but joyous dance, especially grateful as the pattering on the metal roof picks up in volume and tempo. Unlike on my first night, I no longer take shelter like this for granted. Still, finding it out of sheer luck bothers me. Luck here means something didn't go wrong that should have, and eventually it runs out.

A picture frame hangs on the wall with the different colors of *osamefuda* fanned out behind the glass. Sold in packs of two hundred, they all have the same design: a rectangular paper strip with a seated Kukai on top and running down the center kanji that reads dedication: traveling with *kobo daishi* along the pilgrimage to the 88 temples of shikoku. The color represents the number of times the *henro* has completed the pilgrimage. First-time pilgrims like me carry white slips. After five completed circuits, *henro* upgrade to green *osamefuda*, then red (eight), bronze (twenty-five), and gold (fifty). Those who've completed one hundred or more carry brocade *osamefuda*, woven fabric glued onto strips of poster board. Also known as *nishiki,* they're considered such valuable protection amulets that locals will dig through the tin boxes outside the shrines to find one.

I'm envious of the knowledge that spread of color represents. It's experience I want now, downloaded *Matrix*-style into my brain, so I can bypass these beginner mistakes and focus on the deeper reasons I'm here. It's the same envy I felt as a white belt in karate, sparring with black belts like my sensei, or my Japanese classmate Tomo, the polite oak tree. With only a thin grasp of the basics, every move I knew was easily countered, resulting in a regular series of ass-kickings. Even a solid blow, perfectly landed, resulted only in a grunt of "good" before an uppercut knocked the wind from my lungs. Humbled and bruised up, I am a white belt again, using all my skills and still flailing. In karate, advancing to a new color of belt meant hundreds of hours of dojo training each year, and accepting that it would take a thousand more to earn the black belt. I don't have that kind of time here, so this journey will end up as I expected: a lot of walking and not much talking before I return to work.

Predawn, I meditate to ceremonial drumming mixed with the thrumming downpour on the roof, then venture into the rain to watch the end of the ritual. Kneeled before the *honzon* in the main hall, the monk beats the drumhead. The tempo slows, then ends. He bows to the shrine, and I'm free to move again.

The resident priest wanders up while I'm putting in my contacts at an outdoor sink. He fingers one of the three beaded bracelets on my wrist, a jade stone surrounded by dried Bodhi seeds. It was given to me by the priest of Seattle's Shingon temple when I'd stopped by to ask for some pre-pilgrimage advice. After he placed the bracelet on my wrist, where it joined one given by a friend and another blessed by a Korean monk on a mountaintop, the Seattle priest solemnly intoned, in broken English, "It is the journey you need."

I nodded respectfully, thinking about swords.

Here in this temple's courtyard, the priest is more interested in the tattoos on my shoulders. He's pleased by my explanations of the wolf and the cranes, or by my pantomimed barking and flapping. A bow, an *osamefuda*, a scratch behind the temple dog's ears, and I head into the rain with my formerly magic poncho.

On a bridge spanning a sandbar, a heron and I are

the only witnesses to the dawn sky, haunted by the gray specter of rain. After a couple of hours on a road empty of shops and cars I reach Highway 55, where I'll spend the rest of my day and most of my time in Kochi.

Weaving down the coastline, Highway 55 separates the rippling ocean from the towering mountain chain with one cacophonous concrete ribbon. On my left, the churning sea crashes against the sands and carves rivulets into the boulders beyond the shore. On my right, a retaining wall with a tall chain-link fence keeps the lush chaos of vines from pouring across the road into the sea. Hidden inside, monkeys shriek, birds caw, and cicadas hum. Ahead of me is the unchanging view I'll come to know as Kochi, emerald walls undulating into the distance, where a glittering ocean arcs into a cloud-streaked sky.

The other common sight and sound is the diesel roar of road construction crews, breaking the monotony of the walk as they stop traffic to wave me through. Their orange roadwork signs live up to the stereotype of this being the most outwardly polite culture. On American signs, it's men in hard hats fixing the road. On Japanese signs, it's men in hard hats bowing in apology for fixing the road. The road crews are the only people around, and midway through the day I remember being warned about this first stretch in Kochi, that it's seven or eight miles without shops, toilets, or homes. I didn't stock up on extra water as they instructed. Thankfully, it's overcast, so I sip rather than having to chug.

Another mistake, another lucky break.

After hours of ceaseless footfalls on flat concrete, I take advantage of the new scenery and descend the sea-wall staircase to the beach. Interlocking concrete tetra-pods lay half buried in the sand, extending far into the waves. Resembling a scattering of toy jacks thrown by a giant 1940s tyke, they form jumbled breakers to distract the ocean's attention from the shore. Hoisting myself up on one of their concrete arms, I scamper across the tet-rapods. The shifting pack increases the challenge, further breaking the tedium until I return to the sands. There are no stairs ahead, so I climb a worn metal ladder back to the highway. At the top of the rusty rungs, I discover that a frayed nylon rope is all that holds the ladder to the wall, probably not tested for 230-plus pounds. I look down at the hard sand far below.

Another mistake, yet another lucky break.

Eight hours after leaving the temple this morning I reach Muroto City, where, finally, there's something to see besides mountains, ocean, and bright sky. A rock-hewn path cuts through the craggy boulders tumbled across the shoreline, ending at Hotsu-Misakiji Cave. A millennium ago, a man's life changed inside its stone walls.

In 792, an aristocratic youth named Saeki no Mao defied his parents and dropped out of State Confucian College. Seeking the deeper truths of reality, he devoted himself to becoming an itinerant mountain ascetic. At age nineteen, while wandering through his home island of Shikoku, he entered a cave on Cape Muroto. Focusing his meditation on where the sea and sky met, he pledged to remain there until he achieved enlightenment. Three years later, while performing the esoteric Morning Star Meditation[6], he saw the morning star appear in the sky and enter his mouth, and he became enlightened. Taking a new name based on the focus of his meditation, where the sky (*ku*) and ocean (*kai*) meet, Kukai left the cave, dedicating his life to helping all mankind. With further insight gained from his time as the disciple of a revered Chinese master, he would found the Shingon school, which advocates that enlightenment, the realization of the oneness of all things, can be reached in one lifetime through meditation and hard work.

As I leave the same cave on my way to T24, I also look out to where the sea and sky meet. I have neither the time nor the dedication for it to be anything more than a horizon. I'd been hoping for some kind of spiritual epiphany on the pilgrimage, but that was expecting too much. A week and a half into Shikoku, when twenty-one miles ends with eight hundred stairs to the temple, my hopes involve retaining knee cartilage.

The *Nio* of **Hotsu-Misakiji: Cape Muroto Temple (T24)** glow firefly green from the moss creeping across their flowing robes. The courtyard is a sterile patch of crushed rock and carved stone bordered by the Gordian knot vines of a subtropical jungle. A priest leads the last bus *henro* group of the night through the sutras. I stand

---

6 Repetition of the mantra of the bodhisattva Kokuzo while visualizing Kokuzo in the form of the morning star (Venus)

apart, chanting my own, while the jungle's inhabitants compete to be heard over the din. When they begin the long chant of *Hannya Shingyo*, the priest wanders amongst the *henro,* giving each a benediction by rubbing his staff on their backs in a circle. Without a pause, he does the same for me. The group moves on to the stamp office, and I move on to the *Daishi* shrine.

While reciting the sutras to Kukai, a few women from the group join in. Outside of synagogue, I've never chanted in a group. Even joined by three elderly voices— in a new language, in a new religion, in the middle of a jungle—there's a spiritual depth to it. For a moment, this exhausting path is holy again. However, I'll later question if a holy sutra means as much if you lose your place in the middle while killing a mosquito. Shaking the priest's hand in thanks, I bow and descend the steps, planning to bed down behind a public toilet at the bottom of the hill.

Midway down the path, a gazebo overlooking the cape is a much better shelter option. I dive through a swarm of mosquitoes into my tent, hunting down the few that slipped in. Settling in for a night on concrete, I've learned one lesson in Kochi: Lower your expectations enough, and you'll be happy no matter where you sleep.

7
THE WHALING MUSEUM

OUTSIDE MY TENT an army of mosquitoes is assembled, their high-pitched whine hovering above the ocean's distant roar. During the night a crisp sea breeze shut off my sweat glands for the first time on Shikoku, allowing the dirt, oil, and salt from the day's walk to congeal. All morning the mosquitoes' antennae have been receiving an agitating broadcast through my tent's mesh walls. Now they are clamoring for blood. I crouch by the entrance flap, shaking the aerosol can of repellent.

In one motion I unzip the tent and rush headlong through the onslaught, preceded by a chemical storm front. The mosquitoes charge undaunted. I strike wildly as another battalion invades my tent to attack the remaining specter of heat and stink. The first *henro* of the morning wanders by. Our eyes meet as I wallop myself with flailing limbs. Wordlessly, he turns away toward the temple.

Packing my gear, I set out to explore Tosa Bay. Except for the morning's battle, I'm in no rush. Besides a couple of temples, there's only one destination for the day: the Whaling Museum.

I set a leisurely pace along the hiking path to enjoy my new environment. Cape Muroto's subtropical weather stands apart from the rest of Shikoku's humid, subtemperate climate. Blooming red hibiscus breaks the ever-present forest-green. Palm fronds sway in the ocean breeze, and the grasping roots of strangler figs envelop ten-foot boulders like greedy octopi. On the rocky beach, waves swirl around vertical pillars of turbidite, slabs of mud and sand compressed over eons, then shoved upright by the subterranean churn of magma. Offshore, two-story concrete walls shield the fishing boats moored inside the bay, and peppermint-striped lighthouses stand guard on every quay, scanning for a distant pair of eyes to warn.

Returning to the highway, I keep searching for the balance between focus and awareness. With my eyes locked on the road ahead, I enter a meditative calm where time slows. It disappears as I turn my head, not wanting to miss the jade waterways snaking through the locks, docks, and harbors into the open sea. Floating sidewalks bob in the currents, and canals bisect the roads leading to **Shinshoji: The Temple of the Illuminating Seaport (T25)**. Here, fishermen pray for safety to the thousand tiny Jizo statues enshrined beside the *honzon*, each steering a ship's wheel.

According to legend, Lord Yamanouchi of the Kochi Castle was saved from shipwreck by his devotion to the Jizo, who took control of the helm during a storm and steered him to safety. The steep staircase is worth the panorama of the bay, where bonito-fishing boats wobble out of the harbor to find their catch.

On the way to T26, fox-like Shiba Inu and Akita dogs guard the residential shops and homes. Early in the morning they'd be barking incessantly until this white stranger is out of sight, but the midday sun presses them flat against the sidewalks, their tongues lolling in the shade. The soft lap of waves and the muted hum of shoppers is broken by an air-raid klaxon, and I scan the horizon for the danger I keep missing.

The pathway soon crooks behind the mountains through lush rice fields, and a steep hike brings me to **Kongochoji: Vajra Peak Temple (T26)**. The tangled woods add to T26's fairy-tale atmosphere, as does the Yakushi Nyorai statue inside the main hall. It's so ornate and lifelike that, according to legend, it walked to the altar after the carver's final stroke. Given the artisan's skill, this I'd buy. The *Daishi* hall contains a camphor tree where Kukai, talented in his own right, carved his own image after chasing away the winged Tengu demons that had resided inside the trunk for a century. Brass plates on the main hall's wall depict Kukai kicking the Tengu out and meditating peacefully (but in triumph!) inside the trunk. I complete my final prayers of the day.

Now it's time for something completely different: a museum of whales.

Face to face with the stamp office monk, I realize I don't know the word for either "whale" or "museum." With no other *henro* in the stamp office to assist, the monk waits patiently behind the counter as I pantomime scanning the horizon with my leg propped on the imaginary bow of my ship. My hand shielding my eyes from the harsh Pacific sun, I thrust my staff overhand like a harpoon and reel it back in. The monk remains perplexed, understandably, so I take a scrap of paper and draw a picture of sad whale getting harpoon-stabbed by a stick figure in a boat. He nods and draws me a map on the other side of the page.

Eyes locked on the directions, I follow it through the forest.

This area was once famous as a whaling district, and some former whale hunters now run whale-watching tours. Though it's the end of the whales' annual migration season, the entire time I've been keeping an eye on the waves, hoping to catch a slick hump breaching the surface. Whales are one of those creatures my generation was taught to revere by bumper stickers and *Captain Planet*, but for me they go nearly as deep as ninjas. One of my earliest memories is of a family vacation to the San Juan Islands, holding on to my mother's calf as she pointed out the glass doors at a pod of humpbacks cresting in the chilly Salish Sea. The last time I saw whales I was ten years old, in the San Juans again, on a whale-watching tour.

The entire time I had spouted off all kinds of facts to the captain in that way that when you're younger you believe will impress people, but instead signals to the adults that you're not losing your virginity till way past high school. It's another obsession that never really left. If anyone besides Kukai was with me on the slippery, rock-strewn descent through the trees to the seaside museum, I'd still be telling them about how songs sung by one whale pod are mimicked and recited by different pods all over the world, and that their hearts are the size of cars with arteries you can swim through.

The Whaling Museum is a nondescript circle of tan plaster walls. A harpoon gun points me to the automatic sliding doors, where I enter a typical natural-history museum. The gift shop by the exit sells plastic whale figurines and toys for the science kids, anime and plastic nunchucks for their rambunctious siblings, and sushi keychains for the adults.

The effusively sweet women at the counter gesture for me to leave my pack in the lobby. I shrug it off atop a chair that settles with an audible creak, then drop my yen into a vending machine beside the curtained entrance to the main hall. The ticket dispenses along with a souvenir postcard of a majestic heart-shaped tail breaking above the surface, water sluicing off the tips. They tear my ticket, I pocket the card, bid my hated pack adieu for the moment, and walk through the curtain.

An undersea panorama covers the walls of the curving, blue-lit corridor. Blue, gray, and minke whales navigate the tranquil ocean alongside schools of porpoises searching playfully for their dinner. Manta rays flap their wings in pursuit of mackerel, and massive sunfish power their way through the watery expanse.

Emerging into the main exhibit I find that the hallway isn't a diorama, it's a picture menu, and I'm in a warehouse of whale slaughter. Display cases house the giant blades, saws, flensing knives, and hooks used to tear these creatures apart. A shiver crawls up to my neck. I take a deep breath and continue. A blue whale hangs from the ceiling above a reconstruction of a traditional Japanese whaling canoe, the thirty-foot hull brightly colored with orange and red blossoms and green oak leaves. Across the wall hang woodblock prints, illustrating the seventeenth-century style of whaling, where dozens of boats encircle the whale, making a racket to drive it into nets wielded by a second group. Once their prey is entangled, harpooners row up and stab the beast until it dies of exhaustion.

In the first painting, canoes of loin-clothed hunters surround a whale thrashing in the surf, a volcanic spurting wound turning the sea red beneath it. On closer inspection I see another harpooner has leapt onto the whale's head. Minuscule in scale, he grasps for purchase on the slick blubber, stabbing through the colossal skull with a knife as long as his arm. Despite my disgust at the entire painting, I have to admit there have probably been few people as historically badass as someone willing to leap atop a thrashing leviathan to jam steel through its brain.

This takes balls you have to send an extra ship to carry, pure and simple.

In further paintings, the whale carcasses are dragged onto the shore and sliced crosswise into gigantic sashimi. Four groups on the shore push the arms of a windlass, the ropes hooked through the blubber peeling it from the muscle beneath. The entire village has collected to harvest this bounty. Bonfires, lanterns, and torches light the dusk sky. Vendors sell the fresh grilled meat to the geishas, travelers, and families gathered to watch the spectacle. To the right of these prints are photographs documenting the actual sights a couple of centuries later. Atop their kill that rocks listlessly in the surf, whalers flense the blubber with blades on six-foot poles while a crowd watches from the shore. The display cases below the pictures are filled with random whale parts: a collection of the conical teeth, a dried flipper used as a canvas for a ship painting, a bone katana, and a fetus in a jar next to a whale's vagina.

A balcony on the second level showcases the modern, more efficient Norwegian hunting method. It was these cannons and power-driven boats, introduced during the Meiji era, that turned whaling into a profitable business. Red and yellow rubber slickers hang next to a loaded harpoon gun pointing directly at the whale hanging from the ceiling. Examining the blunt point of the harpoon and dull iron grapples, I shudder, imagining the thud and the ragged wound punched into the blubbery flesh. With a newly formed appreciation of the vegetarian mentality, I've seen enough.

I pick up my pack at the front desk, where I'm handed a pamphlet with the title "Let's Cook" above an anthropomorphic whale wearing a chef's hat and licking his lips. A cannibal whale is disturbing, but worse is the cheeriness of the front-desk women, given the charnel house their museum contains. I look around at the gift shop again, hoping to see something reflecting the gruesome display behind the curtain. I find nothing, so I price-check the nunchucks, then pick up my pack, say goodbye to the receptionists, and walk out. I still can't shake the *Futurama* song "Whalers of the Moon" from my head, which has been on repeat since I first walked through the sliding doors. Nauseated, I take a seat on the shore. It's a familiar feeling that I recognize from my time as a student in Spain in 2003, on the day we attended a bullfight.

While the four vegetarians in our small group of liberal-arts majors chose not to join us for this cultural experience, the rest of us were curious enough to sit in the cheap seats high above the arena. We were there to put aside our preconceptions of what some American states consider a felony and discover what the locals see in this cultural touchstone. I liked cows much less than the steaks they provided, so I thought I'd be fine. I soon learned the difference between knowing my meal was at one point alive and watching thousands cheer a harried animal slowly getting stabbed to death. When a weakened bull finally collapsed from blood loss, the matador would jab a dagger into the back of its neck, cut off an ear, and toss it into the adoring crowd. A train of horses then dragged the carcass away, the blood-smeared sand was raked, and the process was repeated.

By the time the third and final matador of the day entered the gate into the arena, a few students had left. The rest of us were committed to seeing this through, still trying to understand the appeal. As each bull was dragged off to the crowd's delight, I was less and less able to see it as anything but cruel in the purest definition: a remorseless celebration of pain.

However, the last fight, featuring the top matador in all of Spain, was unforgettable.

We could see his skill even from high above in our cheap seats. Clad in crimson and gold, he spun with balletic grace away from the horns passing inches from his side, snapping the cape with a flourish. And unlike the others, he didn't wait for the bull to run itself to death. Facing down the charge, he threw his cape aside. Unleashing a battle cry that reached the back row to ring in our ears, he sprang from the earth, twisted in midair above the horns, drew his sword, and buried it to the hilt between the shoulder blades. The matador somersaulted, hit the dirt on his shoulder, and rolled effortlessly to his feet.

Frozen in place, the bull opened its mouth, its final bellow lost in a gush of blood. It slumped into the dirt beneath the locals' deafening roar. Cheers, wineskins, bread, roses, and seat cushions rained down upon the torn sand. The matador guzzled from one skin, wiping his mouth and offering it to his gathered entourage.

Outside the arena, the crowds disgorged as our group collected around our teacher, queasy and lightheaded from our cultural afternoon. The Texan in our group broke the silence.

"I'll be the only one to say it, but that was fucking awesome."

On both accounts, he was right.

The lesson was clear that day. We had just watched an animal get tortured to death, but what did the Spaniards see? The next day our teacher explained the ceremony, that the bulls up until the ritual stabbings have a much better life than the American cows herded in pens and killed with a bolt gun. In Spain, bull's beef is considered premium.

Similarly, from the Japanese perspective, whaling is as much a part of their culture as bullfights are to the Spanish or cattle-ranching is for the Southwest. The oldest surviving Japanese publication has a passage in which the first emperor of Japan eats whale meat, and some tribes, believing whales to be deities of the sea, built shrines to them before the hunt. The relationship was much like that between Native Americans and bison, and there is a famous Japanese proverb: "There's nothing to throw away from a whale except its voice." However, to alleviate the food scarcities following World War II, General MacArthur converted ships to whaling vessels to stop mass starvation in the country he'd just defeated. Thus began Japan's modern commercial whaling industry, which has decimated the species.

I leave the beach by the museum and return to

Highway 55. By early evening I have settled down for the night in a rest hut beside the shore. Until the sun sets I scan across the horizon, as I will every time I'm beside the Pacific, hoping to see that slick dark hump breach the ocean surface. I never do. The only whales I'll see on this pilgrimage are in snack form.

Still, I think back to the painting of the whale hunt, and of the lone man atop a thrashing titan. Armed only with pointed steel, he faces down death so his village can thrive.

And I gotta agree with the Texan: that's kinda fucking awesome.

8
THE WRONG SHOES

MY FEET DANGLE above the concrete as I meditate on the rest hut bench. With my right hand cradled in my left palm, my thumbs form a bridge. Breathing in as the irregular cars whoosh past, I exhale one final time to the ocean crash that fills the silence.

At peace, I open my eyes to another day beside the Pacific.

A monk in brown robes and his layman friend in slacks walk their miniature Dobermans past my rest hut. The layman whips around with a look of disbelief that I've come to know well, the same look I'd give an Inuit bull rider. Given that Westerners comprise about one out of every 41,667 *henro* each year, we are a rare sight. The monk stops to ask where I'm from. I reply, "America." He leaves it at that, and the imaginary baseball bat falls from my hand as they stroll off. Turning back to the Pacific, I take one last look, inhale slowly, and prepare for what comes next.

I slide off the bench, the ground presses into my feet, and all the calm shatters.

A month before leaving for Japan, I road-tested my newly purchased hiking shoes on a stroll circling suburban Mercer Island. They fared much better on the thirteen-mile loop than Murphy, the family dog I brought for company, so I considered the shoe issue solved. My mother, still keeping her eyes on me since the Tar Pits incident, decided she knew better and guilted me into buying another pair of hiking shoes a week before my flight. I left the extra pair with her and resumed the hectic preparations I should have completed months ago. With my backpack already over capacity, I could take only one pair and chose the ones I'd already broken in. But staying at my parents' home the night before my flight, where the untested shoes still resided in their original box, gave my mother one more chance to rescue me from the danger of making my own choices. While I frantically packed, unpacked, and repacked my backpack, she anxiously suggested the new shoes until, after a third argument, I finally broke down and agreed: "Fine, I'll bring the fucking shoes."

Because of "The Fucking Shoes," I wake every morning with cramping arches so intense that I'm scared I'll never run or walk normally again. Mornings are the worst, when the concrete punches through the rubber treads and metal plate into bone with every step. In those first few miles, until the throbbing ache fades into background noise, anger courses through me: at my mother for meddling, at myself for caving in against my better judgment, at the Japanese for not having larger feet. With each step I repeat the second oath of the *henro:* "Do not complain when things go wrong on the pilgrimage. Consider such experiences to be part of ascetic training."

This is a difficult oath to follow, as it directly contradicts my Jewish oath of "Kvetch[7], because, why not?"

I take a deep breath, and temper my temper with compassion. *Mom was only trying to help because she loves you, Dad too, and you love them ... just not right now. One day you'll try to help your children with something you don't understand, like pursuing a career, and you'll screw up too. Being angry now helps nothing, so focus on what is around you.* Then I take another step, and another, and grind my teeth as my metatarsal bones wail.

To my left, waves retreat and charge against the seawall. The narrow concrete span protecting the homes from the churning ocean is a cozy place to walk. Behind the houses, white-tiled patios are filled with buoys, nets, and rods. Others have garden beds, or small family cemeteries where granite posts record the generations entombed in the urns below. I'm used to lonely trees between vast lawns of stories, quotes, years, and pictures in American graveyards, so these compact cemetery plots fascinate me.

---

7 Complain

Most exist on the margins, either between the sea and homes, or on the borders of fields where the epigraphs tell the stone Jizo whom to protect on their journey below. Besides a lone flower tilted in a vase, everything is stone, sand, square, and silent.

So many lives contained beneath a small patch of a small island.

Back on the city roads, modest homes, garages, and shops line the streets, their doors open to the refreshing salt breeze. In Tokushima, every house was in some stage of processing rice. Here in Kochi, there's variety. A lumber mill's screeching blade planes boards for ship hulls. One family peels crates of yams, calling me over for *ossetai* of hard candies and iced tea. Another kills and de-feathers chickens in their garage, the grandfather directing his two middle-aged sons from a chair in the corner. One son tosses whole chickens into a miniature washing machine, where the drum twists in a roiling broth of dirt and feathers. He hands the newly bare, steaming carcass to the other son for beheading at the slick red cutting board. A barefoot child perches on a stool, learning the family business.

It's yet another day of the sun nipping at my shoulders with its sharp rays. Relief only comes in the shadows of the verdant slopes that wind down the coastline for days. But all too soon, I've curved around the foot of yet another mountain back into the penetrating solar glare. Piers provide occasional breaks in the monotony. A dozen workmen in straw hats and long sleeves patch a fishing net stretched out across a concrete dock, dwarfing the trucks that brought it in. It takes long minutes to walk the length of the black nylon. Distant fishing boats trawl the ocean with similar nets, and I can't tell how anything is still left swimming.

Food is, as usual, impossible to find. After five hours on the highway I'm melted across the steps of an amphitheater-style walkway on the beach, filling my lungs in between chugs of water. Waves cast stones that clatter like dice along the shore, and the full moon hangs midday between two lighthouses. All of it frames more road, more mountains, and, beyond, more Shikoku. Nine miles away my day will end at T27, another *nansho* temple. Already hot spots are forming into blisters on my soles.

Shoes unlaced, I go through what has become a three-times-a-day ritual. Removing the duct tape and Band-Aids from various blisters and raw sores, I check for infection, cut away at dangling skin, drain the older blisters, disinfect, then dry and reapply. With one last look at the ocean, I take a deep breath and prepare for what comes next. Feeling has returned to my feet over the break. Gritting my teeth, I beat the nerves back into submission against the pavement toward Nahari Town, two hours away.

I duck into the first ramen shop that appears, my eyes adjusting to the dim light filtering through the pebbled-glass windows. Three regulars and the owner smoke at the bar, awaiting the lunch rush with sweating glasses of beer. I place my order and sink into a couch facing the entrance. Tacked beside the door is a tourist poster with Kochi's famous historical figures in cartoon form: a samurai, his wife, a barrel-chested guy with a wide mustache and dressed in a kimono, and a short man in a red striped shirt wearing a straw boater's hat.

I already know two of the figures, which my friends Miwa and Tomo told me about before I arrived. The samurai is Ryoma Sakumoto, a vanguard of modernization who helped overthrow the Tokugawa shogunate and establish the modern navy. His wife, Oryo Kotatsu, was also active in politics and saved Ryoma's life during an assassination attempt at an inn. Hearing the killers enter while she was bathing, she burst naked into Ryoma's room to warn him and his allies. Ryoma, after seeing Oryo's bravery, and also how she looked without clothes, married her soon after. The other two characters, Japanese Teddy Roosevelt and Hat Guy, remain a mystery.

I lose all interest once the ramen bowl hits the table.

Spicy, oily broth arrives at my stomach with brief notice from my mouth.

My head tilts back, eyes shut, and I resurrect on the cushions. When I rise to pay, the wheelchair-bound regular waves me off with a smile. An *osamefuda*, a bow, and I head off toward another *nansho* temple.

A stream snakes though the field of tall grasses that conceal the concrete upslope to T27. The steep hike levels off by a ramshackle house, where five locals lounge beneath the shady trees on lawn chairs. One raises a half-clenched fist, calling out, "*Ganbatte*," before his hand drifts back onto his belly. Past the house, the *nansho* trail earns its reputation. My lungs work double time as my pack shifts back and forth on top of bruised soles. Still, it's not Burning Mountain. Leaving footprints and gallons of sweat in the dirt behind me, I near the temple. Every descending *henro* offers a reassuring "*chotto.*"

In the early twentieth century, a young mother from a provincial farming family made this same hike to **Konomineji: God Summit Temple (T27)** to pray for the prosperous life of her young son, Iwasaki Yataro—or, as I knew him, Japanese Teddy Roosevelt. She either prayed on the right day or used up the *honzon*'s wish allotment, because her son grew up to found the Mitsubishi Corporation. In honor of this, the multinational conglomerate still patronizes this small mountain temple.

My energy and arches are failing by the time I've finished praying, but a mysterious staircase draws me further above the complex to a Shinto shrine tucked away in the forest. Two stone foxes flank the shrine, messengers of the harvest goddess Inari. I drop between them at the top of the steps, the day's challenges complete. It's literally all downhill this evening. Propped against my pack, I watch gossamer curtains of mist tumble down the ancient cedar trunks, concealing me from the world. Sometimes, in these quiet moments in solitude, I forget to question why I'm here.

Dinner is eaten in the most lively temple shop I've visited. The room clamors with the hopeful chirps of caged birds and the clatter of pots in the tiny kitchen. Amongst the barrels of staffs and tables of *henro* attire, I search shelves filled with treats for tomorrow's breakfast. Seeing a pack of whale jerky, I sigh at the dry white strips. Above the entrance hang photos of the chef with famous *henro*, including a sumo wrestler who'd somehow made the climb here without his heart exploding. Fittingly, there's a charcoal sketch beside the sumo wrestler of Iwasaki holding a sign proclaiming impossible is nothing.

A bowl of udon with thick-cut, fresh vegetables disappears the moment it hits the table. On my way out the door, I graciously accept the cook's *ossetai* of a frozen water bottle. A bow, an *osamefuda*, and I roll the icy bottle on the back of my neck as I descend to a rest hut one kilometer away. As I'm setting up my tent, the chef drives by with a friendly double honk. We wave goodbye.

Across the road from my rest hut is an outdoor sink and toilet, so I won't sleep in my own sweat tonight. It's is more luxury than I've come to expect. Sponge-bathed and contacts removed, I have one last order of business gurgling in my intestines. Swinging open the toilet's door, my eyes grow wide. It's only mosquitoes.

Three fluttering sheets of hungry needles peel off the walls toward me.

I slam the door shut and tell my sphincter that, like it or not, we are literally shutting this shit down for the night.

My feet throb throughout my dreams, so I switch to sandals that morning to give them some reprieve. The sandals blister the balls of my feet against the roasting asphalt and are useless on long distances, but there are no other options. No stores in these rural villages stock size-twelve boots, so it's me, the sandals, and "The Fucking Shoes" until the end. Adding insult to injury, the shoes dangle off the back of my pack, kicking me in the ass with every wincing step down the mountain. To distract myself, and give back to Shikoku in some way, I begin a daily routine of collecting litter in one of the many discarded plastic bags on the ground.

The trail levels off at the ramshackle house, where I toss the litter bag into an aluminum trash can. The five locals are still lounging in the shade, and as far as I can tell haven't switched seats. One of them motions up the hill to ask if I'd slept up there. I nod. He and his friends laugh.

"*Ganbatte.*"

It takes an hour to return to the highway, where a sign announces I'm entering a tsunami inundation area. For the next thirteen kilometers I'm filled with the same unease as driving through Tornado Alley. I know the chances are slim, but the waves to my left do take on a menacing air now that I know what they're capable of. I keep them in the corner of my eye, not that it will make a difference.

Another sign welcomes me to Aki City, the birthplace of Japanese Teddy Roosevelt, with a cartoon dove holding a red umbrella next to a picture of the business executive. So far I've heard nothing of the bird's accomplishments.

Breakfast is spicy udon soup in a seaside restaurant with stained-wood furniture. Outside the window, Tsunami Danger Zone waves roil and smash against the concrete, the drops spattering against the glass.

I don't care.

After two weeks of drinking cans of "Authentic Coffee Flavored Beverage," I've finally found a place that serves real brew. It's a small cup, but filled to the brim with authentic coffee. Pouring in cream from a thimble-size pitcher, I can relate to Gulliver's disappointment at the Lilliputian portions. The owner, who wears the brushed-back pompadour of Kim Jong Il, sees my joy at the black drip and refills it free of charge. A bow, an *osamefuda*, and I pause at the entrance to look over an antique hand-crank telephone. Though tempted to spin it and listen for a dial tone, I abstain. I have a habit of breaking old things.

Caffeine being one of the drugs I'm deprived of here, I'd forgotten how powerful it is. The bright sunshine sparkles as I stride along the seawall. Every photo taken of the surf spattering through the gray tetrapods is Pulitzer-worthy, and every idea I dream up is genius. I'm making excellent time toward Aki's city center, easily outpacing the two *henro* ahead of me. Everything is right with the world until the spices and the coffee reach lower into my bowels, meet with the food from last night, and make it very clear they all have somewhere more important to be.

Two weeks without coffee.

I really forgot how powerful it is.

The growing urgency propels me past scattered houses, cemeteries, and lumberyards. There are no stores or restaurants around, and Aki City is still hours away. Meanwhile, the food grows more emphatic about reaching its next destination. Soon I can't hold it back with pride or muscle control and start making contingency plans.

Squatting in a graveyard isn't an option, so I race down from the seawall along a lumberyard and knock on the doors of three houses lined up beside the fence.

No one answers.

I turn to the stacks of lumber, prepared to ruin some poor workman's day.

Suddenly a door slides opens. A woman says hello and I ask frantically for the toilet. She lets me in. I break speed records removing my shoes, drop my backpack, which takes up half of her entryway, and make it to the toilet in time. After a good ten minutes, I make sure the porcelain bowl is again flawless. On my way out, the woman accepts my bow and *osamefuda* with a look of "*Thanks, now get the fuck out of my house, gaijin.*" From now on, breakfast will be anything bland and coffee will be viewed with appropriate caution.

After that excitement, it's back to the hardest part of Kochi: the long distances. Walking meditation lasts only so long before my attention span runs out, and on days like this, when I'm on a bicycle path weaving beside the ocean for ten miles, there's little else to distract from each aching step. With no distance bollards or city signs to mark progress, there's only forward for indeterminate hours as waves grind against the sand with the regularity of watch gears.

I've never understood how people can vacation on a beach, spending days just sitting and watching the waves. Sitting and doing nothing is essentially how I've spent my entire working life. I don't want the same thing on my break. However, while passing through Kochi, the sea has become more of a companion than an entertainment system. And, as I begin meditation again, it provides yet another benefit: perspective.

The coarse brown sand slows me down as I venture out among the abandoned boats half-buried in the sands, vegetation slithering through their rotted hulls. Silver mirages pool in the dunes ahead and ivory mountains float through the endless blue sky. Watching the waves scatter and regroup for another assault on the rocks, I'm looking at something too grand to comprehend. So large the moon took hold, it arches up from the Earth toward space, sloshing back and forth on a scale where humanity vanishes by magnification. And with this view, I worry less. The distance I'm traveling is minuscule, the hours short.

But this perspective doesn't stop the ground from kneeing my feet in the balls.

My day ends at a plush *henro-goya*, one of the government-funded rest huts. Neighbors have stocked this one with blankets, cushions, and an ice chest filled with coffee and soda cans. I enter my name in the guestbook, then discover a foot massager. As the pebbled wheels roll across raw skin into my cramping soles, I think about the luxuries of home: hot showers, a private toilet, the same bed every night, a common language to share experiences, and a variety of shoes in my size.

Here in Kochi I'm learning to appreciate the little things: the feel of ice on my neck after a long day's climb, a bowl of spicy ramen, a Western toilet when you really need it, and, after eighteen miles, my feet once again freed from the road. There are no easy days on the pilgrimage, but there are moments when I forget how difficult it is.

Then, there are days like tomorrow.

9

DO I EVER TELL ANYONE THIS HAPPENED?

I
T'S ALREADY A good day when I wake atop fluffy cushions at the *henro-goya*. No mosquitoes outside, my hips and back aren't numb from sleeping on bare concrete, and there's coffee waiting for me in a blue picnic cooler. Fishing a can from the icy water, I smile and raise it in salute to a neighbor as he parks his puttering moped beside the hut. After refilling the cooler, he scans the guestbook for the alien loops and lines of my entry. Finding it, he nods, smiles back, and we sweep the *henro-goya*'s floor.

A bow, an *osamefuda*, and I'm off. I'm grateful for these locals' generosity, for the restful night of sleep, and that many of the blisters plaguing my feet have callused over. Lastly, I'm grateful that, after two weeks on Shikoku, today holds such promise.

The only concern this morning, as usual, is food. On any given day the searing hours spent carrying the pack burns between five thousand and seven thousand calories, and I'm lucky if I replace two thousand of them. The only calories available near dawn are from liquor stores, and I've banned drinking on this trip for spiritual reasons, and also to prove that I'm only a borderline alcoholic.

There are no grocery stores along the path as it leads further inland. Deep rivers gush from the mountains toward the marshlands, where tall grasses grow in the lazy, swirling pools. Statues in front of the roadside shops appear in curious combinations. On the same street a six-foot statue of a red rockfish stands in line with a twin-engine bomber plane, a stegosaurus, and a triceratops. Still puzzling over the connection, in midmorning I reach **Dainichiji: The Temple of the Great Sun (T28)**, where the *Daishi* carved a Yakushi Nyorai in a camphor tree with his fingernails. It used to stand beside the main hall, but in 1868 it blew down because sacred trees just cannot get a break here. I bow at the exit and parallel a surging canal feeding the paddies below.

With my stomach roaring, it's especially galling to be surrounded by food at all times in these damp fields of grain. Though none of it is edible yet, I'm close to trying anyway. Everything else is eating. Black dragonflies chase their darting prey over the irrigation canals while fish snack on protozoa below. Cranes stab at snails in the muddy paddy water, and frogs snatch bugs off the algae-covered walls. Pausing at a roadside shrine, where twin dragons snarl in the headboards, I take a seat to meditate and be here now.

And here, now, I'm hungrier than I can ever remember being.

As I gaze across the inedible fields, an email from an old family friend that I read last week at the Internet café pops back into my head. When she mentioned my trip to her mother, who'd known me as a chubby toddler, her mother had replied, "We could always get him to walk for food."

A begrudging chuckle escapes from me. Never before have I walked so far to eat so little. Even when the heat suppresses my appetite, the yawning void in my stomach remains. More irksome, while grocery stores are rare on the path, there are always clothing boutiques or barber shops. This makes the least sense to me. These people can harvest their own food but not trim their bangs evenly?

By noon I've eaten an unripe melon found at an unmanned roadside stand. I'm chomping through the rind when I reach **Kokubunji: The Official State Temple (T29)**. Though it shares the same name as T15, termites haven't destroyed this Kokubunji. Instead, it was burned down by the sixteenth-century warlord Chosokabe. I shamble down the tree-lined pathways of a courtyard that's alive with birdsong, and degrees cooler than the roasting farmlands. Beneath a statue of goddess Kannon is a farmers market sampler of fruit offerings. I place my other melon at her feet in thanks for the merciful shade of her 1,001 arms.

Heading back through the fields on my way to T30 I pause, remembering to appreciate these peaceful moments among the sunflowers. Then I remember I've left my staff behind yet again. A couple of hearty curses later, I retrieve it from the stamp office. Despite it being at least a once-a-day habit, my frustration at forgetting my staff increases each time. Besides exhausting myself further as I lose ten or twenty minutes backtracking, it's a daily reminder of how little I can trust myself here. And there's no one else to point out what I'm missing.

After an hour or two on a rolling highway, the melon has long since burned off with nothing to replace it. No restaurants, no grocery stores, and the gas stations only sell gas. Woozy, I pass yet another mechanic's garage, where an Elvis Presley concert billboard hangs on a brick building.

Elvis is touring Shikoku?

I turn around in confusion. The King faces the entry-way of a vintage 1950s-style diner. In disbelief I rush inside, ready to cause a hamburger shortage in Japan.

The décor resembles a TGI Fridays, with classic Americana covering the walls. Framed photos of Elvis's swiveling hips and Marilyn's billowing dress hang above the checkered tables, and a nickel-fed jukebox loaded with 45s sits in the corner. Behind the front counter, dolls dressed as mechanics, cowboys, and a 1920s "leath-erhead" football player line the shelves. Beside them is a vintage Esso motor oil ad, the anthropomorphic drop of oil saluting the motorist. I ring the bell beside the antique cash register, bouncing with anticipation.

No answer.

I ring the bell again.

A curious mechanic glances through the window facing the garage, then returns to his engine. My stomach whimpers and I have no explanation to console it. I'm surrounded by all the things associated with food: a Big Boy figurine serving a burger on his tray, an STP lunch box, and a Pepsi soda fountain. There are stools with vinyl cushions beneath the counter and metal chairs tucked into the tables. But looking closer, there's no silverware on the tables, no sounds or smells are coming from the kitchen, and everything's covered with a layer of dust. I open the slot of a gumball dispenser on the counter. They've melted solid with age. Then, finally, it hits me.

I'm in a museum.

And arguably worse: the Twilight Zone.

On my way out, I'm genuinely expecting Rod Serling to wander into frame and dramatically intone: *"Paul Barach thought he could just travel to Japan and eat every day. Well, fuck that guy."*

After broiling for a couple more hours inside Shikoku's convection oven, I reach what I think is T30, which must have been built for devout giants. An austere courtyard of white gravel contrasts with the rich brown of colossal cedar torii. A towering pagoda looms over an expansive temple, with pyramids of rice-wine casks stacked along the veranda. While inquiring where to find the stamp office, I learn this is Tosa Jinja, a Shinto shrine right next to T30. Before departing, I eat at their tiny grocery shop. But it's too little, too late.

I pray at **Zenrakuji: The Temple of Everlasting Joy (T30)** on wobbling legs and remember nothing about it. Dreading the long walk to T31, where *henro* can sleep in a viewing platform above the complex, I search for an alternate campsite along the way.

After twelve hours and twenty miles on the road, I plod along the canals on impulse power, envying the animals turning in for the night. Turtles pile atop each other, fighting to claim a two-foot island of grass, and herons group in the shallows, probing the mud for an evening snack. Elementary school students playing on a basketball court pause their games to turn and stare at the *gaijin henro*, who mumbles an *"arigato"* in response to each enthusiastic cry of *"ganbatte!"*

Missing a turnoff across the farmlands, I detour along an access road still radiating heat, then follow the train tracks into town. I've found no place to set up my tent, so the day ends, as always, with a steep concrete path. I climb through an orchard as cicadas and songbirds compete to make their final announcements of the day heard. Farther up, where a few ancient gravestones have sunk into the earth, a small cloud of ambitious mosquitoes attacks. I bat at them with limp limbs. The only relief is that for the first time in two weeks my left arm hasn't swollen from my backpack's weight. The hill crests to reveal a small amphitheater overlooking the town.

I'll just sleep here, I think, unpacking my tent.

Then a security guard passes by.

No, I won't.

Back to my original plan: the rest hut above T31.

Remaining as inconspicuous as six feet of pale skin and overdue laundry can be, I tail the guard. My field of vision narrows as I lurch past rolling lawns of manicured trees, overlooks, and gardens. Suddenly, a locked metal gate appears, blocking my path to T31.

It's too tall scale. I stare dumbly through the tunnel vision at the chain padlocking the gate shut. This wasn't part of the plan. I head into a bathroom, drop my pack, wash my face in the sink, and ponder this conundrum. With the guards patrolling the campus, I can't pitch my tent on the lawn before sunset. I can't stick around here until they leave, but I'm too tired to hike back up the hill after dark. My reflection gawps back at me while my last brain cells finish their murder-suicide pact. Then I notice that the toilet stall doors reach down to the floor, concealing the inhabitant from view.

Kicking my bag into the far stall, I drop onto the throne and cradle my head in my hands. I'm forming a plan of action when the bathroom lights click off. The day's exertions catch up to me all at once. My blinks growing longer and longer, I slide to the floor and think: *This isn't the worst place to sleep.*

A half hour later the lights click back on.

Guard boots resound off the tile and I realize: *This is the worst place to sleep.* Now I'm trespassing on a private property in Japan, one of the most expensive countries on earth. If I'm caught, I'm facing arrest, deportation, and bankruptcy from the fines. Wracking my brain for an alibi, I silently move back to the toilet seat, drop my pants, and press my beaded bracelets into my forehead. If discovered, I'm hoping the indentations in my face and the bleared eyes will make me look like I've fallen asleep on the toilet by accident. I'll sell it by acting really disoriented, which isn't acting at this point.

It's the best idea I have, because I'm in full heart-pounding panic. One bad decision, one stupid unplanned situation, and this is how my pilgrimage ends. After a year of saving and two weeks of pain and exhaustion, I'll return home with nothing. Just more evidence of being the screw-up that my family sees. The guards' boots click past the stall door, then disappear from the bathroom. I stay on the toilet another hour before moving back to the floor, cursing my idiocy. Soon my eyes drift shut.

Guards pass outside the bathroom in loud conversation and I wake with a start, knocking my staff against the porcelain bowl.

Inside the stall, the click is deafening.

The guards fall silent. Breath and time freeze. Boots cross the tile and stop outside the stall door. Blood roaring in my ears, I wait for it to swing open.

And in that huddled terror of discovery, with my future out of my hands, a bloom of compassion opens in my heart. I realize that this fear has been shared by so many throughout history: immigrants hiding from border-patrol flashlights, or the besieged cowering from the soldiers outside. It's the same dread my own grand-parents must have felt as they cradled my infant father in the back of a bread truck, as they were smuggled across the border from Soviet-occupied Poland to American-occupied Germany after the war.

And for a moment, I feel connected to the suffering of so many.

Then, a moment later, I think: *You're none of those things, Paul. You're a twenty-eight-year-old hiding in a toilet stall. Shouldn't you be at home, with a mortgage?*

I can't really argue.

Outside the stall door, for whatever reason, the boots turn and exit the bathroom. It's a brief reprieve in a hor-rible night. Hunched against the wall, I doze for brief snatches in between each passing conversation or car. My heart skips a beat every time I bump the wall or my pack shifts, the end of my journey one noise away.

I'm never discovered. By 4 a.m. it's plausible that the guards would see me as an ambitious *henro* starting his day early, and not some moron who chose the worst place to sleep. My nerves fried, I warily exit the stall and turn toward T31.

The metal gate is still padlocked shut. However, because I've "slept," the tunnel vision has cleared, so I can now see the waist-high stone wall connected to the gate. So I sigh, and put my backpack on the wall, and step over it. And the moment I'm outside it hits me: I'm in Japan, one of the most polite cultures on earth. If I'd been caught, the guards would have spent five minutes apologizing for not letting me sleep in their toilet stall, then driven me to a hotel.

I take a seat on the base of a Kukai statue across from T31, waiting for the temple to open. Jittery from the two cans of vending machine coffee keeping me awake, my focus is broken by the nonstop bark of a terrier, its snout shoved beneath a garage door. I glare at my open journal in odious silence, twitching at each high-pitched yip. The blank page taunts me. I'm committed to recording each day, but after the last twenty-four hours, what is there to say?

Earbuds plugged into my voice recorder, I wince at the optimism of yesterday's early entries, until, finally, I know what to say. Clicking the button of my pen, I touch the ink to the page, and write: *Do I ever tell anyone this happened?*

10

A MURDER OF CROWS

THROTTLING THE BELL cord in my fist, I yank down hard. The gong resounds through the empty courtyard of **Chikurinji: Bamboo Forest Temple (T31)**, covering the volume of expletives behind my gritted teeth. I'm the first *henro* of the morning, for obvious reasons. Climbing a staircase to the *honzon* on rebandaged feet, I complete my sutras to Monju, the sword-wielding boddhisatva of true wisdom, then bow, and say, "I just spent the night hiding in a toilet stall, and I need a break today. Please, help."

It's a selfish prayer, but last night has left me too jagged for altruism. Flinching at every branch that hoves into my periphery, I descend to the courtyard's lush pond to meditate. Across the rippling green pool, dozens of Jizo line the bank. Devout worshippers have tied red aprons around the statues' necks in return for luck on their travels. Having no apron to tie on, I'm hoping Monju comes through today before I snap. Meanwhile, crows dive at my head from the overhanging birch trees, defending their territory.

Opening my eyes, there's a begrudging appreciation at how different each day is here.

The morning before, I sipped ice-cold coffee at a plush rest hut.

This morning, I'm planning to murder several crows.

Along the wide canal leading from T31, coruscations of black dragonflies claim the warming air above me. But there's no time to stop for scenery; I'm running on fumes. Then a road sign appears with a Kappa in a kimono juggling on a unicycle while puppies frolic beneath. An arrow declaring 600 m points down the road, and I have a decision to make. Fifteen minutes later I'm back on the path, grumbling incoherently and wishing any part of that sign were true.

Past a smelting plant and a dirt road torn up by bulldozers is a tiny restaurant. Nodding to the three gray-haired men silently examining their newspapers, I slump into a booth. A few tables over, a young workman in brown coveralls stares into space. A steaming mug of coffee sits untouched before him as he withdraws cigarette after cigarette from a waterproof case.

My blurry gaze rests on the table until I hear the clink of the ceramic plate and savor my first meal in seventeen hours. The other patrons have left by the time I ask for my check, so I'm unable to thank whoever paid for it. I give an *osamefuda* to the women working the grill to pass on to my benefactor. A stranger's generosity, food again in my gut, and there's a genuine smile for the first time since yesterday morning.

Beginning walking meditation beside the wide Katsuhura Pond, I focus on the purple flowers emerging from the islands of algae muck. Over the past two weeks of constant practice, I've been able to keep my attention on one object for increasingly longer periods before getting distracted by other thoughts. However, my ultimate goal isn't to zero in on one thing in view; it's to observe all my surroundings equally. Without the distractions of a computer, a job, a phone, or other people, I figured it would be easy here.

Yet another addition to the "Incorrect Shikoku Assumptions" list.

When the path turns from the pond through a residential neighborhood, where yapping dogs patrol the lawns of stately homes, meditation ends and my mind wanders down the road.

By 10 a.m., I'm at **Zenjibuji: The Temple of Ch'an Master's Peak (T32)**, high above the L-shaped harbors stretching from the coast. Across the Pacific, my friends are just getting back from work. I wonder what mundane days they're finishing up. They're certainly not standing on a bluff, drained yet jittery at midmorning, dousing themselves in sunblock and bug spray since the heat hasn't yet defeated the mosquitoes.

Lucky bastards.

Beneath the *Nio-mon*, a busload of chattering *henro* gather around the priest. Normally I'd roll my eyes as their tour guide strains to lift duffel bags packed to capacity with their stamp books and scrolls. However, I don't resent these tourists this morning. True, they haven't lugged their packs up this steep path to pray, but that's OK, because walking this pilgrimage is really, really fucking hard. My way takes dedication, not smarts.

A few miles later, I'm catching my breath in the shade of a castle-like home. Beneath wing-shaped eaves, I lean against the boulders of the foundation wall beside my pack. A *henro* pulls over in his car and hands me an *ossetai* of vinegar-cherry-flavored pretzel sticks. A bow, an *osame-fuda*, and I wait for him to drive off before looking for a garbage can. Vinegar cherry tastes like I'm being punished for something. Unconsciously, I open the pack and crunch into one. They taste as awful as usual, but I've stopped eating on this pilgrimage and begun to feed. Shaking the last crumbs into my mouth, I throw the container into the next dumpster along with my plastic bag of collected trash. I'm hoping the karma from my daily litter patrol will prevent another night in a toilet stall.

The pretzel sticks tide me over for about three seconds. Even though I'm rushing to catch a ferry that will take me downriver, my hunger's reached Tasmanian Devil levels and must be appeased. At noon I duck inside a small grocery store selling prepackaged snacks and what appears to be one of every fish in the ocean. The owners bring over a stool, watching in amazement as shelves of food vanish.

A bow, an *osamefuda*, and I double-time down the narrow city streets to catch my ferry. On my way, a middle-aged man out with his wife hands me ¥500 "for something cool to drink."

For a place known as Devil's Country, the generosity here grows my heart like the carolers in Whoville. Even if *"Atsui desu ne?"* is all we say to each other, they're content to give me a gift and walk away. The guilt that I can give them nothing in return is quickly forgotten on the pleasant ferry ride downriver. I recline in the cool breeze, watching the land float past with no effort on my part.

We disembark at the far bank and I'm soon at the *honzon* of **Sekkeiji: Snowy Cliff Temple (T33)**, considering whom to pray for. I decide on Taylor, a childhood friend I'd recently reconnected with. He's going through difficult times as his father, Jon, succumbs to Alzheimer's. Making it more tragic, Jon is Taylor's only real family left. Breast cancer took his mother when we were young, and his grandmother died of grief soon after. I complete my sutras for him and head to the stamp office, where the monk confirms something from my lodging guide that I thought I'd misread.

Not only does T34 offer *tsuyado*, but there is a hot shower.

Through untapped reserves of will, I don't hail down a taxi.

With that on my mind, how can I care about any of this agricultural expanse standing between me and some way-overdue hygiene? Still, I gotta try. With a long inhalation beside a canal, I begin walking meditation. When I turn to cross through yet another cultivated tract, suddenly my surroundings come into sharp relief, like turning a camera lens. I become a thread weaving through an unbroken fabric that stretches from the blades of grass waving at my side, past the distant yellow grains surrounding a lone, pine-covered mountain, and over the steel-gray peaks on the horizon. With each individual stalk and far-away summit equally clear, my mind falls silent, replaced by a blissful awareness of my place within Shikoku. The warm air that breezes past me also rustles the pine boughs atop the mountain and bears the weight of the snow-white cranes drifting into the paddies. I see myself briefly intertwined with each distinct strand of this field, creating one unique piece in an unfathomable whole. I've never experienced anything like it, and yet it feels so obvious that I calmly accept this new insight and continue on until thoughts of a hot shower reinvade the clarity. When it dissipates, I acknowledge the change with a smile and continue toward **Tanemaji: Sowing Seeds Temple (T34)**.

A sprawling complex of sea-green roofs, T34 was destroyed by typhoons on several occasions and rebuilt each time by the devout or slow-to-learn locals. I recite sutras to a Yakushi Nyorai, carved by a shipwrecked Korean fisherman in gratitude for the deity's naval rescue operation. The monk signs my book, gives me an Asian pear, and leads me to the *tsuyado*. I drop my bags, place my staff respectfully in the corner, then slide open a panel door to behold Shangri-la: bare concrete walls and a spigot above my head. The monk bows and departs. Seconds later, I'm naked and twisting the H knob.

After a few sputtering jolts, hot water erupts from the spigot and dopamine drenches my body. Good sex and good drugs have felt this spectacular, but I don't remember when. With my hands braced against the wall, the grease, sweat, and dirt from two days, and, really, two weeks, dissolves and drains away beneath my feet. After drying off, I lie on the tatami mats craving a cigarette, and debate calling the shower the next day to tell it how I feel. Ultimately, that seems too needy, so I decide to play it cool. It takes a while to return from the afterglow, and I pray I haven't just ruined sex for myself.

I'm returning to the shower when a college-age *henro* named Emilio arrives just after sunset. Bearing a melon Popsicle for each of us from the monk, he's as happy as I am to find indoor lodging.

His anticipant eyes search the room.

I reluctantly point to the panel door.

He bows and rushes inside.

The faucet handle cranks and I glare suspiciously at the door, worried the shower will like him more and they'll elope. I drag out a soft futon from the corner and distract myself by mapping out the next day's walk. Every rest hut for the next few pages is circled to assure there's no repeat of the toilet-stall incident. Emilio returns from his shower and unrolls his sleeping bag.

"*Atsue, desu ne?*" I ask.

"Yes, very hot," he agrees. "Do you speak Japanese?"

"No. Do you speak English?"

"Yes."

"No fucking way."

While growing up in Kanagawa on Honshu, Emilio waited tables in Italian and French restaurants, where English is the common language. Now majoring in mathematics at Tokushima University, he learned about the pilgrimage from local monks and must complete the journey before his fall quarter begins. Carrying only a light pack and no pilgrim gear or stamp book, Emilio sleeps on whatever bench is closest after the sun sets. Though his running shoes are tattered, he's confused as to why I'd ask about foot pain.

Lucky bastard.

The face-to-face conversation revives me and lasts long into the night. He too is on Shikoku to learn what makes him happy, forgoing electronic distractions to immerse himself in the journey and forge a deeper connection to the experience. I'm glad to meet someone taking this as seriously as I am, and don't mind the laughter about my night in the toilet stall. From there, the conversation ranges to the things we have in common. On animated films, he favors Miyazaki's *Porco Rosso* over my favorite, *Princess Mononoke*, but we agree on *Finding Nemo* as the best Pixar film and *The End of Evangelion* as a breathtaking product of insanity. We trade Jay Z lyrics and, when asked about attending his concert in Japan, Emilio can only reply, "The greatest," still reveling in the experience. Before the miles catch up to us and drop our heads to our pillows, there's time for one final question: "What do you miss most from home?"

"Gorgeous food." Emilio replies.

I can relate.

Eyes shut, I mumble a thanks to Monju for granting my prayers today for a break. After a free meal, a hot shower, some conversation, and a small glimpse of a deeper connection, I'm ready to continue on.

The next morning, I wake up just as Emilio's stepping out the door. Still drowsy, I call him back and hand him a ¥1,000 note.

"What for?"

"Gorgeous food," I reply, and wish him well on his travels.

After stretching and meditation, I bid the shower a longing goodbye and head off for T35. While I'm crossing the lengthy Niyodogawa-ohashi Bridge, distracted by my map, everything begins shaking. Japan's known for earthquakes, and given how my trip's been going, I should have expected one. Instead, I freeze in panic, with not enough thought to unclasp my backpack and prepare for a swim.

When the semi-truck rumbles past, the tension subsides. However, I stay on guard.

One thing no one mentions about traveling in foreign countries is the naked vulnerability in an emergency situation. My first morning in my South Korean apartment, I was awakened at 6 a.m. by an urgent announcement repeating through a mounted loudspeaker. I bolted upright. Whatever they were saying was important enough to alert everyone in the neighborhood. I rushed outside, halfway into my pants, ready to follow my neighbors to safety from fire or a nuclear strike.

Nothing.

A calm morning in the suburbs, the streets empty and the truck gone. This recurred for a week until I finally made it outside in time to discover a flatbed urgently announcing it that had fish for sale, fresh fish, and all the tentacled delicacies of the sea. I bought earplugs that afternoon.

On the far side of the Niyodogawa-ohashi Bridge, I restock my bandage supply in a small town. A mountain path leads to T35, but a flat, shorter path leads to a nearby café. The temple will still be there after breakfast.

I've come to expect a couple of stares wherever I go, but either no one in this café has seen a white person before or "American" is a popular breakfast everyone is ordering at the same time. My booth is beneath a framed, autographed photo of Tomoaki Kanemoto, an outfielder for Hanshin Tigers. Judging by the number of blatant stares, the customers will remember this day as clearly as when he ate here.

Past the mechanic garages and garbage dumps dotting the rice field, the concrete upslope to T35 disappears into the trees. Halfway up, Emilio passes me on his way to T36. We wish each other luck and health, exchange email addresses, and say goodbye for the last time.

The weathered *Nio* at the gate of **Kiyotakiji: Clean Waterfall Temple (T35)** are the most terrifying so far.

Eyeless black holes stare out from decayed faces and blotches of faded crimson paint bleed from their snarling teeth down their bleached wooden flesh. Their outstretched hands end in wooden pegs, where the fingers rotted off years ago. After the bow, bell, wash, pray, pray, stamp, bow, I say goodbye to these grotesque relics for now, certain they'll be returning in my nightmares. Below the courtyard, the panorama of Takaoka Flat stretches into another mountain range. I head toward the Pacific, peeking through the lower ridges.

On the way down my legs slip from under me. My staff snaps into thirds as I break my fall with my ass. Collecting the pieces from the road, I'm surprisingly mournful. Regardless of its symbolism as the *Daishi*, the staff had been my only companion. Since the T1, it had taken every step beside me, and waited patiently for me to realize I'd forgotten it at yet another temple. It had sweated my sweat, soaked up the same grime from the road, and been my weapon of choice against boar and monkey attacks. By tradition, I'd taken care to wipe the dirt from the bottom before resting it beside me in the tent or standing it reverently in the corner if I had a room to sleep in. Not knowing the procedure for a broken *Daishi*, I place the shards beneath a tree by a small graveyard and continue downhill, lonesome for a cheap wooden pole.

Back on Takaoka Flat, I double my walking meditation to re-create the connection in the rice field yesterday. Slowing my pace with my breath, I focus on a hawk perched on telephone wires, a writhing snake in its beak, and zero in on a stunted tree growing from a rock wall, pink blossoms erupting from the jagged sketch of branches. It's not working, and I learn yet again the difference between focus and awareness as I'm startled by a car's horn. The driver, fed up with my lame-cow pace, swerves past with an angry gesture and a parting honk. I give up for the moment and continue into town. Outside a grocery store, an old man flags me down and opens his wallet. I receive a ¥1,000 *ossetai*, the same amount I gave to Emilio and enough to buy a new staff. A bow, an *osamefuda*, and I'm off, thanking him and Shikoku for this instant karma. Without the staff's motion to maintain circulation, my right arm has already swelled from the shoulder straps. My left arm, having adapted to the pressure over two weeks, enjoys some schadenfreude.

After lunch, the path branches from the highway over the mountains I saw from T35's overlook. I'm planning another deep meditation in the silent forest, but instead spend my time swatting furiously at the two black flies hunting me. The path empties out into a series of canals and construction detours, where a caution sign warns me, to my best guess, to beware of overjoyed hippos. I encounter none, ecstatic or morose, along the way back to the ocean. Meanwhile, I strive for the awareness from yesterday to return until my head aches. Still nothing.

The bridge to Yokonami Peninsula describes a massive arc across glittering waves before landing at the tip of a forested ridge. Once back on land, I head to a *henro* shop at the base of Utsaga Mountain and purchase a new staff with my *ossetai*. This one has a satisfying heft, less likely to snap against concrete roads or a charging monkey's head. The familiar metronomic click returns to fill the quiet miles.

The evening's humidity drapes across the marsh's tall grasses leading to T36. My excessive perspiration patters onto the usual steep staircase to **Shoryuji: Green Dragon Temple (T36)**, where I recite sutras to the *honzon* Fudo Myoo. It's yet another guardian of fishermen, who should consider another profession if they require this much divine intervention.

I head down to the stamp office on my last legs, wishing I could trade places with a Fudo beneath a cool waterfall. While my book is signed, an old *henro* beside me points to my face, then hers, jabbering at the stamp lady in the recognizable tone from 1980s stand-up comedy: "*See, white henro sweat like this, but Japanese henro, we sweat like this.*"

I'm gifted two Asian pears by the stamp office, which rest beside me on a covered picnic table as I gaze across Usa Bay. As the sea breeze shuts off my sweat glands, a motorcycle gang stops across the road to preen their high pompadours, smoke, and see who can rev their engine the loudest.

Like Emilio, I'm relearning what makes me happy. Before the trip it was booze, friends, a girl, and good food. Now it's hot water, shelter, conversation, and any food. I'm disappointed that the awareness I experienced in the rice fields hasn't returned, but tonight a cool breeze, a covered place to sleep, and the tart bite of an Asian pear is what I have. The motorcycles roar into the night down Highway 47 as stars reflect in the lapping waves.

Yesterday morning I was planning on murdering several crows on a mountain.

Tonight I'm drowsy beside the Pacific, chuckling at how different each day can be.

11

BOREDOM AND TRAINS

A S ALREADY ESTABLISHED, I really, really didn't know what to expect when I stepped off the train bound for T1. At worst, some long walks and awkward miscommunications.

At best, wizened Japanese men bearing swords.

But never while skimming the *henro* websites did anyone mention the boredom. While my body slowly adapts to the punishing heat and the physical toll of each footstep, staying mentally present only gets harder in this unchanging routine of wake, wash (hopefully), meditate, walk, eat, walk, meditate, walk, eat (hopefully), walk, shelter, sleep. Besides the experience on my way to T34, there's been no real sense of spiritual or physical progress. In this repeating Hanna-Barbera background of fields, mountains, highways, and ocean, my motivation is changing from "Be here now" to "Get done fast." Especially for the next three temples.

Separated by long stretches, T37, T38, and T39 wrap around the fang-like Yokonami Peninsula over the last one hundred and thirty-one miles of Kochi. Ahead lies a week of ten- to thirteen-hour days spent waking up nowhere and going to sleep nowhere, a day closer to somewhere than yesterday. When I reach T39, the first half of the pilgrimage is complete, and it's impossible not to think ahead to the end. However, there's only one way to make it happen.

With my feet dressed in moleskin, Band-Aids, and duct tape, I apologize to them in advance and step onto Highway 47.

Parabolas of sun-baking concrete fill the morning and afternoon, the crest of one gray wave revealing an identical one ahead. Thick foliage mutes the ocean so completely that I can hear each crab scuttling through the dry leaves in the drainage canals. Within these oppressively silent stretches I live for the rare gaps in the tree line, where a saline breeze carries the ocean's hungry roar from below as it gobbles up the mountains bit by bit. Through these windows the peninsula's green ridges end in sheer drops to the Pacific, the series of coves disappearing into the stark horizon. Then it's back to the solitary, endless road, only the tock of my staff against the ground marking the time that passes beneath a stationary sun. Spiders and grasshoppers cling to the undersides of grasses, the only shade for miles, and the air-conditioned flight home pervades my fantasies. The road curves back into view across the mountainside with no shops in sight, prognosticating a half hour into my future, when I'll still be hungry atop shimmering concrete.

After five hours I stagger into an udon restaurant floating in a lake and motion vaguely at the menu when the waitress appears. Another *henro* wobbles through the entrance and drops beside me, motioning vaguely at my food when the waitress returns. Wordless, we compare our maps, pointing out the distances we've already covered since daybreak and nodding to each other woefully. As I leave we pump our fists at each other with a half-hearted "*Ganbatte.*"

More viscous hours return me to farmland. I once found something spiritual in the simplicity of these fields. Now the uniform rectangular tracts and rural homes have disappeared into visual white noise, so when I encounter a petrochemical plant in the fields, it's jaw-dropping.

I gape at impossibly huge metal tubes snaking through the sprawling complex of towers, which dwarfs any structure here by magnitudes. Like the ancient Germanic tribes staring at the Roman aqueducts, I'm so baffled by the titanic scale that "built by giants and/or gods" is a reasonable conclusion. I've seen the skyscrapers of New York, Chicago, Tokyo, and Seoul, but four years later that petrochemical plant remains in my memory the largest structure I've ever seen. I keep repeating "Fuck ..." and shaking my head until I cross a bridge and enter some kind of carnival. The smell of frying dough, sizzling meat, and boiling broth hits my nose, and my stomach has an orgasm.

The food stalls stretched across a park sell meat on sticks, in soup, in bread, and on plates. After ruling out eating everything as unfeasible, the clear choice is Nabeyaki ramen, the local delicacy. Veiled behind roiling steam, the cook drops eggs, green onions, chopped tentacles, and a sliver of raw pork into the bubbling broth before handing it to the drooling *gaijin* with tears in his eyes.

I join local parents slurping their food on long picnic tables. Their children dash about with faces painted like lions and rabbits, winning bags of goldfish at the skill games. The ramen lives up to its reputation and I'm happy with my decision, as well as the decision to follow up with pot stickers.

And chicken skewers.

And ice cream.

I lean against my pack on the lawn with sugar-glazed eyes as children lose their minds on a summer weekend. It's Sunday, but calendars are meaningless to me here. Every day is Walkday, and the highlight of my weekend is soup. Looking back wistfully at the fried dough and wishing for another stomach, I haul my pack and my gut down the riverside.

Tonight's destination is a government-designated rest area known as a *michi-no-eki*, this one located beside a busy port. At the town's entrance, a group of middle schoolers are hanging out on bicycles in the courtyard of the local Shinto temple.

"Where are you from?" they call out.

"Ichiro" I reply, swinging the bat.

They yell back his name and cheer, "*Ganbatte!*"

Whether for Ichiro or a *henro*, any encouragement on days like this is a balm as the last of my energy drains away with the sunlight. Their ovations carry me over the last three miles to the *michi-no-eki*. The rest area turns out to have a variety of seafood stalls, but no place to sleep unless I want to take my chances in the dark alleyway of an industrial port. I make the right decision, barely, and my feet scrape back to the Shinto temple.

The middle schoolers are gone by the time I return, but two elementary school girls are ensconced in a blanketed fort underneath the walkway, reading comics. We regard each other warily, both hoping one doesn't rat out the other to the cops for trespassing. They return to their books and I set up my tent in a corner, out of sight of the main road. As I'm falling asleep, a man looks through the mesh of my tent and walks away. On alert, I unclasp my Swiss Army knife and lay it beside me.

Then everything goes black.

There's no energy left for self-preservation.

The predawn rain pounding on the roof rouses me back to consciousness. My feet are sensitive to the touch, but no new blisters, which is a plus. And I haven't been murdered in my sleep, also good.

I pull out the groceries that I purchased yesterday,

congratulating myself for the foresight to avoid the usual morning breakfast rush. Lounging on my sleeping bag, I snack on thick white bread and bananas in between sips of coffee.

With my tent all packed up, the burst of starch hits as I turn the corner. Above the sloped roof of the temple gate, inky purple clouds bubble over the mountains to stain the morning sky. Witnessing this marvel, I realize how small I am—and how fast I need to find a toilet as the coffee and sugar jump-start my bowels. Racing out of the complex, I pass the potential murderer from last night. He's still asleep on a bench next to his bicycle, a *henro* hat, staff, and bell tied to the frame. Probably harmless.

I make it to a chain restaurant (thank gods) without incident (thank gods). The bathroom doesn't smell of fresh bleach for long. I buy a coffee in apology on my way out and head to the *michi-no-eki* for the morning foot-disinfection ritual.

By the time I'm rebandaged, the dawn clouds have deflated across the peaks. Their sunrise hues have drained away, reflecting my mood as I near the end of Kochi. At this point, my daily goals have shrunk to the basics: food, shelter, and not shitting in public. Having already covered two, I focus on reaching the *tsuyado* at T37, thirteen hours away. In pursuit of a roof, I follow the highway and vanish into the murky sky.

With the map providing only a basic topography, the diverse scenery of the *henro* trail unravels moment by moment. The sea breeze flutters tall purple flags in a graveyard between the highway guardrail and the sheer drop. Beyond the cliffs, small islands dot the waves, punctuation in the ocean's run-on sentence. Within an hour I'm hiking deep into a cedar forest, where rain-fattened streams cascade over rocks. As the path returns to town, the shuddering clang of construction equipment shearing the mountainside bald replaces the muted drips of condensation.

Days like this, my concerns shift from dodging trucks barreling through cramped highway tunnels to avoiding the dew-heavy spiderwebs haunting the low branches. A half hour after sipping *ossetai* green tea in a *conbini's* wood-paneled side room, I return to a forest canopy so choked with mist that it's midnight at midday. Neon-orange fungus glows in the dark as it munches on logs rotted soft. Trapped in these doldrums, it's up, down, over, and through one long obstacle course, with T37 as the finish line.

The woods end abruptly at a terraced rice field that shines yellow and green through the weak sunlight. Black plastic flags putter and snap in the wind wailing down the slopes. Back on flat land, a grassy riverbank is so soaked that I can skate across the slick vegetation. It's the most fun I've had all day. Tiny frogs scatter out of my way as I glide past the roughly built shacks and shrines that line the misty bank like relics of a half-forgotten dream. Returning to the highway for an hour-long race against closing time, I pay no attention to anything besides the blackening clouds overhead. When they finally burst open, I'd better be beneath something solid.

With glaring white eyes and stout, powerful limbs, the fearsome *Nio* of **Iwamotoji: Rocky Root Temple (T37)** protect the five *honzon* within the main hall: Fudo for avoiding evil influence, Kannon for good luck, Jizo for children, Amida for a long life, and Yakushi for overcoming evil. After forever, I finish my prayers to each deity and limp to the *tsuyado* in a nearby garage. Risking tetanus from the ragged metal hole serving as the handle, I hoist the garage door with a piercing screech. A naked light bulb dangles from the ceiling as I arrange the soiled couch cushions into a bed, then lay some cardboard over that to shield me from whatever lives inside. Once tucked into my sleeping bag, my feet regain consciousness from the vicious beating today and begin confessing everything. Strained shoulders, twinging knees, and growing blisters are the cost to sleep on filthy cushions as bold roaches scurry undaunted across the dank concrete. But as the driving rain rattles the rusty door, I'm grateful. Any port in a storm.

The next morning, a fat stone Buddha outside T37 laughs merrily in the downpour. He's the only one. Heavy fog obscures the mountain peaks and dampens the fields' bright colors. Aching from the waist down, I hum songs to keep my feet stepping as my mind flips channels through the haze. Surrounded by nothing I haven't seen a thousand times before, rain an all-day event, my poncho a rustling hassle, I battle an MSG migraine from my pasty ramen breakfast. Nothing of interest lies ahead besides the coast, where I'll stop moving.

On the bright side, I'm another day closer to the end.

My first time in Japan, I was on vacation from South Korea and enjoyed every packed moment. I could stay up all night for the Tsukiji tuna auction at dawn, visit ornate temples midmorning, search through the neon chasms of Akihabara for pillowcases you can marry in the late afternoon, and kick back with a beer in a crowded hostel that night, swapping stories and planning for tomorrow. Now I'm on a solo journey constrained by strict rules, enduring the same routine, and waiting to return home. Waiting for bike rides, drinks, karate, jogging, laughs with friends, long conversations, and short nods that speak volumes. These long hours of monotone motion leave me feeling like Optimus Prime after he's been stuck as a truck too long, ready for the jet packs and laser cannons to come back out. But I'm still committed to this journey, so I return to walking meditation and focus on the dim pathway ahead.

Cries of "*Ganbatte!*" follow me all day, cutting through the synaptic haze. Old women in grocery stores, motorcyclists passing me on the highway, and children returning from school all pump their fists and cheer. It's not a day for anyone to be walking without support. By late afternoon, mud-streaked from an unexpectedly rapid descent through a forest gully, I stop at a coastal rest hut to put on my knee braces and decide I will go no farther. The sky is darkening, and this *henro-goya* will block the incoming storm. Plus, there's a beware of boar sign up ahead, and I'm not going to risk finding out if they're nocturnal too.

After practicing some karate in the soggy grass, I remove my shoes in a bathroom for the disinfection ritual and crack up. It's been happening gradually, but my feet are now so covered in white and brown bandages, it looks like ancient Egyptians have prepared them for burial. I apologize again and put them to bed early for the first time in three days. As I lay out my tent, a lightning bolt throws the trees lining the shore into stark relief.

The rain has ceased around 3 a.m. when I wake to take a leak. Craning my neck, I find Scorpio and the Pleiades, and wish I knew more constellations, especially when the stars are this bright and full. Meanwhile, my feet continue throbbing from the previous twenty-plus-mile days, and in anticipation of all the ones to come. A shooting star streaks above me, and I wish the day's end wasn't all that I looked forward to anymore. I lower my gaze to find that I'm peeing on a crab, who either enjoys it or is too mortified to move.

By 7 a.m., the sun has emerged from the damp curtain of the sky to take center stage as a bright star. Besides the fishermen casting their lines from the concrete harbors, the sweltering beach is empty. Irregular igneous lumps jut from the sandy shore, directing the swirling waves back to the ocean. So much trash washes up here that I fill a bag, look out at the expanse of ragged plastic debris, and give up on starting another.

Henro signs detour me off the highway, beneath a

railroad track, across a field, and beside a graveyard of five-element stupa[8] to a rough shrine that houses a piece of wood. A thin *shimenawa* rope with four straw tails hangs above the offerings of money and booze piled up in front. I'm puzzled why the signs directed me here, but it's a break from the tedium. My map book lists no prayers for wood spirits, so I shrug and bow respectfully to the shrine. An odd feeling wriggles through my chest and I realize that I'll spend all of September on Shikoku. Taking a seat on the steps below to meditate, I gaze at the train tracks and contemplate my time here.

I've spent most of my life waiting for time to fly by, because it's the easiest way to endure onerous situations. Waking up for school or work on Mondays, it was comforting to know that by keeping my head down and powering through, it would soon be the weekend, or a holiday, or summer. But as hard as I try to ignore the pilgrimage, and as much time as I spend fantasizing about being home, time does not fly by here. There are no weekends off, no nights where I can kick back in a bar with other Westerners. From the moment I lift my pack to the moment I set it back down to sleep, it's the routine, the heat, the hours, and the miles of Shikoku.

The day after I arrived it felt like I'd been here forever and would always remain, but in concept I know this isn't true. I'm a watch hand ticking from number to number

---

8 A stone monolith of five stacked geometric shapes, representing the five elements

back to the start. In two days I'll reach T38, in four days T39, and in ninety-five miles Kochi will be complete, the pilgrimage half over. Time passes slowly, inescapably, but it is passing. I can't make this journey meaningful anymore, but I'll keep going through the motions for another month. A final exhalation on the steps and I open my eyes.

A train whistles weakly somewhere between a distant arrival and a distant departure.

12

DRAGONFLIES

BE HERE NOW, I remind myself as the waves curl onto Irino Beach, but all that's on my mind is goals. Besides the usual three of food, shelter, and shit indoors, there are two urgent ones: contact-lens solution and laundry. It's the early afternoon and I've already sweated through what yesterday was my last clean shirt. And after four days of sleeping with my contacts in, my blinks are audible.

Be here now. Kneeling on the talcum-powder sand, I meditate on the distant crest separating two blue tones. Minutes later the sea breeze dries my contacts into sharp ridges.

Screw it.

I head into town.

The pharmacist's yellow Lab perks up with the whoosh of automatic doors. Tail quivering, he dives nose first into the dim sum tray of smells passing through the shop. The pharmacist rises from his desk, I point to my bloodshot corneas, and he hands me contact-lens solution from the shelf. Head tilted back, I'm not expecting the menthol additive.

The moan I emit would embarrass a porn star.

We avoid eye contact after that.

An *osamefuda*, a scratch behind the dog's ears, and my bruised soles return to the concrete treadmill that is Kochi.

A few hours before sunset, I reach the laundromat and empty my dirty clothing bag into the washing machine. The result of the four-day bacterial orgy wallops me across the face. Dumping soap haphazardly onto the reeking pile, I hit the hot water and imagine millions of tiny screams.

Clothes freshly sterilized, I hurry toward shelter past the thousandth farm village this week. Eyes downcast, I pause to observe a wasp laying eggs inside a paralyzed spider, the only new thing in days. Looking up, I'm similarly frozen.

Above a soggy, overturned paddy hovers a galaxy of metallic red dragonflies, the evening sun glittering off their armor plates. Mouth agape, I stand transfixed. In that instant, I know that I'm sharing an experience that's occurred over the centuries as pilgrims, peasants, and holy men stood on this spot, witnessing this marvel and feeling what I do now: lucky.

Lucky to be here.

Lucky to be alive.

And in that moment, I'm chastened. When did this appreciation become so rare? When did I close myself off from these gifts? It's been happening gradually, but I've let myself become immune to Shikoku's beauty, narrowing my focus to the road ahead as I rush toward the evening's shelter. Because I've stopped looking, how many of these ephemeral sights have flown by unseen, forever lost to me? No more. I resolve to snap out of these doldrums and rededicate myself to the pilgrimage.

Then, five minutes later, I see the exact same thing and think: *When the fuck is this road going to end?*

Freed from the distractions of a job, a city, and electronics, I expected my meditation practice to deepen, leading me to some epiphany on this holy path in an exotic land. Instead, focusing on the present increasingly means focusing on pain. As I walk beside a pond of vibrant purple lotus flowers, blood blisters stab between my toes. As I climb through shrouded forests, where stone Buddhas pray among gnarled roots, my thighs cramp and my eyes sting with sweat. It's easier to distract myself with fantasies of iced liquor on climate-controlled flights as I hurry to get off my feet sooner.

By evening I'm passing through a small farming neighborhood en route to the mile long Shin-izuto Tunnel. If there's no sidewalk, I'm preparing for another fun stretch of hugging a soot-caked wall. Then my mantra returns: *Be here now.*

The punch of concrete through my soles intensifies as I slow my pace and my breath. Suddenly, dragonflies surround me. A gushing irrigation canal mutes the traffic, and ravens perched on telephone wires chew through spiders with a crystal-clear crunch. Through the smoke and hissing snap of burning chaff, I see the deep creases in the faces of the farmers as they finish tending their gardens for the day. As I return to the highway, these couple of minutes that I chose to experience are the highlight of my day, excluding minty eyeballs.

Then I enter the tunnel. After twenty minutes spent inhaling the exhaust of bellowing engines, I emerge at sunset and lurch lifelessly to a *henro-goya* beside a long-closed restaurant.

Following a restless night of sleep on a hard-slatted bench, morning meditation is impossible through the mental and physical haze. After checking my pulse to make sure I still have one, I grimly wave aside the countless insects crawling across the soda machine's glowing panel. A can of authentic coffee-flavored beverage spills into my empty stomach.

While I'm applying sunblock a huge moth lands on my arm. Gently unrolling its proboscis to sniff, it flies away with a glob of white lotion protecting its nose like a tropical tourist. The thought of the moth haggling for island trinkets in a bright floral shirt brightens the morning until the rising sun literally does the same.

I parallel a canal on jellied legs, my devastated muscles demanding nutrients I'm unable to provide. An hour later, a *conbini* sign high on a pole comes into view, mocking me with the knowledge that it's another half hour on foot to the town. A wiry, sun-darkened bike *henro* waves merrily, then speeds away at velocities I pray for as blisters sprout underfoot.

At midday I step off the highway and onto Okinohama Beach, my last Pacific beach on the *henro* trail. I cross the chalk-white arc separating the sky-blue water from the forest that stretches unbroken across the faraway peaks. The beach is empty except for a few lounging couples and a fisherman standing waist deep in the waves, his spear poised above his prey. I turn in to the forest. It's a peaceful place. Red crabs scurry through the rocky streambed, snatching whatever morsels drift past, and butterflies flit about, drinking nectar from the flowering vines. I'm sorry to leave it, especially as I emerge to the stench of hundreds of gutted bonita fish, sun-drying on long tarps outside a processing warehouse.

For the first and only time on the pilgrimage, my hunger disappears.

Returning to the highway, behind me is the view of Kochi I've known since I first beheld the Pacific waves pounding over tumbled boulders. Green mountains wind into the distance, one farther than the next, too endless to traverse. Ahead of me, the curves terminate, and there's a sharp pang. I've spent two weeks beside the sea, wishing this would be over faster. Now the lighthouses watch over an ocean I'll soon miss.

Hawks sing just above my head as I crest another foothill, where a young carpenter is building a roadside shack in the hopes of turning it into a *henro* café. J-pop streams from his laptop speakers, and with permission I log into my email. As usual I lie to everyone back home that I'm doing great, then walk another three miles up a baking highway to the penultimate Kochi temple.

A palpable sense of serenity emanates from the courtyard of **Kongo-Fukuji: The Temple of Everlasting Happiness (T38)**. However, the name is somewhat ironic, as its seaside bluff is a favorite spot for suicides. Modeled after the paradise dwelling of the goddess Kannon, past the *Nio-mon* a stream cascades through the mottled pink boulders, feeding a central pond where herons stalk above their reflections in the still water. Statues of Kannon, Jizo, and the rest of the pantheon populate the courtyard, free-standing or perched on kneeling bronze elephants. I wander through gods and rocks to the *honzon*, where a priest leads two separate tour groups through the sutras. Passing among the congregation, he rubs an accordion-folded book of *Hannya Shingyo* on the worshippers' backs. He approaches me with a smile before whacking my back with the heavy tome. The sharp sting into knotted muscle imparts the extra effort put into my blessing.

The sun is a red ember extinguished in the waves by the time I reach a *henro-goya* beside the highway. My feet gnawed up by the late-day race, I limp across the road to overlook the Pacific. Besides the suicidal leaping from the cliffs of T38, some devout monks have ended their lives by sailing west from the shore, bound for the celestial paradise of Kannon. As the sky darkens, I say goodbye to the Ashizura Coast and the last horizon many have seen.

At 4 a.m., a gaggle of old men with flashlights end their predawn stroll on the bench outside my tent. Cans of coffee rattle from the vending machine, reinvigorating their already loud discussion. I emerge from my tent to buy a juice and also alert them that someone is sleeping. They nod to me and only get louder, throwing some "*gai-jin*" into the conversation. A shooting star streaks across the speckled mass above the cove, and I wish for them to leave. The meteoroid doesn't listen, so I return to my tent and shove my earplugs in deep. Three hours later I wake back up, prepared for a grueling final two days in Kochi.

Another morning spent alternating between mountains and sea begins with the aroma of gutted fish permeating the seaside village, which dissipates a half mile into the trees. Zoning out as I hike past naked roots burrowing through crumbly sandstone, I'm thinking about T39 and beyond until a hiss at my feet snaps me back into danger mode. The beady eyes of a venomous mamushi glare into mine before it slithers away with a parting hiss and a flick of its tail. Newly vigilant, I inspect each step of trail ahead, and walk face first into yet another spiderweb.

Other *henro* must have passed through these forests in the last few days, but somehow spiderwebs festoon every few feet of pathway. I tunnel through by swirling my staff, webs wrapping around the bottom until it resembles a cotton candy cone that fell behind the animal pens. The spiders ride the staff to the ground and skitter away, pledging to rebuild. The webs are spaced so regularly on the trail that lowering my staff in a moment's distraction means wiping off another faceful of sticky gauze. By the time I reemerge into another cloud of fish stink, I still can't tell if the spiders lack the reasoning to move their homes, or they're involved in a *Far Side*-esque gambit to snare and eat one weak *henro*.

My lunch break comes outside a small grocery store in Ohama, the entryway brimming with racks of seed packages. While munching on my rice triangle, I puzzle over a mural painted on the seawall that seems to involve a magic fish and Abraham Lincoln. I later discover that this is the story of John Manjiro, the final famous person from the Kochi posters.

A local fisherman, Manjiro was rescued by a whaling vessel after a shipwreck. The captain took him home to Connecticut, where the young man received a decade of Western education. When the Meiji restoration of 1868 opened Japan to outsiders, Manjiro could finally return home, where he was promptly sent back to the U.S. on the first diplomatic mission. As far as I can tell, the magic fish has been erased from the history books.

Further hours of punishment from the sun above and the road below drop me in the shade of a dried-fish shop. Across the street, statues advertise a granite cutter's versatile skill. Jizo pray beside half-moon lanterns, marlins, and minor *Ultraman* villains. All in all, I'd prefer a *kaiju*[9] decorating my yard to a gnome.

---

9 Giant monster

From a pay phone beside the bathroom, I call my father back home.

"How's it going?" he asks. "You're nearing the halfway point."

"I know. It's going great," I reply, having just cut away more blisters in a dingy toilet stall while planning a bicycle theft.

"I'm glad you remembered to call today."

"Why?"

"…You forgot what day it is, didn't you?"

"It's … Walkday?"

"It's Rosh Hashanah."

"Oh, Happy New Year."

There's a drawn-out sigh. "At least you'll be at temple."

It deserves a slow golf clap into the mouthpiece.

"How long you been holding on to that joke?"

"A few days."

After hanging up, I switch to the sandals to prevent my raw pinky toe from rubbing against its neighbor. Now separated from the friction, it sticks out, colliding with my staff.

"Nearly halfway done." I grit my teeth. "Nearly halfway done." Walking meditation lasts until the third time I stub my toe against the staff, when I have to devote my entire body to cringing while swearing.

Leaving the seawall for Highway 321, I hike inland past dry-docked boats languishing in the grass beneath a foothill. Then it's more hours of nothing until the sun sets.

Catching my breath in a covered bus stop beside a

bridge, my first attempt at standing back up fails. With my head hanging below my knees, I dumbly regard the ants blanketing the carpeted floor.

This isn't the worst place to sleep ...

Comfortable as it looks, I decide against it and force myself onto my feet for another half mile to what a liquor store clerk tells me is a campsite. After setting up my tent, I realize it really resembles a lawn on private property. I don't care. If security disturbs me, I'll act confused, repeating "*Camp-jo*" and pointing at my map.

I'm in Japan.

They'll politely drive me to a hotel.

The next morning, a handicapped-accessible toilet stall offers enough space for a luxurious sponge bath. I inspect the raw skin and red-rimmed blisters on my feet, which may be infected, but there's nothing to do but rebandage them and hope for the best. I'm uninsured, and a doctor's bill could derail the pilgrimage.

Wait and see, I think, recalling all the other times I've panicked over some imagined medical issue. *In the meantime, try not to drive yourself nuts.*

Among the many emotions welling up as I near the pilgrimage's midpoint, one of the biggest is relief. Being halfway done means I'm halfway to not worrying about things like infection anymore. I start off toward the last temple in Kochi and soon pass the real campsite. Despite the liquor clerk's assurances last night, it was not "close," at least not in my ragged stupor. It was as distant as the bed at home that I can't wait to sleep in again.

The early morning is abandoned to a solitary man, dwarfed by the field he's hoeing. By noon, I wave to some construction workers, then spend the next six hours trekking along empty highways. With two traffic lanes packed into one car's width, the nonexistent shoulders fall into a creek and butt up against the mountainside. On that thin white strip, every blind corner is an adrenaline rush. The half hours between water breaks fall into a routine. Zone out, fantasize about not being here, meditate so I can be here, hear the birds chirping above the gurgling stream, feel the wind that sways the dangling vines, then break meditation, zone out, and think about the end.

Despite my attempts to be present, my heart jumps as I think about reaching Temple 40 in Ehime and how it's the start of the "lasts." The last I'll see of the Pacific, the last of the three-day walks between Temple 43 and 44, the last of the *nansho* temples, the last two provinces, and the last of my time here. While fighting to be in the moment, I must also accept that while I'm hot, tired, and enduring another drudging hour of nothing on a concrete ribbon, the moment kinda sucks.

And over the hours of this balancing act, I finally come to peace with it. The battle for focus through the dulling monotony. Enduring the sharp strike of the road into my soles. The days laboring up mountains as my legs strain to birth new muscles. These are my offerings to the next temple. Compared to such alms, my *osamefuda*, my coins, and my chanted prayers come cheap.

Nearing sunset, I race over Nakasuji-gawa Dam, feet

aching, knees creaking, and promising myself I'll take it easy once I get out of Kochi. Twenty-six miles ends on a pathway snaking up Red Turtle Mountain toward T39. Passing the corrugated tin farmhouses, I'm so dopey from the day's marathon that I have to ask directions from four people in the space of a quarter mile before finding the *Nio-mon*.

According to legend, the bell of **Enkoji: Emitting Light Temple (T39)** was brought to the complex on the back of a red turtle. The bell would go on to reside in a Tokyo museum as a national treasure. The turtle would go on to harass a stout Italian plumber. I approach main shrine and offer to the *honzon* every step on feet bruised, strained, bandaged, and blistered that brought me here, panting and weak, from T38.

Descending to a bus stop beside the road, I fill out my journal while waiting for nightfall. A spider weaves its web in an empty window frame, struggling through its circumnavigations. When the sky is black I shove everything into my tent, insert earplugs, and prepare for some police harassment. I've never been so open about my squatting, but bus stop or jail cell, sleep is happening now. Every appendage and joint throbs against the cooling concrete, my devotions to T40.

Kochi is complete.

SECTION THREE

EHIME: THE LAND OF ENLIGHTENMENT

13
FINALLY, AN *ONSEN*

STEP BY STEP, the mountains approach. And with a newfound confidence, I think: *Let them come.*

Plagued by nightmares, I've been up since 4:30 a.m., but I've handled tired. I haven't eaten in hours, but hunger's nothing new. New blisters ping their location with each step, more offerings to the next temple. Ahead, the shark-fin peaks slice through the earth. Hikes on a scorcher like today are murder, but after a couple hours I'll be on the other side and praying at T40, the first temple in Ehime and the geographic halfway point. After everything the first three hundred and seventy-five miles have thrown at me, I'm finally prepared for the last three hundred and seventy-five.

Step by step, Shikoku passes beneath me, a series of familiar obstacles.

From a forest slope carpeted with fluffy cedar bark

and sawtoothed ferns, I emerge into the open sky of terraced fields. A few sun-drunk mosquitoes waft onto my
limbs and are easily massacred. In the shade of rough
shacks, where overalls hang to dry above rows of split-
toe galoshes, I reapply insect repellent before reentering
the woods. In the leafy cool a whining squadron attacks,
bouncing off my chemical force field.

On another incline, I chuckle at my frantic memo-
rization of the *nansho* temples that first week as they
replay through my head. Fearing another day like Burning
Mountain, *T12, T20, T21, T27, T60, T66, T71, T81,
T82* became my mantra, reassuring me that this hike isn't
the worst to come. Three weeks in, the numbers have lost
their ominous power. There will always be long, draining climbs up a mountain or highway after a day of long,
draining walks beneath the sun. There will always be the
equally arduous descents that cause what the locals have
dubbed "laughing knees." My *nansho* mantra is ingrained,
but the ground beneath me is enough to worry about at
the moment.

An hour and a half later, I cross the border between
Kochi and Ehime atop Matsuo-shige Pass, clacking my
staff against the thick wall of bamboo. Signs promising castle ruins that I never find bring me to a viewing
platform overlooking Sukomowan Bay. Far below, small
islands near the port sprout metallic growths of industry.
Farther out, forested mounds dot the waves, becoming
vague ideas as they approach the horizon. Hawks wheel
and soar above the sheer cliffs, tracing parabolas that make

you wonder why Superman always looks so serious when he flies. Across the Pacific lies a home I no longer miss. It's become an old friend, waiting to greet me on the tarmac as I disembark the plane. I'm here now, where I belong for the time being. After drinking my fill of the Pacific, I descend into the Dojo of Enlightenment.

While I've adapted to the hiking, the heat remains a menace. As the daily temperature peaks, my synaptic network browns out during the climbs and descents and further climbs through orchards, forests, roads, and rivers. Back in the city and lost in confusion, I slump onto a curb in the shade of a hospital's entrance. I'd check myself in, but given the yen conversion rate, I don't want to go bankrupt for medical care.

Still, this is bad.

While cooling my brain in the freezer section of a grocery store, I nod along to shopper's directions to T40 until words aren't nonsense anymore. Following a red asphalt path through town, I arrive at **Kanjizaiji: The Temple of Kannon (T40)**. I recite sutras to a triad of Yakushi, Amida, and Kannon, carved by Kukai from a single piece of wood, and fireworks go off inside my chest to celebrate this milestone.

Halfway done.

I don't want to be so happy about this.

With reverence, I dip a ladle into a small trough and pour water over the statues of deities carved into the wall. Dark stains run from their laps back to the trough from years of prayers, but my mind is blank. At this point in the day, I have only one wish and wait patiently at the stamp office for it to be granted by the head priest: *tsuyado*.

Stretched out atop four folded blankets, I'm "clean" from another bathroom-sink sponge bath. Tomorrow, the priest will draw me a map to an *onsen* over a dozen miles away. Open late into the evening, it's a certainty that I'll make it. For the first time on Shikoku, I'll be relaxing in the hot pools, my tensions melting away along with this grime pasted to my skin. Buzzing with anticipation, I know sleep will be as impossible as for a kid on Christmas Eve.

I pass out instantly in the quiet room.

An early day of hiking and minor heat exhaustion will do that to you.

Waking from a vivid dream about my childhood friend Taylor, I meditate and prepare for the long day ahead. As an experiment, I forgo socks in my shoes. My feet will never stop hurting, so it's time to mitigate this disaster by taking some pressure off. With the majority of both feet wrapped in duct tape, and using more as hot spots form in my arches, my hypothesis is correct. No new blisters. One more problem solved, kind of. Without socks to absorb the sweat and dirt, new life forms will thrive. Sadly, this means that once I finish the pilgrimage the shoes must be thrown away, rather than taking them home, dousing them in gasoline, and watching them burn to ash with a glass of scotch in my hand.

Past the pilgrimage's halfway point, each step is a subtraction, chipping away at the total mileage until nothing remains. My heart leaps every time I think ahead to the *onsen*, to the final province, to home, so I force myself into another balance. Every thought toward the future requires another walking meditation. There's a lot of meditation today, because if a hot shower felt that good last week...

Through the city, the *henro* trail follows a garbage truck's collection route, then a sewage truck. Their stops are just short enough that I'm gagging downwind for a good half hour. It's a relief when the path branches off, then less so as it leads through the industrial section.

After another half hour of olfactory bliss among rumbling cement trucks and fabrication factories, I gulp deep breaths beside a wooded river. Tucked into the leaf litter is a ¥1,000 note, and I rejoice. This will pay for food and the *onsen*, all I want for today. Scanning the ground for more, I realize I'm living out a *Calvin and Hobbes* comic strip. *Take the ossetai and go*, I demand. *This is time you could be soaking.*

Standing at the foot of another two miles rising into the forest, a new hiking mantra takes hold. *A few difficult hours of your life, and then it's done.* It's of greater use than reciting the *nansho* temples, especially since the hours are no longer as difficult. Over three hundred and seventy-five miles in, my thighs are corded with muscle and my back has doubled in size. While my shoes will always trouble me, in a month they'll be a memory. There will rarely be a day without a punishing slope, but there will never be a day where it's too steep to complete.

At the foot of the trail, the wind picks up, carrying

the bark of a lone dog in the distance, and crows fill the silence overhead: the soundtrack to another battle with gravity. There's an *onsen* on the other side of this mountain. I'll climb over it or tunnel through, but I'm getting to that spa today.

When the path levels off into soft dirt and cedars, a baby boar bursts across the trail. On guard for Mama, I'm glad for the heavier stick and that my daily karate practice has kept my reflexes sharp. No further boars appear, so it's a good second day in the Land of Enlightenment. I take a breather at a cliff-top shrine, where the trees part to reveal another vista of islands and inlets. The wind whispers "*shhhhh*" through the bamboo and I pause, my mind quiet as a library. Even without the dragonflies surrounding me, I feel lucky, appreciating these views again. Maybe that connection I experienced in the rice fields will return. On a perfect day like this, anything seems possible.

After speeding through one more town, finally, finally, finally, I'm inside an *onsen*. I enter a lounge area filled with the contented grunts of old men in thrumming massage chairs, pass by a small café where robed families slurp up salty broth, and hand the front desk the only non-sweaty bill in my wallet. Placing my pack behind the counter, they hand over a key on a plastic tether and point me to the men's locker room, glad to exorcise the powerful stench haunting their lobby.

In the changing room my key twists in the locker door, safeguarding only the essentials: stamp book, map book, journal, voice recorder, camera, passport, and money. The rest of that backpack can go to hell. Out of curiosity I step onto the electronic scale beside the entrance, having recently noticed that the small pudge encircling my waist has disappeared. The digital display chases its tail before announcing the result: 74 kilograms.

There's no "lbs" button on the scale, so I give up on the conversion and step through the steamy glass doors to the tubs. There's an audible record skip as everyone turns to stare at the pale, bald intruder. But who cares? I'm Templeton the rat entering the fair. Hot water in countless basins and faucets, wet and dry saunas, soap and brushes. Where do I begin?

Careful not to rush on the slick tile floors, I grab a handful of rough salt from a bin and scour my skin pink. At a mirrored cubicle with a blue stool and hose, I scrub hard with the sudsy washcloth, douse myself with the provided bucket, and scrub again. Three weeks of stink, sweat, and strain gurgles down the drain. Lathering up again, I shave my head and stubble clean with a disposable razor and hose myself back down until I'm a surgically sterile surface.

I lower myself in the hot saltwater pool first, and the other patrons either blatantly distance themselves or climb out. All night it's tight smiles and tight nods before looking anywhere else. All except for the guy whose full vest and half sleeves of tattoos signal organized-crime membership. He's not smiling at anyone, and I ain't making eye contact with him.

Any remaining cares quickly dissolve in the water. A

few trips in and out of the cold pool, hot pool, cold pool clear out my pores, and strong sauna jets unknot a lower back locked up beyond soreness to immobility. The pinnacle of the experience comes as I stand beneath a pressure hose dumping a heavy stream onto my neck, where apparently I've been storing opium in the cartilage. All I hear is popping and crackling as the water pounds down before I float out of my body. I return to the hottest pool. The temperature barely registers as I lie back in a daze, renewed.

Throughout the evening bodies splash, soak, and reemerge around me. *Onsen* modesty is a strange thing. Everyone covers his crotch with a hand or a small towel when moving from tub to tub until resubmerging, as if water's not as transparent as air. And if balls are immodest, why is there a grinning Tanuki statue outside with a boner and testicles large enough to affect the tides?

My first *onsen* visit ends in an outdoor pool. Muscles pliant, skin fresh, body unencumbered, I'm serene beneath the stars as the chatter of the women in their section drifts over the wall. Mind wandering, I become less serene as I imagine them naked, then my last girlfriend naked, and blood pulses south. There's only one thing that will make this *onsen* more awkward. I distract myself with my weight's metric conversion.

C'mon, you know this. Seventy-four kilograms. A kilogram is … 2.2 pounds? So multiply by two, then add twenty percent?

Blocking out my ex-girlfriend's thighs, I focus

with a mental intensity that should have been applied to the SATs. Blood reverses course up to my brain and the answer appears. Because of my frequent inability to find food, since stepping off the train I've lost about ten pounds a week, dropping from 190 to 163, which I last weighed when I was shorter, chubbier, and twelve. This would explain the veins bulging from my stomach that would gross out Iggy Pop.

An announcement not about monster attacks comes over the PA, and everyone leaves. The *onsen* is closing.

Inside a rest hut in the parking lot, I drift into undisturbed sleep without soreness, fear of infection, or grimy skin. The drastic weight loss is a bit of a shock, but I'm feeling healthy and strong. Sore shoulders and cramping legs no longer wake me at night or greet me at dawn. The backpack's weight demands attention, but no longer pulls me down with it. I breathe hard on the climbs, but air no longer ignites my lungs. The Land of Ascetic Training has prepared me for the next three hundred and seventy-five miles, a series of familiar obstacles.

But in two days, I'll break one of the temples.

Then things get worse.

14

HOW INDIANA JONES LIED TO ME

FEELING TRANSFORMED AFTER my long-awaited *onsen* visit, I'm ready for the second half of my pilgrimage. The sky is bright, my muscles are limber, I'm clear-headed after a deep meditation, and without socks the foot pain is manageable. Also, in five days it'll be the longest I've gone without booze in the past three years, proving that I'm not an alcoholic.

However, knowing that exact length of time is probably a warning sign.

Regardless, I'm enjoying the pilgrimage again, now that I'm halfway toward never doing this pilgrimage ever again. The only moment of concern comes at the entrance to a forested pathway bypassing a highway tunnel. An old mountain farmer in overalls points up the hill with his hoe, relating some urgent instruction or warning. I reply that I don't understand, thank him, and continue up. If there's been a rapid increase in boar attacks over the past few days, he'd do more to stop me. A half hour later the undergrowth behind me rustles and snorts.

I ignored the withered local's advice.

In horror movies, this is how you die.

I freeze. The rustling moves away, then silence. Yet another transformation from this pilgrimage: the amount of time spent fearing boar attack has increased three hundred percent in just one month, up from zero percent in the previous twenty-eight years. I relax once I reach a mountain town, the street lined with bubbling aquariums. Goldfish are safe, or at least contained.

A few miles below the town I enter Uwajima City, where a laid-back afternoon of sightseeing begins with my first Japanese castle, which is surprisingly small. I'd expected something dramatic, as Kurosawa had led me to believe. Instead, each level is the size of a modest two-bedroom apartment. After that historical reality check, I break to meditate in Tenshaen Park, the sprawling vacation retreat of an eighteenth-century feudal lord. Unbeknownst to me, the hundreds of koi fish navigating the central pond have been conditioned over the decades to equate visitors with food pellets. I recoil as a writhing mass of gaping pink mouths explodes from the water onto the grassy bank. While that image processes into nightmares, the rest of the day passes through peaceful farmland. A woman in a skirt hoes a field below an overpass, showing a flash of bare leg with each strike to the earth. A farmer harvests a narrow crescent of rice paddy tucked between the bend of the road and the foot of a mountain. At the end of the day an old *henro* politely suggests that I find another rest hut, anywhere else, by politely jabbing his finger on every other one on the map. I do find a nicer spot a mile down the road, practicing some karate beside a stream before a night of refreshing sleep on soft grass.

The next morning brings me to one of Shikoku's most heavily agricultural sections. Despite the overcast skies, the paddies gleam emerald and gold. A gaggle of elementary school students in rain-slicker-yellow caps toddles to school behind a teenager in black slacks and a pressed white shirt. Ravens clack and caw as they hop about, devouring whatever animal never made it across the road. With new eyes, I see the rice as more than just a landscape. Instead, it's as much a piece of Shikoku's history as the temples and castles. Mentally dividing the fields into *koku*, I imagine the lives, economies, and governments built upon these stalks.

A *koku* is a measurement equal to 150 kilograms of rice, the amount needed to feed one man for one year; the number of *koku* in a fiefdom informed both the taxable wealth of the territory and the strength of the army. Equivalent in value to one *ryo*, the gold currency, both *koku* and *ryo* made up a soldier's salary during the feudal Edo period. The fields surrounding me defended Uwajima Castle, built Tenshaen Park, maintained armies, and sustained the people who lived in the middle of it all. Now the feudal system, the samurai, the castle, and the park are all history, and the rice continues to flourish here in the fertile Mima Valley.

It was also during the Edo period that it became popular to worship Inari, the Shinto goddess of rice and fertility. Over a third of all Shinto shrines in Japan are dedicated to her, and **Ryukoji: Dragon's Ray Temple (T41)** is the nation's head office of Inari worship. Accordingly, it's been patronized by samurai and merchants since its founding in 807.

Inside a lavender-scented stamp office I hand my book to the wrinkled matron behind the counter. With great care, she places a strip of newspaper beneath the page so the ink won't bleed through, and begins the ritual. Pressing the rubber hard into the red ink pad, she rolls the three stamps firmly across the paper before conducting the wand of black ink through elaborate loops and lines. Along with the ¥300, I give her an *osamefuda* and my sincere gratitude. Her doughy face breaks into a grandmother's smile.

Despite costing the same per page, the effort by each stamp office varies widely. Women, especially elders, usually perform the ritual with a patient and delicate grace. With men it's either elegant calligraphy followed by touching the book to their forehead in blessing, or a mad dash of dry bristles across the page. The half-hearted ones are extra disappointing because, in part, these stamps control my pilgrimage.

I almost didn't get the stamp book, having been warned by a few Shikoku websites about the "stamp race": that the focus on receiving calligraphy at the temples can distract from the journey in between them. I don't regret buying it, but on these multiple-temple days it does become a burden. Arriving at a stamp office after it closes at 5:30 p.m. means a night of walking to a rest hut and a morning of backtracking, then waiting until 8:00 a.m. for the office to reopen. It means eating breakfast and lunch on the run, breaking meditation to check my watch, and hustling past scenery at the end of the day. Because of this, I deserve more than a couple quick thuds of rubber and haphazard bristle scratches. But when a bus tour guide heaves a duffel bag onto the counter with a heavy thump, I lose any expectations of solid ink lines. My book becomes yet another off the stack, stamped, signed, and returned without a glance. After wiping the sweat from my hands, I slip my newly signed book carefully into a zip-lock bag before sliding it into my pack. The bus *henro* hand off their books and scrolls to their guide, who restacks them into the duffel bags before lugging them into their air-conditioned transport. I try not to be resentful, but not that hard.

While T41 is dedicated to rice growing, **Butsumokuji: The Temple of Buddha's Tree (T42)** is dedicated to animal husbandry, patronized by farmers and peasants. In the middle of the courtyard stands a rough shrine to Dainichi Buddha, the protector of animals. Hoping for the good health of their livestock, farmers have placed toy cows, chickens, dogs, and horses in front of the statue, like concerned parents leaving pinwheels with Jizo.

Besides their agricultural history, T41 and T42 are

also the first temples on the pilgrimage destroyed by U.S. bombing raids during World War II. There's a tinge of guilt as I pass between the bright red *Nio* with freshly painted blue flower petals on their flowing robes. The majority of these temples have been burned in wars over the centuries, mostly, it seems, due to the warlord Chosokabe, but this was the first time they'd been destroyed by non-Japanese. My presence here feels disrespectful. The monk nonchalantly signs my book and waves me off.

Inari's abundance extends beyond rice in the Mima Valley. Enormous produce, radiation-leak big, ripens on trees and vines along the highway or grows beneath plastic domes. At one roadside fruit stand my mouth waters at grapes the size of robin eggs, but the massive clusters are massively expensive. As I pass by another, the clerk beckons me over.

"*Ossetai*," he smiles, handing me an Asian pear the size of a softball and waving me off.

As I'm crunching through the last juicy bites, two petite farmer women invite me up their driveway for some figs fresh off their tree. I nod to a student *henro* I met at dawn, who's already snacking graciously on the sweet fruit. I'm surprised that he's ahead of me. I've been hurrying all day to reach the next town before sunset, hoping to catch the millennium-old practice of cormorant fishing. A bow, two *osamefuda*, and I'm back on the road.

Despite the many servings of fruit today, hunger gnaws at me. Heading to a *conbini* for lunch, I pass the withered *henro* who kicked me out of the rest hut yesterday evening. The student I can understand, but how did a senior citizen get ahead of me? Are there some hidden warp whistles I'm missing? Combing the store's refrigerated shelves, I'm hungry enough that a yakisoba hoagie smothered in mayo sounds like a good choice. Once the brick hits my gut, I dig for some Imodium.

New food rule: Before eating, say the ingredients out loud to yourself.

Founded more than 1,400 years ago, **Meisekiji: Brilliant Stone Temple (T43)** became the dojo of practice for mountain ascetics. As with T38, I'm entranced by the palpable energy emanating from the courtyard, which is bordered by colossal redwoods. Each cedar-plank hall and shrine looks to have taken root and sprouted from seedlings dropped by the overhanging boughs. The rich, burgundy rooftop of the main hall spreads like wings above me as I complete my prayers. Turning away, I'm transfixed by an elderly *henro*.

In over four hundred miles of pathway, every pilgrim I've seen is dressed the same: a staff, a conical hat, and a white vest like the cartoon *henro* in the stickers. This man is dressed like Kukai from the statues. Sunshine plays across the dark lacquer of his maroon dome hat, and his flowing brown robes sway as he breezes up to the *Daishi* shrine on coiled rope sandals. His right hand grips an expensive elm staff topped with six brass rings hanging from a hoop, symbolizing the six states of existence. Called a *shakujo*, it's used by ascetic monks for *shugendo*, mountain-walking meditation.

Henro-wise, this guy is a pro amongst us amateurs.

Turning back, I see a torii standing on a raised platform of earth, level with the temple's veranda. Previous *henro* have piled wishing stones atop the torii's crossbar, and I decide to add my own. If any temple can make my wish come true, it's this one. A two-foot gap separates the veranda from the rock wall supporting the earthen platform. Instead of walking down the temple steps and up another flight to the torii, I figure I can clear the gap.

In midair between the sharp snap of the wooden plank and the fast-approaching rock wall, I learn that Indiana Jones lied to me: ancient temples are not sturdy leaping platforms.

The stone impacts with a dull thud into my shinbone.

I sprawl on the level dirt, in momentary denial that I just did something that stupid. Hot liquid beads down my leg. I check my shin. Purple skin puckers around an overflowing well of crimson drops. I've had plenty worse. I glance back to the split plank in the dirt beside the temple it was recently attached to, possibly for centuries.

Cold tendrils grip my chest.

I don't know how much ancient temples cost.

I place my stone on the torii and wish that no one saw what just happened, then speed through my prayers to the *Daishi*. Anxiety yells loudly that I run away before anyone notices, but compulsiveness is yelling louder that I finish my prayers and leave no blank pages. As I rush through *Hannya Shingyo*, my legs getting weak again, the maroon *henro* approaches softly on his rope sandals. With wide, concerned eyes he points at my shoe darkening with blood. I repeat, "*It's OK. Thank you. It's OK,*" with a nervous smile, get my stamp, and speed to the bathroom to scrub the gash with soap and water.

While applying the Band-Aids, I'm approached by a young man who brings a translated message, saying that the maroon *henro* is worried for me and has medicine for my bleeding shin. I tell him I'm fine, to thank the maroon *henro*, and then flee into the woods. I'm not going to stick around after breaking a temple a dozen centuries old, sure that the question "Are you all right?" will soon be followed by "Why is that board on the ground?" followed by "How much money do you have?" followed by "That's not nearly enough, *gaijin*" followed by "Are your organs healthy?"

A few hours later I realize I've been going backward, away from Ozu City. I've lost my chance to see cormorant fishing at dusk. It's late afternoon, and now gaggles of children in yellow hats toddle home. Middle school students ride past on bikes with license plates: G for girl, B for boy, followed by their number. My frustration grows at my tight schedule each time I check my watch against dusk, sick of missing local culture because of some little detour. Once the sun goes horizontal, so do I, and I'm tired of the routine. Three more weeks and I'll be finished, but it's three weeks of Shikoku, all day, every day.

I need to see cormorant fishing. In this 1,300-year-old tradition, fishermen throw leashed birds into the water, where they catch fish and bring them back to the boat. Seeing this living cultural thing will break the monotony, if only for a day. I race against sunset yet again, the breeze cooling the blood still trickling from beneath the bandages. Preferring a sterile place to check my wound, I settle for retaping my leg in a dingy porno-shop bathroom of bare concrete and an exposed squat toilet.

Nearing 6 p.m., I enter a long highway tunnel with no sidewalk and dim lights. I turn on my headlamp as cars whoosh by too close for comfort. The ones without their headlights on take notice at the last minute and swerve around me. In fifteen minutes my voice recorder is filled with goodbye messages to my parents, friends, and anyone else I can think of.

Having survived the tunnel and with a new lease on life, I continue down the highway toward Ozu City while the sky darkens. My exhausted body demands I stop for the night at one of the rest huts I pass, but now it's become a fight to detach the end of my day from sunset. I have to free myself from this schedule and walk into unknown territory. By this time on any other day, I would be finishing my journal and preparing to sleep. Instead, I continue on toward the oil-black rivers and distant lights of Ozu City. A scraggly *henro* approaches and we nod, glad that we're not the only ones out this late.

When I reach the city, reality is staring me in my dead eyes. I don't know where I am, where the cormorant fishermen will be, or where I'll eventually sleep. In the ambient light I follow my map book past closed metal gratings and unlit neon signs. Swearing constantly at myself for turning down the previous rest huts, I hunt for an alley to pass out in. Then, through the dark, I hear the lapping of water against stone walls.

Following the sound, I look over the edge of the canal, where firelight sways beneath a bridge. Illuminated by lanterns, the captain stands on the bow of his boat in baggy pants and floppy hat, cradling a cormorant on a leash. The long neck and sharp beak glance around before the captain tosses it into the water. It dives beneath the boat. He reels in another line and a sleek bird bursts from the water, a firelight-orange fish glittering in its sharp beak. The captain grabs the bird's neck, removes the fish, and the bird disappears beneath the surface. I've made it. I broke my schedule and saw something cultural. I've never felt such a sense of triumph while watching repeatedly disappointed waterfowl.

Finding a rest hut in a small park above an *onsen*, I set up my tent before heading to the spa to scrub my leg. It must be cleaner than the porno-shop bathroom. The cut is still bleeding, so I tape it up and keep it dry while I take a load off in the pools. Massaged by the water jets, I allow some self-congratulation at walking through sunset and seeing the cormorant fishing. There's so little on this pilgrimage I have control over. It's always nice to have a win.

As I'm rising to leave, sudden head spins take me to my knees. Noises are too loud and my skin is pulsing. I rest a while longer before returning to my tent. Crawling inside my sleeping bag, I feel clean. Inside my shinbone, my immune system feels differently.

15

DOES THIS LOOK INFECTED TO YOU?

S CRUBBING MY LEG in a public bathroom sink near dawn, I ignore the tinge spreading from the edges of the puckered skin. As an uninsured foreigner carrying weak U.S. dollars, one hospital visit will end my pilgrimage.

It's just part of the healing process. There's no reason to panic.

I dab sunblock around the fresh bandages and venture out to see Ozu's famous castle. Perched on a hilltop overlooking the city, it should be easy to find. After an hour of fruitless wandering through empty streets, I give up on the map. I'll just ask someone. Spotting my tobacco doppelganger outside a liquor store, I wait beside the cigarette machine for the streets to fill. I'm still hoping to be confronted by someone lugging an oxygen tank, blaming me for making smoking so attractive. I remain unrecognized, but once the shop opens, a customer points up to the giant castle looming over us. A bow, an *osamefuda*, and I'm off, reminded yet again how being frequently lost makes me an awful tourist. By the time I find any famous landmark, instead of thinking *Amazing! Think of the centuries of human existence contained within this structure!* I think *Finally, there's that fucking thing.*

Two stories taller than Uwajima, Ozu Castle survived the U.S. firebombing raids that leveled the rest of this town. Despite the morning's frustration, I circle the perimeter with a goofy grin. Whether it's Europe or Asia, I'll never get over how people can walk around with a castle in the middle of town like it's nothing. I'm sure people could say the same for landmarks like the Space Needle or the Statue of Liberty, but to date no pitched sword battles have taken place there.

On the highway outside Ozu is another famous pilgrimage spot, the bridge Kukai slept under when no one in town would offer lodging to a wandering beggar. Unlike with Emon Saburo, the cruel businessman who refused Kukai alms, somehow this didn't end with a town full of dead kids.

Traditionally, because Kukai's spirit still rests beneath the bridges along the pilgrimage, *henro* must carry their staffs across rather than disturb him with the tapping. Beneath this bridge, a polished granite *Daishi* still slumbers. After bowing, I slip my *osamefuda* and coins into a small tin box, then feed the koi in the river from the pellet dispenser. Like the fish in Tenshaen Park, they battle for space to receive their offerings. Looking down at the thrashing mass, I notice the pink flush peeking above the bandages.

In the bathroom of a mechanic's shop down the road, I reapply sunblock to what has to be sunburn. I should have rubbed in the lotion this morning instead of dabbing it around the bandages, but I didn't want them to lose their already tenuous grip on my hairy legs. Patting the seeping gash dry with a paper towel before replacing the Band-Aids, I return to the busy highway.

During the hours flanked by porno shops and humming lights, I zone out, thinking about the term "staycation." I finally understand the attraction: the ease of resting at home instead of traversing an endless concrete strip, worrying about a sunburn that kind of looks like an infection.

Then the path turns off into a grassy forest.

Diesel engines become a memory as birds sing to each other in the tangled undergrowth, promising sex or violence. In a terraced grove, fresh-cut bundles of rice hang from bamboo drying racks, resembling shaggy stick insects. As wind slithers through the rustling stalks of a field in mid-September of no identifiable century, I remember why I hate stay-cations. I've never grown from being at ease, and these ephemeral moments don't happen in a living room.

I can't leave yet.

My leg has to be fine.

Finishing my lunch outside a grocery store in Uchiko City, I nod respectfully to a grizzled *henro* as he pulls his rolling suitcase through the automatic doors. Elderly pilgrims like him are inspiring. It must take true devotion to walk this path a few miles a day for months while strapping young *henro* like myself speed past. As I toss the sandwich wrapper in the trash, a tour guide stops to practice her already perfect English. She directs me to the town's "antique street" of homes and shops dating from the 1700s.

Happy to see more of ancient Japan after all the highway porno shops, I find the detour is well worth it. The slatted plank homes are straight out of a samurai movie set, and dramatic posters announce upcoming sumo matches. In another welcome break, a recording of classical music plays throughout the town at noon, instead of an air-raid siren. More tired than usual, I take a seat outside a boutique toy shop and stretch out my legs. The pink flush has reddened and spread farther past the bandages, where I'm sure I applied sunblock this morning.

My history tour is over as my first anxiety attack in over a year begins.

Grabbing a bar of soap from the shop's bathroom with trembling hands, I slam open the outdoor faucet's valve, scrub furiously, wash, scrub, and wash again, so harried I forget to take off my shoe. Gulping some tea purchased from the clerk for letting me use the hose and most of her soap, I taste nothing. My head is hissing television static with the volume cranked. With one sloshing shoe, I navigate through the tunnel vision to a Shinto temple on the next street. Eyes shut in the tranquil courtyard, I measure my breaths and remind myself that I was expecting this.

Before leaving for Japan I knew I'd have at least one anxiety attack. It happens every time I travel, but I've been dealing with it my entire life. It began with nightmares. Waking from one is my first memory, and they were so constant growing up that falling asleep can still make me nervous. By elementary school it became hypochondria, worrying over any meat that wasn't burned through and washing my hands so compulsively that my parents intervened. Sickness and decay sent such shivers through me that I refused to hug my uncle the last time I ever saw him, uncertain if his stomach cancer was contagious. Partly due to that lingering guilt, by high school I'd gotten it somewhat under control. However, when I'm in a new place and things are in flux, the anxiety comes roaring back to life.

The most frustrating part is the helplessness. Even when I know nothing's wrong, attempting to use reason during an attack is like remarking "I don't think I smell smoke" to someone sitting beside you in a crowded auditorium while a man on the PA system screams, "FIRE!!!!!!" over and over again. He's so insistent that eventually you start coughing and running.

With deep, slow inhalations I remind myself that every other time I've panicked over some illness or infection, it's turned out fine. The sunburn will fade by tomorrow, I'll feel foolish like always, and the pilgrimage will continue. This isn't like Korea, where I had insurance through the school and could visit the hospital twice in a month, to be told it was nothing. Opening my eyes, I see a row of red lanterns leading back to Uchiko's main street. I refuse to succumb to my frantic imagination. On this final journey, things will be different.

I have few clear memories of the day after leaving the temple. My legs run on autopilot, and the world is a jittery blur.

By dusk the highway slope levels off near a Shinto temple. A grizzled *henro* unwinds on a bench near his tent, chaining from one cigarette to the next. Recognizing me from earlier in the day, he gives a friendly wave. I wave back automatically, unable to place him until I see the rolling suitcase at his feet, the same one he'd pulled into the grocery store while I ate lunch. I'd respected him then. But as he savors another drag beside his shelter while I fumble with aluminum poles inside a whining cloud of mosquitoes, I nearly yell in frustration: "How do you old smokers keep beating me here? You're dragging luggage through the woods!"

It's the first time in hours that I'm not thinking about my left shin.

Diving inside my tent, I slaughter the few mosquitoes that follow before checking the wound again.

It'll be fine. It's no redder than the blisters on your feet, and who knows what germs they've been exposed to? It's a small cut and you've kept it clean and bandaged. You tore two inches out of your calf with a bike pedal last year, and that healed up.

My journal opened for the daily entry, I get as far as finding the castle in Ozu City before another wave of anxiety hits and I start shaking.

The pilgrimage can't end here.

Predawn, the grizzled *henro* hacks up every cigarette from the day before and starts off. When the coughing fades into the distance I mash my face into the pillow, willing myself back to sleep.

Within a minute I'm up and shining the flashlight on my shin. It has to be sunburn making it swell hot and red around the crusty bandages. Sunburn is why my heart's pounding and my stomach's in knots.

Feeling wobbly, I rejoin the highway.

By midmorning it feels like I've been walking for days as I whiplash between panic and denial. I finally drop onto a covered bench across from a rocky hillside cemetery. A grandmother parks her motorized scooter nearby and shuffles through the tombstones, gathering acorns in the pockets of her dress. I check my leg again. Squeezing my eyes shut, I focus on the soft breeze and the trilling birds, ignoring my pounding thoughts.

There's a gentle tap on my shoulder.

The grandmother places two handfuls of acorns into my hands. A bow, and her *osamefuda* is forgotten as I rush off.

Below my left knee, my calf and ankle are swelling.

Ragged from another hour trapped inside my head, I

enter the town of Kuma. I'm dimly aware of a local hospital, but my pilgrimage can't end here. The forest pathway from T44 to T45 is one of the *henro* trail highlights. Passing briefly through the next town, it crosses mountain ridges before exiting level with a famous Fudo carved into the cliff above the main hall. I have to see this.

Besides, it's just sunburn.

On my way to T44 I meet Haruka, the first woman *henro* my age. She's striking, and I'm middle school awkward again. Luckily, she never catches me staring. Even luckier, she speaks some English and agrees to walk with me, because at this point my map-reading ability is that of a lightly concussed ox who's dyslexic. Along the way I wrack my brain for questions to ask, happy to be talking to anybody besides myself about anything besides my leg. I learn she's an unemployed fashion designer, praying to each *honzon* for a new job.

Reaching T44 through the picturesque forest takes a while. The branches of titanic cedars catch the sunlight, concealing the path to **Taihoji: Great Treasure Temple (T44)** in murk and mist. The trees are some thirty feet around at the trunk, and Haruka's never seen anything like them. "*Sugoi*"[10] escapes as an awed whisper from her dropped jaw. She hands me her smartphone, and I snap a photo as she hugs the trees. This is most of her photos.

Moss covers everything in T44's courtyard from the *Nio* to the stone steps, and the air is rich with fresh

---

10 Awesome

oxygen. Because we lingered in the magnificent court-yard for prayers and more photos, I set a fast pace along the wooded pathway to T45. There's a lot of ground to cover before their stamp office closes. Haruka and I soon run out of conversation. Puffing hard, she begins lagging behind, then plops onto a stump and makes clear she can't keep up. I'd wait, but nervous energy has been propelling me down the trail one pace ahead of my frantic thoughts and I'm not about to let them catch up now.

Wiping the sweat off her flushed cheeks, Haruka waves me goodbye.

It takes me reaching the next town to realize I've now lost both the only person who can read the trail signs and, worse, the distraction of conversation. Taking frequent breaks to examine my shin, because you can cure any-thing by looking hard enough at it, I miss all the turnoffs back to the scenic forest path across the mountain ridge. Instead, I have to follow yet another highway to the tem-ple. While a yellow crust dries on the seeping bandages, a movie repeats in my mind wherein I arrive at the hospital too late. I'm seated on the examining table as the doctor, who of course speaks no English, peels off the Band-Aids. He clucks disapprovingly at what lies beneath, then nods to the nurse, who jangles some keys to my left. I look over. The sharp puncture of the sedatives enters my arm and I drift off to the sound of them firing up the bone saw.

Then I finish the pilgrimage hopping.

I tell myself it's irrational, but there's no one around to

argue that it isn't the most likely option. So I keep walking to T45, a bone saw in my near future.

Red and blue flags shift slowly along the staircase winding up the bumpy foothill to T45. Eyes downcast, I'm unable to meet the nod of each departing *henro* as they pass. I resent all of them for the ease of their pilgrimage. Of course they found the forest pathway. They can read the signs, ask directions, and visit the doctor. I'm alone here, stuck in my head and terrified of a sunburn. Turning a corner, I raise my eyes and can't believe my luck. Descending the steps, cheeks ruddied with the day's exertions, is a Westerner.

"Holy shit! A white woman! Do you speak English?"

"Yes," she smiles, somehow taking this in stride.

I plop my leg on the railing. "Does this look infected to you?"

"Yes," she nods, somehow still taking this in stride.

"OK, so I should go to the hospital."

"I should say so."

And with that, the denial disappears. My worst fears are true. I have an infected leg that will end my pilgrimage. But also, there's a white woman who speaks English. We strike up a conversation on the steps. Half-German, half-Australian, Elizabeth is traveling with a smaller Japanese woman she met along the way who smokes, laughs, and strides with spark and purpose. Never learning her name, I come to call her "The Nurse." They're staying at a nearby hotel and offer an invitation. I'm initially reluctant due to my tight budget, but Elizabeth's siren song of comprehensible syllables seduces open my wallet. I agree to meet them there and continue up to **Iwayaji: Rocky Cave Temple (T45)**.

Built in three levels on a mountainside, Kukai carved T45's two Fudo images: a stone one kept in a cave at the rear of the temple, and a wooden one enshrined in the main hall, where I pray desperately for my own health. As the priest signs my book with a flourish, Haruka bursts out of the forest pathway with minutes to spare. Panting, she joins me at the stamp office. It turns out she'll be staying at the hotel as well. After we finish our prayers she glides down the hillside. I don't attempt to keep up.

Drained from two days of fighting both an anxiety attack and an infection, I plod to the hotel. Located across the road from the Fujiwara Rocks, a sandstone bed of former sea floor thrust vertical, it's easy to find. Elizabeth is waiting for me at the front desk and offers to pay. I lay down my card. If I'm going broke anyway, I might as well cover my own lodging.

My tiny room holds a short-legged table, a TV, and a sink. Outside the window, the sunset plays off the colorful seashells embedded in the Fujiwara Rocks' gritty sandstone matrix. I splash water on my face. Panicked eyes stare back from the mirror. No wonder Elizabeth is taking pity on me.

Pull it together, man. You've got your pride.

There's an *onsen* in the basement and dinner will be served in an hour. Popping a Xanax, I decide I'll relax for a bit in the pools and eat a good meal before figuring out how I'm getting to the hospital tonight. Wrapped in my complimentary cotton robe with blue stencils of the Fujiwara Rocks, I head to the baths. Even without vests and hats it's clear which guests are *henro* as we peel tape off our pounded feet. I sweat in the hot water and try not to think about bone saws or Haruka naked. I succeed with one of them.

Haruka, Elizabeth, and The Nurse have saved me a place in the dining room. Gathered around the table in our complimentary robes, we dine on a multicourse meal of grilled fish, miso soup, and pickled vegetables. After dinner, we gather around my leg. The Nurse removes my bandages, clucks her tongue, and gathers fresh wraps and disinfectant from the front desk. Haruka pokes at my swollen ankle while I search my Japanese phrase book for "infection." After learning how to ask when to begin our round of golf and where to check my bags at the train station, I find it.

"*Kansesho?*" I ask Haruka, testing the pronunciation.

"*Kansesho,*" she agrees.

Haruka and the lobby clerk call around to find a hospital that is open on a weekend and find one in Kuma. Despite the Xanax and the soak, I'm on edge. When I learn my options are a $750 taxi ride tonight or backtracking to Kuma tomorrow since buses run only on weekdays, I crack. There are no phones in the hotel to call my bank and no Internet to let me check if I'll overdraw my account. Haruka's smartphone can't download my email app, so there's no way to contact anyone. Seething, I ask

Haruka why a taxi costs that much and why hospitals here expect you to get hurt only five days out of the week. She shrinks away as I loom over her.

Sputtering curses under my breath, I twitch uncontrollably. I can't overdraw my account, but what if tomorrow the infection's gone too far? I can see myself entering the hospital where no one speaks English. I can hear the bone saw. The clerk gives me extra bandages for my leg and prints a map, marking the path to the hospital in yellow highlighter. The kanji is impossible to decipher. I take it roughly, thank everyone for their concern, and return to my room.

Defeated, I rest on the floor with a bleeding scalp because my hands were too shaky for a clean shave. Another Xanax finally grants me perspective. Tomorrow my pilgrimage will conclude at the hospital in Kuma because I didn't want to walk down some steps at a temple and refused aid because I was scared of the consequences. I stare at the ceiling, worried for my health and ashamed at how I treated people whose help I desperately needed.

I'll apologize to them tomorrow.

It's the one mistake I can fix before my pilgrimage ends.

16
SAD NEWS

FTER AN EARLY breakfast at the Fujiwara hotel I leave behind my *osamefuda*, my gratitude, and some guilt, both for how I acted toward everyone the night before and because I'm stealing one of the robes. Haruka presses a handwritten note to the doctor into my palm and Elizabeth says goodbye with that pained concern only mothers can express. She'll be staying with Haruka and The Nurse at the *ryokan* by T46 and offers to pay for my room there.

"I'll be fine," I reply, and leave with no idea if that's true or where I'll be sleeping that night. If it's bad, the hospital. If not, I'll find a rest hut near T51 in Matsuyama. The next morning I'll sightsee in the last big city on the pilgrimage, then use whatever's left in my bank account to change my plane flight home.

The Fujiwara Rocks recede in the distance as I limp to

back to Kuma, thinking about the phone call home. Out of pride, I'll tell my parents that I injured myself falling, leaving out the two-day anxiety attack and the potentially criminal property damage. They'll be too relieved that I've finally come to my senses to ask for further details.

Unable to understand why I came to Shikoku in the first place, their concern over what has already gone wrong means every phone conversation revolves around the valid question: "Why are you still there?"

"Because I need to finish this" is my reply through gritted teeth.

I used up my savings to come here. I spent a day collapsing from dehydration and a night cowering in a toilet stall. In record-breaking heat I've traveled over four hundred miles, hiking steep mountains and traversing monotonous rice fields in these fucking shoes. After all this struggle, there has to be some epiphany waiting for me at the end. I deserve it.

But I've screwed it up.

When I get home, I'll be asked "Was it worth it?" If they're my friends, I'll have to swallow my pride and admit that no, it wasn't. As high as my expectations were for Shikoku, my family was right. It was just another way to delay adulthood. I should have stayed home and saved the money for my future. When my contract renews, I'll sit at a desk for years where I'll be alternately stressed and bored, slowly gain weight, and leave feeling sick. And every so often, I'll grind my teeth and think back to that time in Japan when I should have taken the stairs.

The trek back to the hospital in Kuma is a depressing hindsight tour. Highlighted signs pointing out the famous forest path to T45 are mockingly clear. Amplifying the sense of defeat, student pilgrims with bedrolls strapped to their backs and elderly *henro* dressed head to toe in white continue their journeys past me. As each retraced step erases my progress, I look back on the thousands of near misses that passed without incident, and how each time I reminded myself to be more careful, that luck runs out. Mostly, I wonder what else I could have seen, and how bad my leg is.

Despite Haruka's note to the doctor, I spend hours repeating "*kansesho*" to nail the pronunciation. I can't risk pantomime with amputation on the line. Returning to the woods by T44, where I left Haruka behind, I'm snapped out of the vortex of self-defeat by the ancient temple hidden among the majestic cedars. If my days are numbered here, why not enjoy the time I still have?

Back in Kuma there are lawn ornaments for sale at the shops. I debate getting a Tanuki statue for my parents, whom I'll be seeing soon, but the giant balls sway me against it.

I'll hold out for something less cultural.

By 10 a.m. a bilingual nurse points me to a seat in the waiting room. It's an hour's wait amongst the young, old, and oldest, all engrossed in the manga comic books spread across the table. I flip ahead in my map book through the distances I'll never travel and sigh, repeating "*kansesho*" under my breath. They call my name and point to the exam room, where there's no circular saw in sight. The doctor looks at my leg, nods, and announces in heavily accented English:

"In-fec-shon."

I nod back. "Yes, I know 'in-fec-shon.' What do we do about 'in-fec-shon?' "

"How did you hurt your leg?"

It wasn't by breaking an ancient temple, if that's what you're asking!

"I fell…" I lie.

He nods solemnly, buying it.

"…So what do we do about 'in-fec-shon?'"

He swabs the wound, bandages it, then hands me more swabs, antibiotics, and ointment. The bill prints out behind the front counter. I suck in my breath, waiting for my bank account to disappear.

¥4900.

About $58.

Fuck the American medical system.

Back on the road to Matsuyama and beyond, my amputation and overdraft fears are gone. Even though my leg has swelled further since last night and pus is already dripping through the bandages, I walk to T46 with a spring in my step, mostly in the right one. Knowing my pilgrimage will continue is a B12 shot for my spirit. Everything is cartoon bright as I whistle a happy tune. Poppies sing back in vibrant purples, and I expect birds to flutter down from the phone lines and land on my shoulder to become pals. After visiting T46, where hopefully the millennium-old gingko tree is still alive, I'll stop by Elizabeth's *ryokan* and give her the good news. If I keep going, I may even reach the *tsuyado* at T51 by nightfall and have a full day to explore the big city.

Today anything seems possible.

Emerging from the bamboo grove crowning a mountain peak, I'm treated to an unobstructed view of Matsuyama. The gentle downward slope should be a relief after so long in the mountains, but missing the forest path to T45 still gnaws at me. I snap out of it quickly, having already spent two days stuck inside my head. Yes, I should have waited for Haruka so I could find the forest path. I also should have 'fessed up and accepted the maroon *henro*'s medicine when I broke the temple. Or maybe not have broken the temple at all. I can't let what I didn't do in the past distract me from what I'm doing now. Besides, it allowed me to meet Elizabeth, Haruka, and The Nurse. Without them, I could have been in deeper trouble. Two rope sandals hang from a low branch along the path, a dedication from one *henro* to the rest.

The path branches near the city and I choose to go right. An old woman motions that I should return to the other route, but I've had it with backtracking. I end up on a thin highway shoulder, dodging cars against the filthy concrete divider all the way into town.

Still not listening to the locals, I admonish. *Gotta learn that skill.*

In between cars, I daydream about city life. With an entire day to sightsee, I'll leave my backpack at the *tsuyado*, tour the massive castle, soak in the 3,000-year-old *onsen*, and catch up on emails. It's Christmas in late summer.

Haruka is halfway across a bridge near **Joruriji: Pure Emerald Temple (T46)** when I hail her down, surprised that I caught up to her. She must be missing those warp whistles too.

"Your leg?" she asks, motioning to the bandages.

"It's fine," I tell her, believing it for the first time in three days. In simple English I thank her for all her help. She offers me her smartphone to check my inbox, now able to download the email app. For the first time in over a week, I log into my account. The first message that pops up is from my mother with the heading sad news. It's a phrase I know well. I shake my head in disbelief.

Goddammit, Mom, why can't you keep the dog alive when I'm gone?

When I studied in Spain I got the sad news that my then-ancient dog Sid's last remaining brain cell had given out. He had two when we adopted him. Our next dog was Theo, a lively, gluttonous yellow Lab I had trained myself. I was prepping the lesson plan for my third class of the day in Korea when I got the sad news that Theo's liver had failed after he ate raisins off the table. Upon returning from Asia I was greeted by a boisterous yet cowardly Labradoodle named Murphy whom I'd grown to love.

I open the message.

It turns out that Murphy is fine, but Taylor, my best and sometimes only friend from elementary to high school, has killed himself.

A yip becomes a wracking sob. The ground jolts beneath me, and a perplexed, then concerned Haruka watches me slump against the highway guardrail. The outside world disappears as memories from a distant decade flash before my eyes: meeting Taylor in second grade while playing tag on the wood-chip-covered playground. Taylor and I laughing for two hours after the credits roll on *Army of Darkness*, a movie we'll trade quotes from for years after. Sprinting up the steps to his parents' room frantically searching for his mother's medication as she went into another coughing fit, breast cancer slowly shrinking her inward until there was nothing left to take. Shooting homemade monster movies in his backyard. My first beers at a house party, the world tilting as I fell against the refrigerator and began to understand what "too drunk" meant. His father, Jon, at the last Christmas party, eyes filled with a weak flicker as Alzheimer's removed all memory that we'd ever met.

Still sagged against the guardrail weeping, I hand Haruka back her phone. There's no need to read further. I already know why he did it, what gun he used, and it's still a complete shock.

Taylor was my oldest friend. Since meeting in elementary school, we'd spent nearly every weekend together up until high school. When I changed districts, we began to naturally grow apart, pursuing our diverging interests with new friends. Over the next decade, we kept in infrequent touch. However, before I left for Japan, I made a point to invite him out for beers. I'd been hearing secondhand about the stress he was under and knew he needed all the friends around him he could get. Beneath the dim bar lights, I filled his pint glass and slid it across the table to a transformed man. Taylor had always been the energetic one, which made the exhaustion and bitterness on his face all the more striking as he spoke about his legal battles with distant relatives. Smelling profit from Jon's deteriorating mental state, they were swarming in to claim that Taylor's adoption discounted his inheritance.

"You think you can trust family," he said, shaking his head in disgust, "but once money is involved, look out."

Making matters worse, a con artist had gained his father's trust over the past year. Besides stealing Jon's wealth, the con artist had turned an increasingly paranoid and violent man against his only son. It was then that Taylor told me about the rifle, and how he used it to chase off the thief when legal action had failed.

I sat opposite Taylor and listened through all of it. We weren't as close as we used to be, but I could still make him laugh, get him drunk, and reassure him that things would work out. As our evening ended, I signed off on the tab and told Taylor we needed to hang out more when I got back. He agreed that it had been too long. We embraced, exchanged two hard back slaps, and said goodbye for what I didn't know would be the last time.

Outside T46 I regain composure and press off the guardrail. Haruka understands that my friend is dead, but there's so much more than that. Unsure of what to do, I go through the routine at T46 with Haruka close by, bowing, washing, and praying while my sunglasses drip. Shoulders heaving silently, I get my stamp. A tanned, freckled hand gently clasps my forearm. Elizabeth asks what happened. I tell her my friend is dead. She nods, knowing there's so much more than that.

With her arm around my shoulder, we sit beneath the temple's ginkgo tree. The *henro* milling through the courtyard keep their distance as the tall blond woman consoles the sobbing cigarette spokesman in a foreign language beneath their geriatric plant. Elizabeth listens as the story pours out, ending with Jon in the hospital, forever questioning why his son doesn't visit, and distant relatives picking over the estate Taylor fought so hard for.

Elizabeth tells me I'll meet him again. I respond that I don't believe in an afterlife. Taylor is gone and that's the end. She doesn't press the issue, instead offering to pay for my room in the *ryokan*. This time I accept. The thought of going onward, praying at more temples while my voice catches before spending a night alone in my tent, is too much.

While Elizabeth makes arrangements at the front desk, I borrow Haruka's phone one more time and read the entire email. My parents will be attending the funeral the next day. I thank them for telling me and ask them to give everyone my condolences, then hand back the phone. Haruka asks if I'll leave the pilgrimage. I tell her no. Anything I could have said or done for Taylor is pointless now. I wouldn't even return in time for the burial. There's no way but forward, so I'll shove this sadness inside and visit his grave when I return.

I drop my pack in my room and flip on the television, where sumo wrestlers battle for the championship semifinals. A baby-faced Japanese fighter wins the round by dropping the gargantuan Westerner on his face. The crowd erupts in cheers. In the second match another foreign contender sidesteps the charging Japanese wrestler, who belly-flops onto the mat. He accepts the judges' decision with downcast eyes. The final match pauses as the wrestler in blue stands in the center ring, beating his chest to get the entire crowd chanting. Despite their energetic cries, he's tipped off his feet after a furious back and forth, and slammed to the ground. I gaze blankly at the contest, waiting to run out of tears so I can go to dinner.

Elizabeth and I speak more in the dining room. Her mother's inheritance afforded her time to travel, so she came to do peace work in Hiroshima and Nagasaki after completing the Camino de Santiago pilgrimage in Spain. She believes we can feed everyone in the world because we put a man on the moon, and I keep my mouth shut. She let me have my atheism, so I'll let her have her false equivalency. Like me, she prays to the *honzon* for others in her life, and I hope her efforts are more successful than mine. When she asks why I came here, I tell her I came looking for adventure and answers. There's been plenty of the former, and I'm still hoping to find the latter. Elizabeth suggests a slower pace. Having injured her foot early on, she tells me this has been the key to her pilgrimage, allowing her to savor every moment.

After sharing so much personal background, we move on to what we've already seen. We speak of boars, which haven't troubled her, and I don't speak of snakes, which terrify her. For cultural experiences, I have little to offer besides the Whaling Museum and some exploited cormorants. They're easily trumped by her participation in a *Goma* ceremony held inside a cave.

A traditional Shingon ritual dedicated to Fudo, the *Goma* ceremony begins with a priest kneeling in front of a brick fire pit, feeding the roaring blaze with strips of wood bearing the worshipper's sins. Behind him, monks pound heavy *taiko* drumheads as a circle of worshippers chants *Hannya Shingyo* and prayers to Fudo.

I'm envious. It was an overwhelming experience in 2009, seeing it in an enormous temple in Tokyo. Entranced by the concussive ritual, I knelt on the stone floor for the entire ceremony, having to crawl to a bench afterward and pound feeling back into my legs. Performed in the intimate confines of a cave, with the chants and drums echoing off walls animated by firelight, it sounds epic. Accordingly, Elizabeth's face lights up as she recounts the experience. We talk until the emotional and physical exhaustion of the past three days catches up with me.

Excusing myself from the table, I return to my room. Beyond missing flames and chants to sword-wielding demons, what sticks with me most from our conversation is the benefit of Elizabeth's leisurely pace. It's impossible not to question what else I've missed. Would I connect to the landscape again by walking slower? By limiting the distance of each day, could I see a fire ceremony?

Taking my last antibiotic for the night, a laugh catches in my throat as I remember my grand plans this morning of arriving at T51, thinking nothing after the hospital could stop me in my tracks. I swab the wound, replace the bandages, and lie on my futon. Staring up at another unfamiliar ceiling, I'm troubled by a vague guilt. At every temple I've prayed for the health and happiness of those back home, but have I appreciated them enough? Is there more I can do for these three women who came into my life recently and have given me so much? With nothing to offer them in return, my words of gratitude seem paltry.

Despite everything, I'm relieved that the pilgrimage will continue.

And that I won't finish it hopping.

17
MOVING ON, PART 1

THE PREDAWN LIGHT has not yet warmed T46's empty courtyard, and the granite block engraved with the Buddha's footprints chills my bare feet. Standing on the engravings is supposed to heal all injuries, but Buddha has only so much power. When I step down, my feet continue aching and the infection throbs deep into the bone.

After praying for those Taylor left behind, I head to the thousand-year-old ginkgo tree. I took no notice of it yesterday and can't miss a rare survivor of Shikoku's sacred tree blight. Beside the gnarled trunk, last night's conversation with Elizabeth replays in my head. Maybe I've been doing this pilgrimage wrong. A nagging guilt remains that I'm missing something important. Today I'll slow my pace and see what I find.

Back at the *ryokan*, Elizabeth, The Nurse, Haruka, and

other *henro* fuel up for the day ahead. Loud slurps of rice gruel fill the dining room, where a scroll with eighty-eight red stamps hangs among idols of worship: ink paintings of Kannon, statues of Kukai, and a beer ad with Ichiro Suzuki. Hunger momentarily muted, I bow to The Nurse and give my thanks to Elizabeth again.

"Continue to grow into your full potential," she replies.

"I'm working on it."

"I can see that."

I can't, but don't question her as we embrace one last time before I leave for T47. In the shade of the *ryokan's* entrance, Haruka chats with a chubby *henro*. Overdressed in the draping sleeves, puffy pants, and thigh-high split-toe boots of an ascetic, he constantly pats his bearded cheeks dry with a towel draped around his trunk-like neck. His partner arrives, similarly attired and rail thin, so of course they become the Laurel and Hardy *henro*. Haruka introduces us and the Hardy *henro* breaks into a wide grin of porcelain tile teeth. He wishes luck to "Paul from Cee-ah-tu-ru," with a "See you again." The Laurel *henro* bows politely as Haruka and I depart.

Having teleported past us, The Nurse relishes her morning smoke outside **Yasakaji: The Temple of Eight Slopes (T47)** in sensible khaki trousers and a pink fleece vest. Haruka stops to chat while I pray to the *honzon* for the three most important women in my life this week. Outside the stamp office, Haruka and I wish each other luck and go our separate ways. The last I see of her, she's praying for a better job below the white rolling clouds carved above the main hall's entrance.

Elizabeth is half right about the pace. The details of my surroundings are clearer, but they remain surface level. Moseying to T48 with my new contemplative gait, a stupa-lined pathway in the middle of a field catches my eye. I follow it into an empty Shinto temple filled with paintings. In one, samurai rush out the doors of an open dojo into a pitched winter battle, swords clashing in snowy gardens and atop frozen ponds. In another, samurai discuss matters over cups of tea. In a third, two geisha kneel in prayer while a passing noble gazes lustily over the fence. They're cool to see, but besides epic winter battles that may involve ninjas, the rest of the meaning is lost. Back on the sweltering concrete path to T48, a woman's lilting voice carries through the plank walls of her home, chanting a sutra I'll never know.

Given the past week, I should approach **Sairinji: West Forest Temple (T48)** with some trepidation. The second barrier temple, it's said that evil pilgrims will fall into hell upon reaching the *Nio-mon*, which is a pretty drastic escalation from T19. There I only had to worry about an egret pecking out my eyes. Here it's eternal torment. How will the next one top that?

According to a less extreme temple legend, the courtyard's central pond will remain full in even the worst drought due to Kukai's protection. I bow to the heavenly guardians and remain in the temporal world, so either the pond isn't drought-proof or I'm forgiven for the temple thing. The Laurel and Hardy *henro* also passed the damnation test and rest their feet beside the gate. I nod to them as I leave, and Hardy calls after: "See you again."

My leisurely amble is easy to maintain when the day ends at noon. It's a short walk between **Jodoji: Pureland Temple (T49)** and **Hantaji: The Temple of Great Prosperity (T50)**, where I wait patiently in a long line of bus *henro* for the monk's careless scrawl. An older man juggling five scrolls in his arms lets me cut ahead. After replacing my book in its zip-lock bag, I drop my pack onto a bench and call my parents from the courtyard's pay phone. They fill me in on Taylor's funeral and I hold back tears. The *henro* with the five scrolls begins tapping on the glass. I ignore it, making him more insistent. Finally I turn and glare. He's holding my staff, forgotten at the stamp office. An embarrassed bow, an *osamefuda* that he receives gratefully, and I return to the call.

When I come back to my pack, I find some asshole has thrown trash on it. The trash turns out to be crumpled cellophane containing a frosted star cookie, and that asshole was Elizabeth, who also left her card. Beneath a smiley face, she's written *You're a star*. I leave blushing as the bus *henro* finish their prayers. The priest clapping the wood blocks together slows the rhythm as the last four syllables of *Hannya Shingyo* fades out behind me. My full potential requires a lot less assumption.

While asking directions to T51 in a bakery, my eye catches a moist, golden rice cake. The baker waves off my wallet with a smile that multiplies the light creases around her eyes, and motions to a table by the window. After the cake and a glass of iced tea, she receives my *osamefuda*. Her brow furrows, puzzling over a signature that's illegible to most English speakers. While my handwriting has always been atrocious, in this place where calligraphy is an art form, it's become an embarrassment. I rise to leave and she catches me at the door, pressing three tart, speckled satsumas into my palm. I don't deserve such kindness, not for a strip of paper and being lost.

A King Kong–size Kukai peers over the rooftops in the courtyard of **Ishiteji: Stone Hand Temple (T51)**. According to legend, in the early seventeenth century, the chief priest was summoned to Yuzuki Castle to cure the lord's son. From birth, the infant's left hand was clenched shut, and had remained so for three years. The priest performed consecrations and prayers over the child until, at last, his tiny fingers unfurled. Out fell a stone that read: *Incarnation of Emon Saburo*. Kukai had granted the dying wish of the repentant *henro* crumpled at his feet on Burning Mountain. Reincarnated as a lord, the rehabilitated Emon could treat Ehime's peasants with fairness and mercy.

Steeped in the legends of the pilgrimage, the sprawling courtyard of T51 is one of Matsuyama's main tourist destinations. Vendor stands lead to a *Nio-mon* flanked by ten-foot-tall woven rope sandals, replaced every century. Since it's my final temple for the day, I take my time. The crowded courtyard is filled with incense smoke, Buddhas, demonic festival masks, and colorful paintings of the heavenly kings. I pause the longest at a wood statue of the first emaciated Buddha I've seen. He sits cross-legged atop a lotus, robes draped across the sinewy arms and prominent ribs of a body weak from extreme asceticism. This is the Buddha who sat in meditation for forty-nine days beneath the Bodhi tree, prepared to starve until he gained enlightenment.

It's expertly carved, but there's only so long I can spend appreciating the artwork.

There's a city to explore.

Stowing my pack and *henro* gear at T51's *tsuyado*, by early afternoon I'm at the entrance gate to Matsuyama Castle, perched high above the city. After so long in the solitary countryside, I gaze in amazement at the angular, packed thrum below. The kiosk hands me a ticket and I'm finally inside a satisfyingly immense castle. Unlike those efficiency-apartment-size ones before, there's more than enough room here in between the towers and ramparts to stage a climactic battle. I pore over the display cases of weapons and armor, especially the crested helms with tall feather plumes and face masks with horsehair mustaches, flamboyant displays of manliness to strike fear into their enemies. But when I look out the window, I see the next two temples in the distance and can't help wondering what will happen in between them. Turning from the view, I've got my fill of samurai swords and fearsome mustaches. It's bath time.

En route to the *onsen*, I pop into the lobby of a posh hotel to watch a mariachi band perform. Live music is yet another thing only a big city can provide. After two songs, the front-desk clerks make it clear that a grimy, injured *gaijin* in basketball shorts is not their preferred clientele.

You wouldn't be so rude if Kukai was here, I think, exiting the pristine glass doors. But all evidence of our close relationship is back at T51. Right now, I'm exactly what they see.

Inside an appropriately ancient-looking building, Dogo *Onsen* is the most expensive and least impressive of the spas I've visited. Two hot pools beneath a tile mosaic of cranes stalking through ponds, and that's it. No cleansing salt scrubs or opiate-releasing pressure hoses to be found. Still, it's worth the price to be naked in a structure that predates Christ. Unless I can somehow streak the pyramids, this will be the last time. The novelty soon wears off and I'm bored.

Two Dutch men soak beside me and I strike up a conversation, knowing it may be the last one in English for a while. They're incurious about the pilgrimage, which I can't blame them for. The few Europeans I've met are here on holiday to see a castle, a temple, and an *onsen*, not to hear about some unprepared American's long walk in the wrong shoes. I struggle to find another topic, so we discuss politics a little, the Muslim situation and the right-wing resurgence in Holland, Obama's "secret Muslim" situation and the right-wing resurgence in America. They soon leave and I soak alone, thinking about tomorrow's mileage.

The sidewalk glides beneath me as I return to the

tsuyado through a surreal world of colorful buzzing neon advertisements, churches, and a giant robot crab waggling its legs above a restaurant. Young professionals window-shop at the feet of skyscrapers beside Lolita girls in thick white makeup and frilly Victorian skirts. Bright street-lights illuminate the wide sidewalk, where passing cars present no danger. This alien world is so reassuringly familiar, but I'm off-balance without the pack and I keep grasping for my staff. I've had my day of English conversations, music, swords, and prominent grocery stores. Tomorrow I'm back on the trail.

What a relief.

After morning meditation, I scan through my map book as robed locals head to the *onsen* for an invigorating soak. Back in pilgrimage mode, the weight on my back is as reassuring as the staff in my hand. A magnetic pull draws me down the path toward the next temple. It's not the strongest pull in my body, and I'm soon stopped in my tracks by a German beer poster. A Teutonic goddess of all the best curves wrapped in Daisy Duke shorts bends over in front of a refrigerator. Mist cascades past flawless breasts, a lucky undershirt caressing rosebud nipples. She removes two frosty beers and looks back at me with an enticing smile that says, *Paul, we were just thinking about you. It's been so long. Haven't you missed us?* She's right, but not enough that I'll visit the liquor stores or brothels ringing the *onsen*. One infection on this trip is plenty.

Outside of Matsuyama, streaks of antifreeze-green algae cover Yoshifuji Pond. The stagnant waters have bleached a fallen tree on the bank and I'm keeping an eye out, ready to run if mutated tentacles breach the surface. A van pulls over with the hazard lights blinking. The driver emerges and gifts a bottle of frozen black tea wrapped in its own thermal sleeve. A bow, an *osamefuda*, and she motions for me to wait. Another trip to the car and she returns with rock-salt hard candies. I thank her again but reserve a second *osamefuda*, in case she's somehow inspired to return with the van's keys.

A half hour later the highway dips into another city, and I'm struck by the odd contrast of white cranes perched on power lines. I've only seen them gliding gracefully over rippling fields or stalking prey in the paddies, so I'm feeling a little betrayed that they're slumming like common pigeons. It's like the first time I saw a bear rummaging through a dumpster and thought: *Shouldn't you be batting salmon out of a glacial stream while Sir David Attenborough expounds on your hibernation cycle?*

On the long path of cedars and marble obelisks leading from the stamp office to **Taisanji: Big Mountain Temple (T52)**, I run into The Nurse again. She tsks at the bandages drooping from my calf like an old cotton sock and makes clear she'll be waiting by the stamp office to fix them. No longer refusing the advice of my elders, I take her up on it.

The ornately carved main hall is worth the long walk and steep staircase. A national treasure of richly polished zelkova wood, it's fitted together like a puzzle box without the use of nails, cleats, or pillar connectors. It's dedicated to yet another divine search-and-rescue operation, when the goddess Kannon saved a wealthy merchant from shipwreck. Washed ashore, he climbed toward a bright light on the mountain's peak, where he found a statue of the goddess. According to some, he built the shrine there that night. According to me, that's impossible. Still, it's a damn impressive sight. I want to spend more time here, but it's rude to make a lady wait.

The Nurse pats the steps beside her and settles my foot into her lap. Shifting a glowing cigarette to the edge of her lips, she unfurls my bandages to reveal a caldera of raw tissue centered atop a swollen mound. Producing new bandages and wraps from her shoulder bag, she swaddles my shin snug in the span of one cigarette drag. I'm partway through "*arigato*" when insistent fingers grip my bicep. Pulling me to my feet, she races off to T53 with me in tow. As I lag behind, The Nurse looks back and jokingly pantomimes Elizabeth's languid hobble. It's a relief that my fast pace isn't unique. Finally, my muscular tobacco doppelganger makes sense.

The Japanese don't need warp whistles.

Cigarettes are their performance-enhancing drug.

En route The Nurse laughs constantly, smokes constantly, and greets everyone she sees, asking for directions or chatting briefly about the trip. When we reach **Emmyoji: The Temple of Circular Illumination (T53)**, she pokes fun at my traditional Kyokushin cross-armed bow before passing between the *Nio-mon*. Over my four years of karate training, it's become an automatic gesture before anything requiring concentrated effort. Here, that's hourly.

In the courtyard, a *henro* with a drooping paunch glances over at me. He speaks briefly to The Nurse before approaching with a jovial "Hello." An electrical engineer, "Ted" is on his fifth pilgrimage, going in reverse this time. Since Emon went counterclockwise on his last circle of the island and found Kukai, it's considered the holier path. It's also more difficult, since the signs are in reverse. Ted's polite but adamant about drawing me a map to T54, despite my telling him many times that I already have a map in English. The Nurse rolls her eyes at him.

With The Nurse in the lead, I puzzle over Ted's map of all wrong turns before figuring out it's written in reverse and tossing it. After a brief stop to buy lunch at a *conbini*, I'm forced to eat on the run since The Nurse can't lose her reservation at the next *ryokan*.

Had I known this, I wouldn't have gotten soup.

I dump the rest and focus on overtaking The Nurse, hoping to reach the *tsuyado* at T54. Gaining the lead, I'm chased down by a businessman in a full suit who gifts me an icy bottle of tea. A bow, an *osamefuda*, and he falls back. I glance over my shoulder to see him give one to The Nurse, who stops to chat. Crossing a bridge, my chest twists at the first view of the Seto Sea. I never expected to reach the ocean so quickly. With mountains to my right and waves to my left, I realize how much I miss Kochi, now far behind me, and how soon Ehime will pass beneath my feet.

I stop racing.

As I snap a picture of a café sign with a faded Western sea captain exclaiming nice taste coffee, Elizabeth waves to me from the window. As glad as I am to see her again, it stings that a middle-aged white woman with a half-busted foot beat me here.

Where are these warp whistles hidden?

The bell rings above the entrance and I sit across from Elizabeth, thanking her for the star cookie, amongst everything else. The Nurse speeds past our window to her next *ryokan*. It's the last I'll see of that compact puffing locomotive.

Elizabeth is burned out on the journey. After chatting with her daughter online, she's questioning what's to gain from being so far from family and friends. As it turns out, walking slowly doesn't provide all the answers either. I tell her what I'm telling myself after reaching the Seto Sea so abruptly.

"Whatever happens, there's only two to three more weeks of this. It'll be over faster than you realize; then you have the rest of your life to be home. Savor this now."

She cheers up, and I'm glad to give her something back. After our final embrace, for real this time, I've gotta reach T54. I'm halfway to the door when she calls out.

"I nearly forgot. I met some *henro* in the *ryokan* last night. They asked if I was the only white one and I told them there was one other. They said, 'Paul from Seattle?'" She smiles and I laugh. Now we are legend.

I return to the seawall. Unlike the Pacific, the air

beside the Seto is pungent from the bands of seaweed rotting on the shore, carried by the gentle lapping waves. A group of skateboarders laze on the wall, drinking from a keg of Asahi Super Dry. Their shaggy dog prances below, licking at their heels. They all lift their red cups in salute as I stroll by, and one offers a fresh pour. I want it nearly as bad as the woman on that German poster, but I'm committed to remaining present, which means remaining sober. I'll have the rest of my life to drink with friends.

By early evening I stand on the tip of one of the thin stone fishing piers that stretch like tan fingers from the shore. The ocean breeze tugs at my clothes as I stare into my map book yet again. Despite my advice to Elizabeth, for the past hour I've been thinking ahead, planning how many days to Kagawa, how many weeks till home. Turning around, I take in the stretch of land I just traversed. The towering green slopes freckled with red and yellow leaves that plunge into the plowed fields. The thin asphalt strip that separates the stalks from the modest homes lining the seawall. The concrete steps that brought me to the sandy shore. And all of it a small fraction of the eleven hours I've spent walking across Shikoku today. My days are limited here. I need to take my time and appreciate it.

Then I remember that I still don't know where I'm sleeping tonight.

Better hurry.

As shadows lengthen I speed through a seaside town famous for producing the clay roof tiles that decorate the nicer homes and temples. The sunset casts its fiery rays across the stacks of demons, dragons, and magic fish spilling from the factory warehouses. There's no hope of reaching the *tsuyado*, or of finding anywhere safe to pitch a tent. To my right is a solid block of ceramic factories and garages. To my left is the seawall. Prepared for another night of racing through the dark, I turn off course to watch dusk end from a long pier. Fishermen young and old spear their hooks through tiny squid, casting their lines into the wine-dark ripples. The clouds ignite as the burning ember drifts through them, disappearing behind the trawlers on the horizon. In a few days I'll reach the final province. My Shikoku sunsets are numbered. However, I still have to find a place to sleep.

On my way back to the highway I discover a covered croquet court beside the pier. In the dark I set up my tent beneath the awning, then practice karate as usual in the gritty dirt. Afterwards I shower with a short rubber hose in a bathroom smelling of gutted fish and rotten curry. Multi-legged arthropods scurry across the moldy concrete, on their way to a Guillermo del Toro casting call. Still, it's the most sanitary place around me. I pat myself dry and avoid touching any exposed surfaces on the way out.

Inside my tent I swallow my antibiotics and examine the wound more closely. It still hasn't scabbed over, and the mound gives like wet clay when pressed. Distracted by my search for a Band-Aid, my fingers unconsciously massage the bump harder and harder. Suddenly it collapses. A clear stream of watery pus squirts out like a pressure hose onto the door flap.

The tent fills with the stench of seaweed rotting on the shore.

Eyes wide in a queasy horror, I hear myself say in a calm, removed voice: "There's a napkin in the fanny pack. Take it out of the fanny pack, dry your leg, put on a bandage, clean the door flap, and throw the napkin away."

I repeat this over and over again until all the steps are completed, keeping the contents of my stomach internal, then shove it out of my mind by calculating the next distances in my map book.

Since it's the only control I have over the pilgrimage, I've become obsessed with it. Planning ahead and setting goals have always been a struggle, but here it's simple. Positioning for one day affects the entire next one, and the one after, and so on until the end. Where I'll sleep, how much time I have in the day to eat or explore, it's all beholden to mileage. But I've begun staring at the map book constantly, distracting myself from the pilgrimage as I calculate where I'll be in the future.

It's yet another lapse as I try to figure out how to do this better, bringing me to the same conclusion as always: mistakes and all, this is my pilgrimage. The Nurse's is fast, Elizabeth's is slow, Ted's is backwards, Laurel and Hardy's is together, Haruka's is professional, and mine is still going as I rush through the brutally hot summer in the wrong shoes, practice karate each night, and search for answers in between boar scares and minor property damage. I just wish there was more balance. I've taken so much assistance, with nothing to give back besides a bow, an *osamefuda*, and a goodbye.

I put the map book away and take out my *osamefuda*, deciding to put some real effort into my embarrassing signature. Lifting my hand from the paper like the monks writing their calligraphy at the stamp office, I focus on the whorls and curves of my name for each one.

Seeing how everyone reacts to these *osamefuda*, it's time to give them the attention they deserve.

18
FIGHTING MONKS

THE RISING SUN warms my back as I meditate on the pier, my focus split between following my breath and not slumping unconscious into the ocean. Returning to my tent, I'm the kind of exhausted that makes merely rolling up my sleeping bag take minutes of planning. With that Herculean task accomplished, I probe my wound with the last medicated swab. The lump is gone, but the scab remains open. This is acceptable as long as I don't have to drain it like a fire hose again, at which time I will promptly lose my shit. I lift the tent off the ground, shake out the last of the ants, take a seat on the bench, and try not to slump unconscious into the dirt.

Practicing karate every night means fighting off fatigue the next morning, but there's no choice. The half hour of strikes and combinations has become as important a part of this journey as meditation or my journal. Since the first day's climb up Big Mountain, I've fallen back on the will and discipline Kyokushin has instilled to continue on. Beneath each labored breath on the steepest hikes, I still find myself repeating the Kyokushin pledge: "We will train our hearts and minds for a firm, unshaking spirit." Having never been tested like my days on Shikoku, I had no idea how deep the years of training had reached. I only began Kyokushin so I could fight.

I'd wanted a black belt since age five, because ninjas and Bruce Lee had them. However, attaining one required discipline and commitment, so that was out. Having tried and quit many styles throughout my life, I devoted myself in the fall of 2006 to getting a black belt. This meant finding a dojo I wouldn't get bored with. By October that year I'd already visited a dozen martial arts studios. Seattle Kyokushin karate was next on the list. Wearing my T-shirt and basketball shorts in the back of the room, I punched and kicked alongside the students dressed in their weathered white *dogi*, the traditional cotton jacket tied closed by a colored belt. The class was fine, one of the top three contenders for sure. At the end we kneeled, bowed in thanks to the instructors, and rose. Then the sensei uttered the six words that would change my life.

"Who wants to stay and fight?"

Kyokushin's founder, Mas Oyama, believed the full-contact, bare-fisted sparring known as *kumite* to be the center of karate. This I could instantly relate to. While never violent, I'd always been drawn to the real-time, adrenaline-fueled chess game that is *kumite*, studying every boxing match, mixed martial arts bout, and martial arts film for new moves. When I began class, I'd learn how closely Mas Oyama's life resembled the kung-fu movies I'd grown up on.

A Korean who traveled to Japan at age fifteen to enlist in the air force, Mas Oyama had become a black belt in judo wrestling as well as in Shotokan and Goju-ryu-style karate by the time World War II ended. Having never seen combat and frustrated by the deaths of his friends and his adopted home's defeat, he became well known among the U.S. military police due to their frequent altercations. Bereft of purpose and at a crossroads in his life, he took the advice of his Goju-ryu sensei and left to train in hermitage. Oyama chose the forests of Mount Minobu, where the undefeated sixteenth-century swordsman Musashi developed the martial arts philosophy that would become his famous *Book of Five Rings*. This treatise was a major influence on Oyama, and one of the few books he would read during his seclusion.

While living alone in a cave for eighteen months, Oyama strengthened his mind by meditating beneath icy waterfalls and toughened his body by racing up the steep slopes, breaking river stones with his hands, and kicking tree trunks. Emerging from the wilderness in 1947 to win the All Japan Karate Tournament, he still believed his skills to be lacking and left again for the forest. Following another year and a half of solitary mountain training, he returned to society capable of wrestling bulls to the ground, chopping off their horns, and punching them in the head to death with his fists. This earned him the understated nickname "Godhand."

That none of this was mentioned that first class was sheer negligence by the Seattle Kyokushin dojo.

Still, I came back. We got to fight.

By the time those first bruises faded to yellow patches, Kyokushin was in my blood, studied with more intensity than any college class. This religious fervor, coupled with my obsession with Japan (and the ninjas residing therein), spawned an inside joke amongst my friends. They'd tease that I was waiting for a wizened Japanese man to emerge from a bamboo forest, hand me a sword, and say in a heavy accent: "You are ready." Then he'd point me to the ogre threatening his village.

"Beats office work," I'd shrug, withdrawing the blade.

I had joked that this was the secret reason for going on this journey. The old man hadn't shown up in Korea, so I had to visit his home.

However, no wizened sword-bearers have appeared this month on Shikoku, and I've stopped joking about it in the emails home to friends. Right now, I'll be happy if nothing else goes wrong in these final weeks. I rise from the bench. A symphony of crackles and pops plays through my joints, the opening sonata of another long movement.

The empty road gives me time to reflect, and the time in between walking meditation is spent rehearsing a eulogy for Taylor that will never be delivered. I'm hoping to process through the nagging guilt that keeps memories of a long-forgotten decade spontaneously flashing past my eyes. Over the hours I get no closer to an answer, or to an open shop serving breakfast. I pass a Korean barbecue joint, the windows cruelly shuttered. Across the sign a pig dances beside a sizzling grill, and my growling stomach reminds me of one of my favorite parts of South Korea, as well as the idiosyncrasies of their restaurant signs. If it were a barbecue joint, the pigs would be cavorting in joyous celebration, but if it were a chicken joint, the birds would be fleeing in terror, fear sweat flying off their brows. I never found out if the pigs were supposed to have a more Buddhist acceptance of their fate, or if the chickens just knew what was coming.

Spotting a *henro-goya* on the beach, I recover in the shade. Across the waves, apatosaurus-like container cranes move cargo from red-hulled ships to concrete piers. A matronly *henro* crosses the sands to greet me with a polite bow.

"Are you Paul from Cee-ah-tu-ru?"

I nod. That's the extent of her English, but having slept at Elizabeth's *ryokan* last night, she's delighted to complete her game of white *henro* bingo. In silence we continue on to **Emmeiji: The Temple of Long Life (T54)** and pray side by side. On our way out I stop to examine the courtyard's three-hundred-year-old bell, a historic target for thieves. It's unimpressive, a studded iron dome that oxidation has turned Statue of Liberty green, but my appraisal is meaningless. I've no grasp on the economics of Shikoku's underground gigantic bell trade.

We soon reach **Nankobo: The Temple of Southern**

Lights (T55), where the four heavenly kings who guard the entrance have been slacking in their protection over the centuries. Rebuilt on a smaller scale after Chosokabe's warriors torched the original structure, T55 was later blown to pieces by B-29 bombers. Currently more construction is under way, and we pray to a tarp-covered main hall before bowing out.

The path to **Taisanji: Peace Mountain Temple (T56)** takes us across the notorious Killer River. Named for the seasonal flooding that regularly decimated the surrounding towns, the river was tamed when Kukai performed secret rituals on its banks that summoned Jizo to appear.

Also, factually, he built a levee.

We part ways after reciting the sutras at **Eifukuji: The Temple of Good Luck (T57)**, where elephant-like, nightmare-eating creatures called Baku are carved into the main hall's roof supports. From the stamp office I watch a tan minivan pull into the parking lot. A family of six disembarks, the frail grandmother carried through the *Niomon* by her son and gently lowered to the dirt before the *honzon*. The family kneels behind her, and they recite the sutras in unison.

With all the *henro* I encounter at every temple, chanting in groups, wandering alone, or queued for calligraphy, it's easy to forget that these temples aren't built for us. For *henro*, each one is a page in their stamp book. For the locals, it's a permanent fixture of their lives. A place to celebrate festivals, bless their dead, and gather with family to pray for a little more time together. Turning from the stamp-office window, I slide my ¥300 across the counter, slip the book into its zip-lock bag, and leave for T58 to collect the next calligraphy in the series.

By early evening I've hiked past the enamel white *Nio* and ascended the concrete staircase winding up the rocky forest slope to **Senyuji: The Temple of the Hermit in Seclusion (T58)**. In the seventh century, the mountain ascetic Abo recited sutras here for forty years before mysteriously vanishing one day. Whether this involved a theatrical puff of smoke or simply heading back into the woods with an Irish goodbye is unclear.

Standing in the spare, dusty courtyard, I instantly like this sequestered mountain temple. A refreshing breeze sways the branches of the unruly maples that shade the two-story belfry. From the edge of the complex, the darkening Imbari Valley and the island-speckled Seto Sea spread out a thousand feet below. I've been waiting to purchase a beaded bracelet on Shikoku and decide that this is the temple to remember.

Finishing the sutras to the *honzon*, I turn to the folding table in the corner that serves as the stamp office. The resident priest's brow furrows in concentration as he signs my book. Shallow creases line the eyes of a softening face. Placing a strip of newspaper between the pages, he closes the cover and brings it to his forehead in blessing.

"*Hannya Shingyo* very good. Where did you learn?" he asks in broken English as he hands it back.

This is a common question, since at this point I've got the sutras nearly memorized. I open the map book and show him the phonetic syllables. He nods, then points to my shoulders.

"Why are your arms so big?"

This is another common question, since at this point I look like Bane with cancer. I give my standard answer.

"I do Kyokushin karate," I say, raising my fists in our traditional fighting stance.

"Ah, I do Goju-ryu. Black belt," he replies with pride.

I bow respectfully. Another hard sparring style, Goju-ryu shares many of the stances and techniques of Kyokushin. Some of the toughest fighters in my dojo studied it, including Tomo, the polite oak tree. The priest isn't lying. Even in his late thirties, his thick athletic build has lost definition but not yet power. I purchase a bracelet of cedar beads from the table's display case and we chat about my pilgrimage while he leads me to a basement *tsuyado* of concrete walls. Wiping the bottom of my staff, I place it in the corner before dropping my pack onto the wood pallet beds. The temple is now closed to the public, so with permission I may be able to train in the empty courtyard before nightfall.

The priest sweeps out the main hall in preparation for the evening ceremony, still wearing his brown robes and loose cotton pants. Perched on the cliff across from the shrines are the residential quarters, where the bus *henro* stay overnight. The priest's slender wife appears in the doorway, cradling their newborn son. Holding the door open with her free hand, she turns back and whistles. Three German Shepherds burst forth. Jostling and nipping at each other, they tear through the courtyard before quenching their thirst in the sacred wash basin that we all drink out of. She joins her husband for the temple chores, and the priest introduces her to the Seattle *henro* who studies Kyokushin. I bow to her and waggle my fingers at the baby, who coos back happily. She asks about the journey and makes the same pained wince that everyone does when I mention hiking to Burning Mountain Temple. When asked about my ranking, I tell her I'm a brown belt. She gives an impressed bow. Pointing to herself and her husband, she replies, "Shotokan green belts."

I turn to the priest.

"Oh, I thought you practiced Goju-ryu."

"No," he replies with a resigned shrug. "Now I practice Shotokan, with my wife."

I understand the slight dejection in his voice. Shotokan sparring focuses more on control and technique than heavy impact, and the point system in their tournaments is based on the amount of damage you would have inflicted. In Kyokushin tournaments, points are awarded if your opponent can no longer stand and fight. Once you've done true, bare-fisted hard sparring, anything else is a letdown.

Our eyes meet. I recognize that look. It's the same one I must have had that first karate class upon hearing those six words from my sensei. As I moved up in rank, I would see the look many times in the dojo. Watching the faces of those new students dressed in shorts, sweats, and yoga pants after they got hit, I knew which ones would soon be wearing a *doji* and a beginner's white belt. The ones who just figured out what's been missing from their lives: a real challenge.

Facing the priest, my rear foot automatically slides back into position as I sink into my stance and raise my fists.

"*Kumite?*" I ask.

"*Kumite,*" he grins.

As his wife continues sweeping out the main hall and the dogs throw each other into the dirt, we square up, bow with crossed arms, and begin.

Shotokan has taught him speed and control that I still lack. Worse for me, he's an inside fighter. My long limbs are neutralized as his granite fists slip past my blocks to jolt my ribcage. I slide back and we circle each other, leaving smeared arcs across the courtyard. Deft feet slip him past my darting jabs and two solid hooks below my armpit hunch me to the side. He feints another hook and I swing a wild block, opening myself up for a rear cross to my solar plexus that nearly winds me.

He's controlling the fight with speed I can't match.

I need distance.

Leaving my jab overextended, he takes the bait and slides in front of me. I launch a knee into his sternum to shove him back, ram his gut with a straight kick to keep him off balance, and land a roundhouse into his thigh with a heavy thud. He steps back, shakes the knot from his quadriceps, and nods. We bow in again, raise our fists, and continue.

Breathing hard with exertion, the match goes back and forth. Puffs of dust fly from our shoes with each kick as attacks are received, parried, and blocked with an errant grunt or sharp "*Kiai!*" He slips in to punish my center with uppercuts and hooks, and I counter by attacking from outside his range with jabs and roundhouse kicks. Initially, I can hold my own. But rusty from a month without training, and distracted by five-year-old Paul's ecstatic applause inside my head, I get sloppy, falling back on the same combinations. The fourth time I fake a hook into his shoulder to sneak a left roundhouse kick into his ribs, he sees it coming from a mile away. Intercepting the blow, he swings a hammer fist block that connects dead center into my infected wound.

The resounding pain shudders through my skeleton to explode with deafening clangs inside my skull.

Falling to one knee, I swallow vomit.

I rise quickly to my feet, refusing to show my opponent any weakness, like throwing up. Ears ringing, I make clear that he hasn't won, but the match is over. We bow out and shake hands. He invites me to attend the *Goma* fire ceremony later that night, and I hand him my new cedar bracelet to be blessed during the sutras.

He rejoins his wife at the main hall. The *Goma* preparations complete, they return to the residential quarters with the dogs trotting behind. I practice karate beside the belfry, just as I've done beside rivers, in parks, and inside *tsuyados*. The high-pitched buzz of adrenaline pumping through me dulls my aching shin and sharpens every black outline as I go through basic strikes and combinations. After twelve hours on the trail, each punch and kick is an act of will. However, in return for tomorrow morning's fatigue, I'm gaining the discipline to overcome whatever obstacle that day presents.

Especially if fighting priests is going to be a regular thing now.

By the time I've finished, an opaque shroud blankets the Imbari Valley. My body steams in the night air as I bow and return to the *tsuyado*. I'll need to wash up quickly before the *Goma* ceremony.

Inside the main hall, the elderly bus *henro* coo at the baby as he crawls near the shrine. I kneel within the semicircle, where a rattle has been placed in front of each of us. The priest nods to a *henro* at the edge of the circle next to a *taiko* drum. The *henro* picks up the sticks. Heavy bass pounds through me from the wide drumhead. Shaking our rattles, we follow the beat. The priest slips my bracelet beneath a pillow in front of the fire pit and kneels to fan the glowing embers. As we chant *Hannya Shingyo* and praise Fudo, he feeds the growing flames with wooden prayer strips, cleansing the worshippers of their sins and attachments. The chants, rattles, and thudding percussion blend together into one vibrating mass, spiraling around the fire pit as the radiant heat laps at our cheeks. Propped against his mother, the baby is awed to silence by all this noise and movement. He searches our faces for how to react.

Folding the accordion pages of the Heart Sutra back

into a heavy paper block, the priest rises. Passing behind the semicircle, he swats each *henro* hard on the back. With me, the smack is audible above the cacophony. It stings deep into the muscle, but I'm not going to show my opponent weakness. What's one more bruise today?

When the fire dies down the priest begins his lecture, mentioning me a few times since I am the very white elephant in the room. When he concludes his speech, we're served green tea and red-bean pastries. After speaking to each *henro* individually, the priest returns my bracelet with its new blessings of health and wealth, one of which I expect to have. We shake hands before one more cross-armed bow. This is the last I'll see of him. Tomorrow is another marathon day through the mountains, and I'll have to leave before sunrise if I don't want to be stuck in the woods for the night.

Lying back in the *tsuyado*, I think back on the fantasies I'd had for this pilgrimage: fighting monks, enlightenment, senior citizens bestowing weaponry. I'd given up on all of them, focusing instead on being in the moment as I trudged toward the end. And now I'm wearing a bracelet blessed in a fire ceremony to a sword-wielding demigod after a mountaintop karate battle with a priest beneath the twilight sky of Shikoku Island.

But even more surprising, after thirty-three days on the pilgrimage, something finally happened that I was prepared for.

19
LET IT GO

THE MOIST MORNING air in the mountain forest outside T58 hangs thick and heavy, slowing time. Completing the illusion, a crinkled red leaf spins at eye level, levitating via an invisible strand. Meditating with an oddly clear mind, I center my focus on it.

Then I walk face first into a spiderweb.

Spitting the sticky strands out of my mouth, I'm still finding that balance between losing myself in the moment and seeing what's ahead of me. There will be plenty of time to practice during today's marathon hike to T61. Shoving away the knowledge of what walking that distance will be like, I turn to the panorama below me. The dawn sun dyes the fields of the Imbari Valley golden-red. Beyond the shore, a solitary barge trawls the silvery waters of the Seto Sea, disappearing behind a billowy curtain of salmon-pink clouds. I raise my camera to my eye and capture the moment with an electric click. On the digital window, a washed-out dot hovers over the dark blurs of land and sea. So little of this experience comes across in pictures, and there is so much I need to remember.

As I emerge from the silent woods into an empty town, a hillside graveyard snaps me out of my walking meditation. With a focus that has grown stronger daily, each crystal speck and chipped edge of these polished granite slabs is in high definition. The difficulty is looking beyond the details to see this graveyard as unique among the thousands I've already passed by. Framed in the window of a nearby house, a mother prepares breakfast. She glances up at me, then returns to her cooking. Through that glass pane she's seen thousands of *henro* pass by her graveyard. Like every one, I have my own distinct story, but to her we all must blend together into the same transitory object, briefly noted and quickly forgotten.

Today I'll take in the remarkable details of these everyday sights, acknowledging them as unique as I consider myself. Of course, while focusing on this mental challenge, I can't lose sight of the physical one: getting past the *nansho* T60 to find lodging beyond T61. Luckily, **Kokubunji: The Official State Temple (T59)** is a quick stop on the side of the road. My first temple of the day is also the third Kokubunji of the pilgrimage, due to Emperor Shomu.

In the eighth century, during a time of famine, smallpox, and military upheaval, Emperor Shomu became

Japan's first devout Buddhist ruler. Believing that pleasing the gods would solve all these problems, he used up the nation's bronze supply to build a five-story Buddha statue in Nara. The gods' opinion of this remained unknown to Shomu, but after he nearly bankrupted the country, a couple of military coup attempts made his subjects' attitude unmistakably clear. In a more popular decree, due to not spending all of everyone's money, Shomu ordered a system of provincial temples constructed throughout the nation. Thus, in Shikoku's four quarters, T15, T29, T59, and T80 all share the same name.

This early in the morning, T59's head priest and I are the only people in the courtyard. Yawning, he breaks from sweeping out the main hall to sign my book. I pay my yen, he returns to his chores, and I return to the road.

A mountain range soon emerges on the horizon, where T60 is perched some 2,340 feet above sea level. Beneath a bright, overbearing sun, the *henro* trail runs through a series of small agricultural villages. Into my voice recorder I catalogue the differences from home, like a tan-phobic driver wearing a bonnet, visor, and mask behind the wheel. Suddenly it hits me: I don't actually know how different this is. I've become familiar with Japanese rural towns, but have no American version to compare it to. Some things could be happening anywhere, such as elementary school students in bright costumes waiting on a balcony, about to perform in front of their parents' video cameras. However, a clerk practicing his golf swing in the back alley of a liquor store is probably the most wholesome activity ever done in that location.

Leaving town, I enter into a long walking meditation through the recently plowed fields. Harvesters are parked inside roughly built garages, the dried stalks hanging from the machinery's maw like whiskers on the Lorax. Completing the breaths, my mind resumes chattering, filling the void where music piping from ear buds used to go. Then I hear: *Shhhhh.*

In the distance, sunbeams cut through the gathering clouds to illuminate the grays and blues of the jagged range. It's the best view today, and I kneel to take a picture across the rolling farmland.

After the electric click, I glance at the digital picture window.

The mountains are indistinguishable from the last ten photos of them I've taken.

Still kneeling, I look over the viewfinder and remind myself to take in the scenery I just photographed. A digital camera is a devil's bargain here, as capable as a smartphone or MP3 player of removing me from the experience. With the ability to easily capture every moment, the attitude forms that documenting the journey is enough. Because why wouldn't this be just as meaningful when shared with friends on a computer screen back home?

It's another precarious balance, because I don't want to forget something important here. In South Korea I became lazy about journaling, and six months after I returned home most of my time there had faded from memory. The few entries I made were frustratingly incomplete glimpses into such a difficult, crucial year that I committed to keeping a complete record of Shikoku. So much has happened in the past month that I've become obsessive about each entry, spending over an hour a night writing down everything I can recall, then adding notes from my voice recorder, and finally reviewing my photos from the day. It's easy to forget to also live through the journey I'm trying so hard to remember.

Be here now, I remind myself for the thousandth time as I follow my breaths and absorb the view. I straighten up, and the open blisters between my toes shift and begin rubbing together. Each step is a fresh paper cut into the webbing. Fantasies of home disrupt my newfound focus: a sweaty glass of scotch in hand, my feet propped up on pillows, the ashes of my shoes smoldering in the garbage. Some things will never get easier.

"I will have my vengeance," I tell the shoes gnawing up my feet. "In due time."

Tempestuous clouds creep over the summits ahead, threatening rain. My hat wobbles in the strengthening gusts, teetering faster and faster until it sails backward to garrote me with the elastic chin strap. After too many escape attempts, I carabineer it to my pack. I'm concerned less about a sunburned scalp and more with the clotting sky turning Shikoku's steepest *nansho* path into mud and gullies, where I'll slide down again and again over sharp rocks like cheese on a grater.

Ducking into a post office en route to mail a gift to

a friend back home, I chat briefly with the mail lady. She asks how long I've walked. I tell her the kilometers and days, then slump onto the bench beneath the whirring air conditioner to express the rest. I've covered a dozen miles since 5 a.m. and have spent the last hours with T60 on the horizon, waiting patiently for my footprints and sweat. Head cradled in my hands, I stare at my pack and the loneliness hits deeper than ever before.

No one who sees me carry this pack can ever understand the depths of hatred I have for it. I've grown past the soreness, but my shoulders still tense as the thin straps bite into the muscle. It's my heaviest traveling companion, dragging me backwards on the upslopes, pounding into my knees on the downslopes, and refusing to carry its own weight even for a moment. My life is contained in this pack, but if I left it behind I could breeze through the rest of the miles. Time is so short with every English speaker I meet that there's no point in complaining about this.

I don't regret walking alone. It forces me to be present with my surroundings. If any of my friends were foolish enough to quit their jobs and join me here, we'd have spent the entire time talking. There would be no time for meditation or contemplation. However, in these weak moments I want comfort: a friend to bounce ideas off or to assure me his backpack is also an asshole, or for future Paul to appear and tell me there is a big revelation waiting at the end that changes my life, and that they're looking for hoverboard test pilots. Instead, there's just this gray and black nuisance I lug around, with the loose webbing that drops my tent, and the metal frame that digs into my lower back, and the constant unbalanced jostling, and how it always, always falls off any bench I set it on. I glare at it for a long while, then sigh, slip my arm through the strap, hoist it to my straining shoulders, and continue on to the mountain.

High across the valley, katabatic winds press the bamboo groves flat, the branches rippling like algae in a rapid stream. But here at the foot of the highway curving up the sheer mountainside, it's a refreshing breeze. I pick a tomato-red persimmon off an overhanging branch, and the ripe flesh gives against my tongue with the flavor and texture of a late-summer apricot. The rest in the shade is pleasant, which this hike will not be.

Beside the guardrail, a wide stream gurgles through the forest, splashing over a smooth shale riverbed. Aquatic plants whip and pulse in the current and a dead trunk undulates behind the glittering curtain. Steadying my hands on the guardrail, I snap a picture. In the display window appears a maddeningly lifeless representation of what is still in front of me. None of my pictures have come out today. And then, the truth hits me: no matter how hard I try, I won't remember most of this journey. It's slipping past moment by moment, and I have to let it go.

Suddenly each rush and purl of the stream spilling over the rocks becomes distinct. Every note in the birds' songs is as significant as the silence that follows it. A calm spreads through me and my chattering mind falls silent. Unlike the connected experience in the rice field, here I feel transparent, as if my body has dissolved. I put the camera away. Tranquil, I float up the rest of the sharp rise. Every sight, sound, and sensation is acknowledged as it arises and allowed to pass on unhindered. At one point I instinctively reach for my voice recorder to explain what is happening. Instead, it remains in my pocket as I watch clouds' shadows chase the sunlight off the peaks and enjoy each creak and groan of the trees in the rushing wind.

The sensation disappears when I crest the highway and stand at the foot of the forested path to T60. I let it go and return to the Kyokushin mind-set, which demands I drive unceasingly through whatever stands in front of me. Stepping over a brook, I'm grateful the rain held off. These slopes would be impossible in the mud. For an hour the weight of my pack grows exponentially as distance markers mock the progress of each grueling step. I grin at the extra challenge, refusing to stop until I've attained the summit and stepped onto the flat earth of T60, the third barrier temple. Sweat erupts from me as I pump my fist in celebration, then drop panting on a bench. Next to me a cigarette smolders in a brimming ashtray and I've never been happier that I quit smoking. Even The Nurse must have been sucking wind on this hike.

Then again, probably not.

In 651 a *shugendo* ascetic founded **Yokomineji: Side Summit Temple (T60)** as an affiliated temple of the one on the holy mountain Ishizuchi, the highest peak in western Japan. When Kukai converted this temple from Shinto to Shingon, he placed the statue of Zao-gongen, the three-eyed god of mountain wanderers, inside his carved *honzon*. Across the valley, Ishizuchi towers at 6,600 feet above sea level, nearly three times the height of T60. Thank gods Kukai wasn't feeling more ambitious about temple conversion that day.

With my book signed, six miles stand between me and T61. Even if I speed the entire way, I still may not arrive before the stamp office closes. Just off the path an irregular tunnel of rough-hewn log torii leads through the woods, and I'm curious to see what stands at the end. It turns out to be a small shrine dedicated to harvest gods. I'm not sure what I was expecting to find, but something more rewarding than a couple sticks and a satsuma inside a birdhouse. Returning through the torii to the main path, I check my watch and recalculate.

No chance to reach T61 in time.

I'll have to sleep in the woods.

A gravel service road curves down the mountainside. Standing on the edge of the decline, where a chilly night in the forest awaits, I think back over my rules. For thirty-four days I've restricted myself to walking. By slowing down, even in my version of it, I've strengthened my meditation and awareness of my surroundings. But despite all the benefits, it's remained chafing. There's always the same calculations of distance that I can cover given the hours in a day, and the same subtle regret of decisions when I don't reach my destination before sunset. Ten brief minutes spent walking through torii means I won't reach T61 in time. Down this gravel road lies another few hours enduring the sharp strike of each step, only to settle into an uncomfortable night. I'm tired of traveling in slow motion. With my toes hanging an inch above the decline, I let go. Deep within, permission is granted.

Run.

Eyes shut, I tip forward over the edge, savoring the weightless instant of free fall. My heart's first heady thump of anticipation pulses through my chest into my ears. With the first jolt through my heel, my inner ear sits up from its newspaper, spewing its coffee and urgently calling down to fast-twitch muscles that the vacation is over. The second and third strides are euphoric. I'm laughing uncontrollably as I slalom down the path, my backpack shimmying. Adrenaline courses through burning veins, dampening the knowledge that one slip means my flesh scraping across gravel and stone until inertia decides it's through with me. My surroundings blur, each pounding footstep accompanied by the screams of every blister as distance ticks off below me.

I slow for the clearings. Far below, tectonic shifts have rumbled the landscape, bunching up the green sheets where the slumbering mountains startled and rolled over. Once past the views, I furiously pump my legs, seeing how loud I can make the wind howl in my ears. After a few miles of freedom, with a thudding chest and a dry mouth, I return to the flat road. My staff resumes its metronome clicks on the concrete and I check my watch. I've bought myself a little time, which is good, because there's a Fudo statue on a streambed. As with every time I see swords and flames, I halt to investigate.

At the top of the waterfall, an iron Fudo sits on a boulder backed by a fiery halo, an immovable throne for an immovable being. Perched below are the statues of his chief attendants. On a boulder to the left of the falls stands Kongara, the youthful personification of tempered obedience, dressed in a robe with his hands together in prayer. Crouched atop a higher boulder on the right is Seitaka. His hair tied in five topknots and armed with a golden sword, he's the personification of expedient action. At his feet are offerings of beer, the beverage of reckless action. Fudo waterfalls like these exist all over Japan and are considered the personification of the demigod. Meditation and prayer beneath one is believed to purify one's soul of desires and attachments, just as the flames do during the *Goma* ritual.

A black hose attached to the top provides the water plunging down the sheer rock face, filling in for the gushing torrent absent in these dry summer months. I meditate as the flow pours onto my shoulders, happy to have finally found my waterfall, even if it may be coming from a spigot somewhere. It's not the cascade from the Shikoku documentary that I saw myself beneath, but there are demons with swords. If I've learned anything from this pilgrimage, it's "Good enough."

Sopping wet, I hurry off to T61.

The priest signs the temple's calligraphy with a minute to spare, then draws me a map to his favorite ramen shop and shuts the counter window. Now that my stamp book and dinner plans are taken care of, I can explore.

From the outside, the main hall of **Koonji: Incense Garden Temple (T61)** looks like a Western convention center. The church-like interior is lined with pews facing the *honzon*. I've worshiped in both Jewish and Buddhist temples, but I feel oddly out of place praying in such a Christian room.

Guided by the ramen-shop map, I navigate the streets in a daze of hunger. Where I'll sleep is of secondary concern, and a gently sloping riverbank beneath a bridge seems like a good fallback spot. Worst-case scenario, I somehow knew I'd sleep under a bridge here. The lanky ramen cook sports a salt-and-pepper goatee, and his unruly hair breaks free of the gel after a long day of boiling broth. He asks how far I've walked today. I announce the kilometer total in triumph, then slump onto the counter, expressing the rest. I'm the final customer of the night, preventing him from closing shop early, so I make up for it by devouring a large bowl of ramen and twelve pot stickers.

While waiting for the cover of night to set up my tent beneath the bridge, I fill in my journal at a corner table so the cook can wipe up. When I rise to leave, he waves off my cash and hands me another hand-drawn map. This one leads to a small motel, where he's already called ahead to confirm my room.

I'm too tired to argue.

The barrel of staffs in the motel's entryway and the sedge hats hanging above the door tell me I'm in the right place. In the living room, I politely inquire about my reservation, disturbing the owners from their TV show. They flick their hands impatiently at their daughter, eyes never leaving the screen. Her exasperation at the unfairness of being dragged away from the program is evident as she points out my room, the showers, the laundry, and returns to the living room without varying her scowl. I dump my backpack in my room, my clothes in the washing machine, my body in the shower, and wait for everything to become clean. The room is nearly fifty dollars, and there's almost enough room between the bed and the wall so that I don't have to slide sideways. I flip on the ceiling fan and crawl beneath the covers of a Western-style bed. My eyes shut fast, a wide grin across my face.

I was wrong this morning. I don't know what these marathon days will be like. After a transcendent experience and standing beneath a demon-infested waterfall a day after fighting a priest on a mountaintop, I'll be keeping my eyes open in the bamboo forests for a wizened sword-bearer.

Anything is possible.

20
MOVING ON, PART 2

IRREGULAR BURSTS OF rain spatter against my hat as I trudge through the morning fog toward **Hojuji: The Temple of Wealth and Happiness (T62)**. Droplets stream down my glasses, blurring the road ahead. Yesterday, some microbe in the waterfall took up residence inside my only pair of contact lenses. Even after throwing them out and dousing with the menthol solution, my eyes are smoldering. My shin wound throbs, but unlike my bloodshot eyes, there's no sign of infection. Every muscle is achy and sluggish, and my brain is faring about as well. My longest walking meditation has lasted almost three breaths, interrupted by fantasies of hitching a ride inside every passing car. Ehime, and maybe the pilgrimage, should have ended on yesterday's high note, when everything was so clear.

Today it's all about distance.

And praying this isn't brain damage.

It's still early when I reach T62, another temple commissioned by the devout Emperor Shomu. I lean my staff beside me and bow to the *honzon*, a goddess Kannon carved by Kukai to resemble Shomu's devoutly Buddhist empress. Mid-prayer, the staff falls over, ricocheting off the step into my open wound. I double over, cringing in front of an empress and goddess carved by a holy man as an Internet comments board's worth of obscenities sputters through gritted teeth. The inanimate wood is incapable of malice, but it's too direct a hit not to take personally. Even Kukai wants me gone.

The courtyard is devoid of people, secular or official, so I'll have to return here to get my stamp. After praying at nearby **Kisshoji: The Temple of Laksmi (T63)** and backtracking, I continue on to T64. After so much distance this past month, extra walking is glumly accepted. What's another two miles out of two dozen?

In contrast to the dark clouds, a three-story metal torii gleams candy-apple red near the entrance to **Maegamiji: The Temple of the Front God (T64)**. Built at the base of Mount Ishizuchi for the worship of the three-eyed god Zao-gongen, it's the headquarters for a small, mountain-worshipping sect of Shingon. A bronze phoenix roosts atop the main hall. Doused by rain, it overlooks the scattered worshippers who pray beneath floral umbrellas in the muddy courtyard. The shower picks up as I leave my last temple for the day. Puddles grow and spread on the pitted road.

A few miles later I duck into a restaurant to wipe my glasses clean. A blurry mop of blond hair shines like a beacon from a far table. Replacing my glasses, I introduce myself to Greg, a clean-cut ex-Mormon from Salt Lake City who looks like he belongs on the BYU athletics pamphlet. The only Western teacher in this small town's private school, he's equally happy to talk to another American. At first we commiserate on the boredom of foreign small-town life. Unable to reach bigger cities on a school night for entertainment or socializing, you're responsible for finding ways of making the monotonous days worthwhile. And then there's the burnout, the frustrating cultural clashes, the loneliness, and the constant downloading of movies and shows for a new distraction. When I ask how it feels coming to the end of his time here, he gives the response of nearly everyone I know who has lived abroad: "I'm glad I did it, but I'm ready to go home."

He's curious about the pilgrimage, having never spoken to the many *henro* he's seen passing through the town. Starting with the rituals, I fill him in on where I sleep, how far I walk, what I eat, and what's happened so far. When I'm finished, he says what everyone at home has already told me.

"That sounds amazing. I would never do something like that."

I think the same thing, hearing of Greg's excitement to apply for law schools and his readiness to move on with his life. It's what I thought I would be doing when I got back from Europe, and especially when I returned from Korea. And now I'm on Shikoku, hoping the same thing.

Greg's lunch break is up, for which he apologizes before putting my coffee on his tab. He receives my *osame-fuda*, and I wish him luck finishing up his year. As I sip my coffee in the booth, I think back to my coworkers over the years. Like Greg, they had their one big post-college excursion before beginning their careers. Most traveled in Europe, but some had more thrilling trips. One spent a summer importing luxury cars for his uncle by driving them from Zurich into pre-unified East Berlin, at one point having to outmaneuver the Stasi tailing him. Others had built water systems for Habitat for Humanity in Africa, or lived out of a van as they bummed around Australia's beaches, but each story ended the same. With travel out of their systems, they went back to school and began their careers, finally becoming adults. Every time I returned from a trip, I'd think I was finished wandering. But after a few months of entering numbers into a spreadsheet and resenting employers for paying me for it, I'd begin saving up for the next one.

Rain streaks down the diner's windows as I thumb through the next pages of my map book. Tomorrow I'll reach Kagawa, and before I know it I'll return to pray at T1, where a different person will be standing in my footprints. I'm hoping he'll finally know where he wants to be. Groggy, achy, and my shin throbbing with many damp miles to go, I'm ready for that to be a desk permanently.

My coffee drained, I stretch the poncho over my backpack and head out the door.

Two soggy hours later the caffeine has woken one thing up and I need a toilet. Since there are no residential homes nearby to make it more awkward, I settle for a dingy bathroom in a run-down convenience store. Every surface in the store has the same dull sheen of old lunchmeat, including the limp fried snacks that look smeared with lipstick beneath the heat bulbs. The two shelves of groceries exist solely to direct people to the many racks of pornos along the wall. The clerk agrees to watch my bag, her limp hair stuck to her cheeks with sweat and oil from the fry vat. The porcelain toilet's as clean as the store, but I still prefer it over the squat toilets, which are like balancing on a tightrope above a sewage vat. With my business done, I search the racks for something to support theirs and buy a Royal Milk Tea–flavor Kit Kat bar. Outside, I take a bite and enter flavor heaven.

Royal Milk Tea is one of the eighty different Kit Kat varieties for sale in Japan, including Soybean, Grilled Corn, Lemon Vinegar, and Baked Potato. Their popularity exploded here due to the same phonetic-based destinies that make people tie bad fortunes to pine trees. Since Kit Kat sounds like the good-luck wish "*kitto katsu*," parents give them to children before big tests. Out of curiosity I've already tried Green Tea (delicious), Baked Potato (odd), and Camembert Cheese (don't). Royal Milk Tea tastes like creamy Earl Grey and is the best candy I have tasted in my life. If I'd known I'd never find them again, I'd have cleared their shelves.

There must be some truth to Kit Kats being good luck, because as I leave the store, I glance back and let out a celebratory whoop. Beside the entrance stands that legendary Japanese combination of perversion and convenience: a panty vending machine. Supposedly they were banned in the 1990s, and I never thought I'd see one. On the top shelf are packages of tissue (fitting), next row is condoms (normal), on the third row is gardening gloves (kinky), and on the bottom, folded panties wrapped in cellophane. I buy a pack of the panties and condoms as evidence of my discovery, sinking them deep into my bag so I don't have to explain this to Customs. It's my last clear thought as I return to the road.

I don't stop again until nightfall. I set up my tent in the courtyard of an abandoned temple, twenty miles closer to the end than where I woke up. At the bottom of my sleeping bag, my left and right feet tell me about every step along the way.

My alarm wakes me at 4:30 a.m. from the dream I've been having all night: repositioning my tent, climbing back inside, then repositioning it again. As rested and clear-headed as if I had actually been up till dawn playing Boy Scout Sisyphus, I pore over my route for the day. Flipping pages ahead in my map book, past Ehime to Kagawa, I laugh out loud. The farthest I'll have to walk between temples in the final province is a paltry seven miles. After all the endless roads and steep hikes of the last three provinces, it's like a Navy SEAL getting an assignment to infiltrate a dictator's yacht in middle of the South Pacific and make sure his kitten has enough food in her bowl. Having undergone so much intense training, Kagawa seems like a bizarrely simple task. Scanning further ahead, I'm shocked when the pages run out. Within a week, I'll return to T1.

My days on Shikoku are down to single digits.

A light drizzle greets my final morning in Ehime. T66, the first temple in Kagawa, lies twenty-three miles away. At three thousand feet above sea level, it's the highest *nansho.* I grin with masochistic pride. As wiped as I am, I can still reach T66 in time for *tsuyado.* At the start of Ehime, after walking more than forty miles in the past two days, this would have been impossible. Now it's simply inadvisable. But if I'm this brain dead at the end of the province, I might as well do something dumb.

The path to Ehime's final temple leads through the residential neighborhoods of Mishima, where the elderly zip by on mopeds with folded-up walkers strapped to the back, and into the industrial sections, where dark clouds pour from smokestacks into the sky. The temperature climbs as I hike up Ghost Mountain along a tropical pathway, where palm fronds bob above a brook. Just before entering the forest I turn back for one final glance across the town. The rotting-seaweed-infused ocean breeze mixes with the musty manure spread over the fields and the carbon gushing from the smokestacks before reaching my nostrils. It's a scent that will only be familiar for another week.

I don't linger.

Spongy moss blankets the stone steps, walls, and stupas leading to **Sankakuji: Triangle Temple (T65)**. The complex was historically haunted until Kukai, like a Buddhist Egon Spengler, busted the ghost. The triangular altar where he performed the three-week *Goma* ritual that cast out the spirit is still in the courtyard, but any ectoplasmic residue is long gone.

A baseball game blares from the portable radio in the corner of the stamp office, where the monk stares into the speakers as though they were HD screens. Fashionable black plastic glasses frame his boyish face. With one ear still tuned to the radio, he quickly signs my book without glancing up. An announcement interrupts the broadcast. His face lights up and he turns to me, noticing my complexion for the first time. When he hears where I'm from, he stumbles over his words, telling me that Ichiro is nearing the record. He assures me his nation's idol will soon make it to two hundred hits for his tenth consecutive season, and then wants to know if I also believe Ichiro will accomplish this historic feat. I tell him I believe it and he pumps his fist with a "*Ganbatte!*"

As I descend from the mountain temple through the clouds, my poncho's rustle and the smell of wet leaves make it feel like fall already. My breakfast long gone, I fantasize about thick stews and bread fresh from the oven, steam erupting from the ruptured crust. As in Kochi, the curving highway offers hours of prognostication. Where the road bends into view across the slope, I see myself ten minutes into the future, more tired and hungry. Winding down toward the valley, I gaze into the hazy lands beyond the waves and shed sweaty layers as the sun burns through the mists.

The only town in the valley consists of a red Shinto temple and a few ivy-covered homes beside a river. My stomach whimpering, I enter a tiny shop consisting of three shelves lined with individually wrapped red-bean pastries and sacks of rice below. It's connected to a home, and the owner/resident, a Japanese Estelle Getty, sits in her living room watching TV. Oblivious to her customer, I call into the living room until I reach the volume she can still hear. She shuffles through the hallway into the shop and taps the worn brass keys of an antique register. The tumblers in the glass dome pop up with the total. As she's counting out my change from the pocket of her apron, her equally ancient friend arrives holding a bag of freshly gathered acorns. They shuffle back down the hallway to the TV.

Outside the shop, I chew fast as I look up the sloping highway, then unzip my awesome gray fanny pack and withdraw my sweat-soaked map book. Gently peeling the crumbling pages apart, I recalculate time, distance, and sunset. There's no way I'll make it to T66 tonight. I'll camp out at the base of the mountain instead and give my legs a rest. Farther up the road, an arrow points to the "traditional" pilgrim route. It's a much shorter path, since it leads straight up the mountainside. I'll still have no guarantee I'll make it to the temple in time, and I may get stuck in the woods when it gets dark. It would be stupid to go this way, and harder.

I start hiking up. Sometimes I don't know why I bother reasoning with myself.

My legs already shaking ten minutes in, I drive unceasingly past the red *henro* tags dangling from the branches. Far above me is the end of Ehime province, which I entered thirteen days ago, confidently prepared for what lay ahead.

Then I broke a temple.

Then things got worse.

Then things got awesome.

Briefly.

It's been a chaotic two hundred miles of highs and lows, along which I fought an infection and a priest, both unsuccessfully but only one enjoyably. I spent days worried I'd be unable to complete the pilgrimage and spent yesterday wishing it were already over. And after everything that happened, there should be some revelation as I approach the end. Instead I'm finishing Ehime as I did Kochi, brain-dead after days of long walks. But there is one major difference. After traveling over sixty miles in the last three days, this hike should be impossible. And two weeks ago, it would have been. Today I can walk forever, filled with a primal compulsion to press on through the exhaustion, and keep pushing myself past what once were my limits.

Eventually the branches unfurl their grasp from the open sky and I stand higher than ever before on the pilgrimage. Whatever I gained from Ehime, I made it through. Nothing compares to this feeling of triumph, exhausted atop yet another obstacle on my path. Each resounding thump in my chest is a blissful reminder that I'm alive. As I stroll along the spines of mountains into Kagawa, a captivating overlook drops me onto a grassy knoll. The lumpy ridge commands a view of the Seto Sea three thousand feet below. Wind whips past my ears, tugging at the grass in swoops and whorls. It's an inspiring view, and I'm not the only one who has thought so.

At the close of the sixteenth century, the lord of Kochi province, Chosokabe Motochika, stood on this mountain ridge, newly galvanized with purpose: to conquer all four provinces of Shikoku. Thus began a decade of war that incinerated most of the pilgrimage temples (and I assume many other structures), as Chosokabe gained control over the island. And with the earth and sea spread beneath me after such an intense climb, I can relate. Even lacking a loyal army of retainers, up here I already feel as though I own the world. Then, like Chosokabe, I turn toward T66. The pilgrimage's final barrier temple peeks out from a woody grove on a cliff's edge.

The head priest of **Unpenji: Hovering Clouds Temple (T66)** was the first to hear of Chosokabe's newly hatched conquest plans and begged him not to go to war. Impressed by the priest's bravery, but obviously not by his argument, T66 became one of the rare temples Chosokabe spared. A couple of centuries later, I follow a cedar-lined pathway to a row of granite lanterns, where I bow and enter the first temple in Kagawa with the less ambitious goals of praying and sleeping.

Two Tanuki statues stand beside the washing basin, their testicles as large as the priest's who stood up to Chosokabe. One is more devout. Cloaked in a robe, underpants, and a pilgrim's hat, he carries a begging bowl with a rosary draped over. His cousin, alternatively, is balls-out drunk, with a flask in his hand. Unable to avoid his lecherous grin, I rewash my hands. I get my stamp and drop my pack in the *tsuyado* before heading to the *honzon* to pray for everyone who helped me in Ehime. It's going to take a while.

After reciting sutras to the *Daishi*, I turn from the shrine and stand astonished. Beyond a metal gate is the most remarkable sight so far on Shikoku. Mesmerized, I climb over the barrier. In a gravel courtyard are hundreds of life-size granite statues. Each individually carved and numbered, the assembly gathers around a reclining Buddha. Lit by the sunset filtering through the trees, their exaggerated, distorted features express five hundred different personalities in animated detail. Armored warriors strike fearsome poses beside hunched ascetics in robes, their eyebrows and beards of equal length. A dragon slithers around a monk with his hands in the mudra of prayer beside a court official cradling a snake. Beside them an elder sits astride an elephant, hand raised to interject a point, and a drunk with lolling eyes guzzles from a flask.

I wander through this grotesque menagerie as the pooling shadows spread, refusing to leave until I figure out what I'm seeing. When the stars emerge, I still have no clue. But the temperature's dropping, so I return to the *tsuyado*.

I'll later learn these are the *Rakan*, the five hundred original followers of the Buddha who achieved enlightenment. However, as I lie huddled in blankets and all my clothes in the freezing *tsuyado*, I chalk it up to one more mystery here. Yesterday I wished that the pilgrimage had ended that night after the waterfall because it would have felt complete. But days like that are highlights, not conclusions.

My night ends as most of them do: alone, hungry, tired, uncertain, and surrounded by something amazing with more miles to go.

SECTION FOUR

KAGAWA: THE LAND OF NIRVANA

21
DAIJOUBU

M Y FIRST MORNING in Kagawa: The Land of Nirvana, I laze my way to the valley below T66. Certain that I'll reach the *zenkonyado* past T71 with time to spare, I'm daydreaming about home and girls when a hiss startles me out of my imaginary bed. A mamushi the length of my arm slithers underfoot before bolting into the undergrowth. Lesson learned: the pilgrimage isn't over yet. There's still plenty of time for another hospital visit. The rest of the descent I'm focused on the present, where there are more important concerns. Like fangs.

The path bottoms out onto a highway, and I soon ascend the tree-shrouded stairs to **Daikoji: The Temple of the Great Growth (T67)**. While signing my stamp book, the head priest compliments my sutra pronunciation. Despite the number of times this has happened recently,

I still have no idea whether this is genuine or just a polite bromide, since I need to name-drop Ichiro when he asks my birthplace. A bow, ¥300, and I'm off.

In the fields outside T67, geriatric farmers work the land on their hands and knees. Given that my grandparents can barely leave their nursing home, I'm astounded as liver-spotted hands wield mini-scythes and grip walkers for support while yanking weeds. The routine has settled into their bones over the better part of a century, as unconscious as a heartbeat. By this point, I'm certain that I could bring in the rice harvest through sheer osmosis, but the concept of doing this or any work for a lifetime remains unimaginable. Immersed in their task, or possibly just blind from cataracts, they take no notice of a transitory *gaijin* passing beside their lives.

T68 and T69 share a courtyard near the seashore, where in 703 the monk Nissho saw the ship of Hachiman, the Shinto god of archery, floating in the waves. The divine protector of Japan, Hachiman promised Nissho he would stay at **Jinne-In: The Temple of God's Grace (T68)** to protect Buddhism and the emperor. Centuries later, perhaps he overheard Emperor Kameyama's prayers at the adjacent **Kannonji: The Temple of Kannon (T69)** for protection from a less benevolent shipload of archers. Whether by divine intervention or meteorological luck, sea storms prevented the Mongols from reaching Japan on two separate occasions. Thus, T69 became the temple of choice for victory prayers. Shikoku and Japan owe their current existence to these two storms, since there is little doubt the Mongols would have easily conquered the nation. Chosokabe may have burned much of the island, but even he could be defeated, as I find out at **Motoyamaji: Headquarters Temple (T70)**. During Chosokabe's arson tour, T70 survived the torch thanks to a swarm of bees that chased his warriors from the compound. Since beginning the pilgrimage there's been maybe a day in which I didn't visit a temple wrecked during Chosokabe's decade of conquest and pyromania. Imagining these fearsome killers flailing cartoon-like as they flee an aggressive hive is endlessly amusing. Central Asian nomads who fed on horse blood while wiping out the populations of a few subcontinents wouldn't have been so easily repelled.

Crossing a wide bridge into the next town, I'm starving again. There's only enough money in my wallet for the stamp at T71, so I reach into my awesome gray fanny pack to draw out my cash reserves.

It turns out my wallet isn't lying.

I only have enough for T71's calligraphy.

I've learned that post office ATMs are the only ones that accept foreign debit cards. After shaking the locked door, I also learn that they close midafternoon on Saturdays and reopen Monday. I should have kept a better watch on my money. The idea of continuing to T71 and fasting for a day is dismissed almost as quickly as it arises. Even after a big lunch this afternoon, my revving metabolism is still sending danger signals from an insatiable stomach. I'll sleep in town tonight, eat as lightly as possible tomorrow, and get cash on Monday.

I return to a sports park that I passed earlier, where an overpass separates the parking lot from the turf. The dry embankment beneath will be a perfect place to camp once the cars clear out. In the meantime, I'll lounge in the grass and fill out my journal. With the gravel lot at capacity, I'm expecting a neighborhood soccer match. Instead, past a perimeter of crackling torches, an audience surrounds an arc of *taiko* drums.

I pump my fist, celebrating my luck.

Since I first heard *taiko* drumming at an Asian festival in Seattle, the fast, concussive bursts have resonated deep within me. Meaning "big drum," *taiko* are known for their powerful, booming tones. Originally used to issue feudal generals' commands across hectic battlefields, they later became holy instruments, the thunderous bursts carrying Shinto priests' prayers into the heavens. Modern ensemble performances began in 1951, when a jazz drummer named Daihachi Oguchi assembled a group to play the many sizes and types of *taiko* like the jazz arrangement on a drum kit. Using the higher-pitched drums as a snare to carry the basic rhythm and fatter drums as a bass line to ground the pulse, the medium drums' propulsive riffs push the music along. All together, the ensemble sounds exciting, holy, and joyously free. For once, my irresponsibility has paid off. If I'd kept a watch on my funds, I'd be filling out my journal by now somewhere near T71. Instead, on my first day in Kagawa, I'll get fire and drums. Two things I love separately, together at last. Now, how can I stay and watch for free?

Rice-paper lanterns border the picnic area, each deco-rated with a grass stalk backlit by a yellow sun. Within the perimeter, a few dozen families sit on wide straw mats with a clay tureen in the center, the soup boiling atop a portable gas range. Canvas tents line the edge of the field, where volunteers hand out plastic bags of meat, vegetables, and noodles to be thrown into the roiling broth. Hoping to enjoy the show sans ticket, I move quietly behind the tents to find a clear view.

I'm quickly discovered by a volunteer in a red kimono, who guides me to a bench beside the tents and hands me a cup of sweet tea. As I'm enjoying my beverage, Red Kimono Lady ushers a woman in waist-high jeans and wire-frame glasses to sit beside me. Yui speaks a little English, and as we sip our tea I do the Ichiro swing, hand her an *osamefuda*, and tell her how long I've been walking. She lives in town, delivers newspapers, and is here with her family to watch the performance. Our cups empty, she asks if I have a place to watch the performance. I point to the bench I'm on. Motioning that I follow, she seats me at her family's mat and announces: "Paul, Cee-ah-tu-ru *henro*."

I'm introduced to her daughter, Mika, a young bar-tender with auburn highlights, and her son, Yuki, a plump programmer who's my age. Yui's mother and sister speak no English, and spend the night kneeling ramrod straight, as if they're posing for an eighteenth-century daguerreo-type. From the moment I'm seated, five people enter into a contest to see who can make the *gaijin* burst. As soon as Mika's grandmother has handed me a bowl of ramen, Yuki has a plate of yakitori chicken skewers pushed into my chest. I eat one to be polite. Meanwhile, Yui's sister hovers an open bag of rice crisps beneath my other hand. I give up trying to refuse and am soon nostalgic for those early weeks of starvation.

A lone drumbeat resounds across the lawn, quieting the crowd and distracting the family from their human foie gras experiment. High school students dressed in blue tunics cross the lawn in two lines, carrying drumsticks as long as their arms and nearly as thick. Bowing to the audience, they arrange themselves beside their instruments. The performance begins in the back as they wallop the big fat drum, a four-foot-diameter barrel carved from a centuries-old tree and covered with the skin of an entire Holstein cow. The deep, rumbling tempo builds momentum and the arc of performers in front join in, leaning back with their drums between their legs to give themselves striking distance. In the center, the star of the show braces himself in a wide stance parallel to his drumhead. His hands blur into an ellipsis as the pulsing beats gather, mix, then explode. I prop myself against my pack on the grass and let the sounds that commanded battles and summoned gods wash over me.

Midway through the performance, Tetsuo arrives at our picnic mat. Mika and Yuki's stepfather, he's back from his camping trip with a cooler of gutted fish and stories of shooting boars. Jovial, gaunt, and weathered, Tetsuo is a man who's enjoyed every night of the hard living that's aged him a decade early. I like him instantly, and not just because he's lowered my chances of boar attack. He and his cooler drop to the mat at the same time, and moments later an ice-cold, cracked beer rests in my hand. Tetsuo holds his can up for *kampai*[11]. Well versed in all forms of drinking etiquette, I show respect to my elder by colliding the rim of my can well below his. While chugging the first beer down, he reaches into the cooler with his other hand and cracks a second one. I sip on mine. Technically I'm breaking my rule about drinking, but realistically there's no way any alcohol is penetrating this wad of food in my gut.

In between sets, Mika, who knows the most English, teaches me a few phrases I've been missing, includ-ing "*dozo*," the informal version of "please," and the most important phrase unmentioned in my guidebook: "*Daijoubu.*" Directly translating to "Don't worry about it," this is the magic word I've been looking for since I arrived that cuts off the five-minute monologue of apol-ogy. In total, I've probably spent at least a day so far nod-ding while someone begs forgiveness for not speaking English, or not having white bread at their shop, or not letting a total stranger into their home to use their toilet. I'll never take the simplicity of "no" for granted again.

The final song crescendos, and afterwards I lean back in the silence, staring up at the full moon. Mika points out the rabbit that the Japanese see on the surface and

---

11 Cheers

remarks that Australians see a crab. I tell her Americans see a face and point to the eyes and mouth. Mika looks at me incredulously, then furrows her brow at the slate-gray craters. I do the same, searching for long ears or pincers and finding neither. Behind us the family packs up and Yui interrupts my lunar safari to ask where I'm sleeping. I point to the bridge.

"Like *Kobo Daishi*," I joke.

She frowns in concern and offers up her home. I politely decline. I got a free meal and a *taiko* performance. It's been a good day. She asks if I'm certain. I thank her again and hoist my pack to leave. Besides my fear that the force-feeding will continue, I'm always uncomfortable staying in someone's home. Even if it's a friend's apartment, I feel guilty because it's the one thing I can't reciprocate. Having spent my twenties living in small rooms in cheap places so I could afford to travel, I've never been able to invite someone over, and have occasionally crashed on couches for a month or four in between jobs or destinations. To make up for being a burden, I'd always give cash, clean, or buy groceries, and still felt like a mooch. Since I can't offer Yui's family anything after sharing their food and company, I'd rather curl up like a python beneath the bridge to digest and see if rice-crisp poisoning is a thing.

Red Kimono Lady returns as I'm saying my final goodbyes to the family. Translating through Mika, she asks if I enjoyed the show. Nodding enthusiastically, I thank her again and give her an *osamefuda*. She was a bus *henro* years ago and follows up with the regular pilgrimage questions about distance, days, and where I'll sleep. I reply twenty miles, thirty-nine days, and point to the bridge again. She frowns and speaks rapidly to Yui, who offers her guest room once more. Red Kimono Lady won't let this go and it'll look like Yui's refusing hospitality, so I agree. Contented, she smiles and continues ushering the audience from the field.

In the parking lot I throw my bag into Tetsuo's minivan and Tetris myself into the backseat between the tackle boxes, coolers, and cases of beer. We follow behind Yui's car and soon pull into the driveway of a modest, two-story suburban home.

Moments after I've entered my first Japanese home I nearly offer to sleep in the yard. Hearing the door open, Yui's grandmother shuffles down the steps in a thin cotton nightgown and scowls at me. I pick out the word "*gaijin*" in her croaky voice, which gets repeated with more and more invective as Mika slides open the doors of the finest guest room I've ever seen. Embarrassed, Yui quickly shuffles her grandmother back up the stairs. I'll learn later that the "guest room" is the *tokonoma*, a traditional recessed alcove filled with art and reserved for honored guests. All I know at the time is that I agree with the grandmother. A grimy *gaijin* should not be stinking up a place this nice.

Waving off my assistance, Mika hauls in futon mats and blankets to make the bed while I stand awkwardly by, gazing over the ornate decorations. A vertical silk scroll hangs in the corner, with a painting in the center of a seaside village beneath a mountain. Below the scroll is a vase of *ikebana*, artistically arranged flowers, and an *okimono*, a small piece of decorative wood. Carved into this crimson block, a band of wild horses charge up a hillside. In the far corner is a black lacquered cabinet containing a shrine to Kannon, with offerings of potato chips and flowers placed in front. It's not the first time I've noticed potato chips placed as offerings before the gods, or that it tends to be the same brand every time. Maybe it's a promotional thing.

Mika asks if I'm thirsty and I walk ahead of her into the kitchen, needing to do something to help, even if it's filling my own water glass. Across the kitchen island is the TV room, where one yapping mini-Doberman lives above another in stacked metal crates. Both immediately decide they hate me. The top one is so furious that pee dribbles through the crate, only making the bottom dog more enraged. Tetsuo carries the top one over to me, holding a napkin to collect the drops, and offers me a chance to hold her. Thankfully, she snaps at my fingers so I don't have to impolitely refuse or be peed on. Yui suggests a shower, and I figure it's the only gift I can give to this family.

Dressed in my last pair of clean clothes, I return to the dining room. Everyone has assembled around the table. Having invited such an unusual guest into their home, they're curious to hear my story.

There's so little I can tell them.

Interspersed with awkward silences, Mika translates their questions and I can reply only with facts about myself or the journey. This is the worst part of the night.

I'm embarrassed to be accepting this family's charity with nothing to give back. I have no money until tomorrow, and no possessions I don't still need or haven't sweated on. Since it's basic English, I can't even tell a joke to make them laugh or an anecdote to entertain them. I have nothing to add to their lives, and tonight something that's been bothering me this entire pilgrimage becomes blatantly clear:

I only take.

And because I didn't pay attention to my money, yet another obvious mistake, I've ended up taking more. Finally, I can't be at the table anymore. Feigning exhaustion, I ask Mika to tell them how grateful I am for their charity and ask if there's anything I can do for them.

"*Daijoubu*," she replies, directing me back to the *tokonoma*.

As I lie down in this room reserved for honored guests, I think back on one of the only lessons to stick with me from Hebrew school: the levels of *tzedakah*, the mandatory act of charity. The lowest level is giving to a beggar out of pity, because one becomes beholden to the other. The highest is anonymous giving, leaving both the giver and the receiver free of obligation. Accepting a stranger's *ossetai* on the road hasn't bothered me. It's like being given water or sucrose packs during a marathon, a small thing to help you on your way. If I didn't need it, I could pass it on to another *henro*. This is different. I can't give shelter to anyone, so I'm beholden. The futons and pillows are comfortable, though, and much appreciated. Soon I'm snoozing.

After morning meditation, I perform the entire temple ritual at the small shrine, asking Kannon to protect this family especially. In the kitchen, Yui pours me coffee while the dogs attack their cages, yipping furiously as this intruder takes more. Yui's found an ATM open on Sundays and will take me there after her morning newspaper deliveries. In the meantime, she'll drop me off at Mika's bar to wait.

Mika's just opened the doors when we arrive. The only other patron is Mika's boisterous Australian Shepherd puppy, Aruma,[12] whose bowl scrapes across the floor as she eats. I scratch this much friendlier dog on the rump and take a seat at the bar. Finished with her kibble, Aruma beelines for my shoes, rolling on them while they're still on my feet. Her scent masked with mine, she prances around the empty bar. Mika hands me a photo album from her trip to Guam, which I flip through as she makes me breakfast, trying not to linger on the bikini pictures. In the photos her boyfriend holds a watermelon to his face with a goofy grin. In a church they stand together with eyes raised, hands clasped together in mock prayer to a foreign god. In another photo they pose on their motorcycles in racing gear, helmets cradled under their arms. Cute couple.

Cheering erupts from the TV and fireworks explode

---

12 Maiden

across the screen. I look up to see Ichiro rounding the bases at Seattle's Safeco Field. Familiar players pile on as he crosses home plate. He's done it. With two hundred hits this season, Ichiro now holds both the record for most hits in a season and the record for most consecutive seasons with 200-plus hits. The ecstatic announcer narrates a montage of highlights: Ichiro throwing from the outfield, his narrow stance at the plate, knees together, feet tamping the ground as he settles in before his swing. If Japan rioted over sports, today would be the day that cities burned down.

Yui pulls up outside. I thank Mika one last time, hoist my pack, which Aruma has been rubbing against, and climb into the van.

Withdrawing cash from the ATM for the final time on Shikoku, I take out extra and offer it to Yui one last time. She smiles and shakes her head. Having run out of conversation last night, we return to T70 in silence. As the landscape slips by, I wrack my brain for one thing I can give to her and come up short. Climbing out with my pack at T70, I thank her a final time. She hands me a plastic grocery bag through the window.

"*Ganbatte,*" she says, and drives off. I open the bag. There's a fully packed bento lunch. I turn to call after her. Then I hear it.

Daijoubu.

I stop worrying about it.

22
GOOD ENOUGH, PART 2

O N THE PATH to T71, I've returned to that serene state of awareness that erases the separation between me and my surroundings. With my mind silenced, everything is close and clear. Sunlight glints off each rice grain's facet as the clusters bob in the soft breeze. When a heron takes off from a roadside pond, the rippling surface is as familiar as my own skin. For hours on the long, flat miles through fields, towns, and canals, I feel the same warm contentment as being surrounded by loved ones. Or my family, sometimes. Even the strenuous climb to the high vantage point of **Iyadaniji: Eight Valleys Temple (T71)** doesn't break this clarity. For a moment, in my final days in the Land of Nirvana, I let myself believe it's permanent.

Past T71's impish *Nio*, the concrete walkway of three hundred and seventy steps snakes through a dense forest past thousands of Buddhas. Perched atop warped earth, bulbous roots, and craggy boulders, or carved into the limestone walls, they silently observe the passing *henro* like *Princess Mononoke* tree spirits.

Inside the main hall I chant sutras to the *honzon* Kannon beside a pile of discarded crutches and medical equipment, left behind by worshippers miraculously healed by the grace of the goddess. On my way out, a column of bus *henro* files past me up the stairs. A few grip the railing tightly as they limp to the *honzon.* I do the same on my descent, wincing at each footstep. By the time I'm at the exit, I can't help laughing at the irony. After praying at all these temples famous for healing powers, I may never walk normally again.

The wind flows through the bamboo forest outside T71. Light dapples the floor of dry leaves through the fluttering branches, which silence the forest with a soothing "*shhhhh.*" Once free from the hushed two-tone surroundings, the world explodes into birdsong and color. Reflected in a pond's surface, silver mountains, pearl clouds, and turquoise sky glitter among amethyst lotus petals. For once, I'm traveling at just the right pace. I've figured it out.

It's a breezy bow, bell, wash, pray, pray, stamps, bow, leave at **Mandaraji: Mandala Temple (T72)** and nearby **Shu'Shakaji: The Temple of Sakyamuni Buddha's Appearance (T73)**. I leave with my back to the famous Cliff of Jumping looming above the temple. According to legend, a millennium ago, a seven-year-old Kukai stood on the edge of the bluff, declared, "Will my desire to save all beings be achieved? If not, I offer my life to the Buddhas," and leapt. Sakyamuni Buddha appeared and caught Kukai in his divine robe, returning him to the ledge with I assume a stern talking-to.

In a later, more verifiable story, upon returning from his studies abroad, Kukai used the latest Chinese engineering techniques to supervise the construction of the nearby Manno Reservoir, the largest in Japan. Surprisingly, local farmers still use it a dozen centuries later. Even more surprising, Kukai built it without any gods showing up to help. In gratitude, the local government funded the construction of **Koyamaji: Armor Mountain Temple (T74)**.

By the time I reach T74, the transcendent feeling, which began to fade after T73, is gone. Like every other time, I don't know what triggered it, and have to let it go. I'm so distracted by the vague emptiness left in its place that the retired schoolteacher praying beside me has to tap my shoulder twice to get my attention. She is dressed head to toe in laundered white *henro* attire, and her jaw drops when I confirm that I've walked the entire distance.

Placing my *osamefuda* into her floral shoulder bag with care, she takes my arm and pulls me over to meet her father. He is cloaked in the brown robes of a *shugendo*; his callused thumb pushes rosary beads through a gnarled fist as he murmurs sutras to the *Daishi* shrine. Sharp eyes study me intently beneath a domed hat as his daughter breathlessly describes how far I've traveled, both across an ocean and across an island. He takes this in with small twitches at the edge of his frown, then digs into his brown shoulder bag and hands me a brocade *osamefuda*. I finally use the word I've kept holstered in case of unlikely events, such as giant monster attack.

"*Masaka.*"[13]

Only those who have completed over one hundred pilgrimage circuits may carry brocade *osamefuda*. Unavailable at the temple shops, their purchase requires a letter of certification from a temple priest, which is then forwarded on to a second organization that mails a stack to the *henro*. Rare enough to be considered protective amulets, some locals will dig through a prayer hall's metal boxes trying to find one. I turn it over in my hands. Sunlight plays across the swirls of gold strands woven into the blue and pink petals. The orange fabric is pasted onto a sturdy posterboard backing, where a red square stamp gives his name. The *shugendo's* expression is inscrutable, but for whatever reason, he shared something valuable with me, earned over his lifetime. A bow, my flimsy *osamefuda*, and I depart for the *zenkonyado* near T75 to sleep.

The next day flies by beneath an overcast sky. I wave to the Laurel and Hardy *henro* at the exit of Kukai's birthplace, **Zentsuji: Right Path Temple (T75)**. "See you again," they reply in unison, for the last time. After that, **Konzoji: Golden Storehouse Temple (T76)**, **Doryuji: The Temple of Arising Way (T77)**, **Goshoji: The Temple of Illuminating Local Site (T78)**, and **Tennoji/Koshoin:**

---

13 Impossible!

Emperor's Temple (T79) pass in quick succession. The rain picks up at dusk and I take cover beneath a bridge, sleeping next to a pen of braying goats on the riverbank.

Powered on by an *ossetai* breakfast of tangerines and green tea from the goats' owner, I'm in good spirits when I reach the final **Kokubunji: The Official State Temple (T80)**. A group of matronly bus *henro* in long blouses and prim white gloves recite sutras to the *honzon*. The *Daishi* hall isn't in the courtyard, so I ask one of the group for its location, bending low to hear her response. When I straighten up, she points inquisitively to my backpack and my arms. Penciled eyebrows jump when I confirm that I have walked the entire way.

"*Ganbatte*," she exclaims, pumping her fist.

Her thick red lipstick forms an "O" when she receives my *osamefuda*. She turns to the group and hoists it triumphantly with a bold announcement. I make it two steps toward the *Daishi* hall before I'm mobbed by a frantic, squirming pile of thick glasses and sedge hats. White gloves gasp open like koi mouths, searching for my hand to shake and a slip to take. My stack of *osamefuda* depleted, they disperse. The one man in the group, who waited patiently in the back for the commotion to die down, gives me a somber handshake and bow. Still disoriented from the scrum of matriarchs, I sit down outside the temple and sign a new stack of *osamefuda*, placing them next to the brocade one in my map book to keep them handy.

I'll never understand why people here value my

osamefuda so much. It's probably just the novelty, evidence that they encountered a statistical anomaly: a Westerner among the half-million *henro*. But throughout the pilgrimage, while people have been interested that I'm from where Ichiro now is, they've been astonished that I've walked the entire trail.

And maybe that's it.

It's the other rarity, an *osamefuda* from one of the few hundred *henro* who've placed their lives on hold because they know the answers they're seeking are worth struggling for. Maybe it's because the people of Shikoku all know what I'd only learn on Burning Mountain: that it's not about strength here, it's about dedication. Maybe that *shugendo* gave me his brocade *osamefuda* out of respect. Because whether one circuit or one hundred, there was one thing we both knew about this journey: that walking it is really, really fucking hard.

Or maybe it's just exciting that it's a white slip from a white guy.

I don't speak Japanese.

The ability to ask questions would also have helped me understand the historical significance of the next temple, which is connected to the fall of one imperial dynasty and the rise of another. From my map book I know that **Shiromineji: White Peak Temple (T81)** contains the mausoleum of Emperor Sutoku of the Taira clan, who was assassinated near T79. Only later do I learn the deeper story of betrayal and revenge from beyond the grave.

Enthroned in 1123, Sutoku ruled the royal court in

Kyoto for only eighteen years before losing the throne to his half brother. When their father died, the ruling Taira barred Sutoku from visiting the grave. Enraged by this slight, Sutoku led a failed revolt to regain the throne and was exiled to Shikoku in 1156. While cloistered for three years at T81, he devoted himself to monastic life, copying numerous scriptures and sending a few scrolls to Kyoto to be interred in his father's tomb. Upon their arrival, the court refused to accept the holy texts, fearing they were cursed. Snubbed again, Sutoku decided to show them what a true curse was. Casting the rejected scrolls into the Seto Sea, he vowed upon his death to become an *onryo*, a powerful ghost fueled by vengeful rage, to throw all of the emperor's territory into disorder.

After Sutoku's assassination in 1164, his *onryo* was born. Over the next two decades, everything from the rise of samurai power in the courts to droughts and earthquakes was blamed on his supernatural wrath. Even after the royal court restored his title to "emperor" in 1181 and elevated him to a Shinto god three years later, the Taira fortunes continued to fall. In 1185, they would lose the final battle of the Genpei War against the rival Minamoto clan, led in part by General Yoshitsune, outstanding duelist and friend of ogre men. The last of the imperial Taira, Emperor Antoku, would drown in the Seto Sea, where Sutoko had flung the rejected scriptures all those years ago.

Shikoku Tourism Board, if you fail to mention a

vendetta-fueled super-ghost wiping out an imperial dynasty, you're doing it wrong.

Farther along the plateau's ridge is **Negoroji: Fragrant Root Temple (T82)**, where, in a much shorter legend, an archer shot the head off an ox demon who'd been terrorizing the mountain villagers, and placed it in the main hall. Sadly, the ox-demon skull is lost to the ages, but there is a pretty awesome statue of the monster lurking in the foliage beside the entrance.

It's a long descent to the foot of the plateau, where I wait at the stamp office of **Ichinomiyaji: First Shrine Temple (T83)** beside the bus *henro*'s guide. He shrugs apologetically at the tower of books, vests, and scrolls on the counter, midway through the assembly line. The stack is keeping me from finding shelter before dark, and this late in the day I don't hide my exasperation well. But there's nothing either of us can do about it, so we lean against the counter and enjoy the approaching dusk. The dry scratch of bristles and the sticky kiss of rubber on the stamp page mixes with the sharp clap of the priest's wooden blocks as he leads the assemblage of bus *henro* in prayer.

Over the last two days the transcendent connection I felt outside T71 hasn't returned, despite my frequent attempts to force it. Each time I come back to the same lesson as always: *Be here now.* This is the pilgrimage, both the high points and the low ones. Accept it. After tomorrow, I'll never again be waiting at the end of an exhausting day to get dry, splayed-out calligraphy, and never again stand in a crisp evening breeze as elderly worshippers' croaking voices merge into harmonious song.

It takes an hour dodging cars along the dark highway shoulder before I reach the next city. I set up my tent in a public park, fill in my journal, and conk out.

By late morning, I'm halfway up the three hundred nearly vertical feet of a concrete trail leading to T84. Locals huff past me in jogging suits, checking their heart rate against their watch to keep it ideal. I'm out of place on this *henro* trail in my worn straw hat and dingy cotton vest, my heart rate way past ideal. Spindly trees grasp for purchase on the sandstone walls, and above them sits the historic battle site of **Yashimaji: Roof Island Temple (T84)**. In the center of the courtyard sits the Pond of Blood. According to a nearby plaque, the pacific pool of lotus flowers spanned by a stone bridge earned its Kurosawa-worthy name during the Genpei War of 1185. After General Yoshitsune's soldiers defeated this Taira clan stronghold, they turned the waters crimson cleaning their foes off their blades.

Thanks to Yoshitsune's prayers for victory at Big Mountain Temple near T5, and the mighty wrath of Sutoku's ghost, and standard military tactics, the battle of Roof Island was a turning point in the Genpei War. Emperor Antoku, the last of Taira's imperial line, was forced to retreat with his forces to the harbor below T84. Beside the shore where the Taira sailed off, another plaque recounts the legendary "Incident of Yoshitsune's Fallen Arrow." When General Yoshitsune rode out into the shallow waters in pursuit of the fleeing ships, enemy soldiers nearly toppled him from his horse, causing him to drop a fletched arrow. Fearing dishonor, he risked his life retrieving it so the enemy would not see what poor-quality weapons his clan used and ridicule him. I can't imagine what missile-related taunts could upset a general whose best friend is an ogre man with berserker powers, but again, language barrier.

Nearby is the tomb of Sato Tsugunobu, who, upon taking a higher-quality arrow to the chest meant for Yoshitsune, died in his general's arms with the words "My only regret is that I won't live to see your victory."

Score one for the Shikoku Tourism Board.

It's another hike up to **Yakuriji: Eight Chestnuts Temple (T85)**, followed by a descent to the shore. My heart skips a beat at the salt and seaweed wafting in the air. This is my last time beside the ocean. Fishermen cast their lines into the gentle waves from the tips of finger-like stone piers. A few glance back curiously at the *gaijin henro* lingering at the shore. One nods before turning back to the narrow sea bordered by mountains that he'll see again tomorrow.

I don't stay long at **Shidoji: The Temple of Fulfilling One's Wish (T86)**, since its famous landscape garden, an intricate masterwork of flowing streams, stones, and stupa dating back to the 1500s, has been torn up by backhoes.

C'mon, temples: first you can't keep your sacred trees alive, and now your landscape gardens are dead?

I'm the final *henro* of the night at **Nagaoji: Long Tail**

Temple (T87), and the priest wishes me luck as he closes the stamp office. I bow at the exit, turn toward the dam where I'll sleep, and think for the last time in my life: *Just another couple miles left today. Then you can rest up for the twenty-six miles tomorrow. After T1, you're home.*

I take solace in that word. "Home" doesn't mean Seattle yet. There's still the required journey to Kukai's mausoleum on Mount Koya, where I'll report to the *Daishi* on my pilgrimage. After that, I'll be a tourist in Osaka, Kyoto, and Tokyo for a week and a half before my flight across the Pacific. Instead, "home" means ease. A place where I can leave my pack behind and wander stress free, knowing where I'll sleep that night. "Home" is a shower always in my near future. "Home" is being done. So I speed along, my feet like panting dogs straining at the leash, the front door in sight. Still, there's a lump in my throat as I think ahead to T1. Sooner than I know I'll be back at my desk, the pilgrimage an occasional fond memory. But my legs don't feel nostalgia, just exhaustion, and they power me forward for another hour until I'm resting beside the ebony waters of the dam.

I wake early, the overcast skies unable to dampen my excitement for the day ahead. Besides the dog-breaking-for-home instinct, I'm eager for the catharsis of closing the loop. As I return from the final temple to the first one, I'll be going over the past forty-two days through the Land of Awakening Faith, Ascetic Training, Enlightenment, and Nirvana, finally understanding what it all means. When I pray to T1's *honzon*, a different person will stand in my same footprints, knowing where he wants to be. With the pilgrimage complete, I'll catch the first morning train back to Tokushima Transit Center, buy my ferry/train ticket to Mount Koya, and inform Kukai what I learned here. Then I'm on vacation. Packing up my tent for the last time, I head off.

The highway climbs the mountainside in tight arcs. Saturated by the cascading mists, the oily concrete bleeds rainbows. Rounding a sharp bend, I startle a boar midway through its roadkill breakfast. It squeals and darts into the trees before I can do the same. I tighten my grip on my staff and stay on guard as the path turns in to the forest, becoming a series of steep dirt switchbacks and stone steps. When it flattens out, I think the worst is over. Later, as I'm lugging myself up sheer, mud-slick boulders, I know it isn't.

Shikoku makes you earn every last bit.

The short celebration I had planned upon reaching the peak is thwarted by the leaden clouds obscuring the mountain vista below. I shrug and descend into the fog, which has condensed into a sodden downpour by the time I reach **Okuboji: Large Hollow Temple (T88)**. It was here that Kukai interred his staff upon returning from his studies in China. In a large glass case topped with the iron rings of a *shakujo* staff, many previous *henro* have done the same. I keep mine, both as a souvenir and in case there are more boars on the way down. I pray for my friends and family to the *honzon*, ask Kukai to protect the people of Shikoku at his shrine, and set out on the highway. Across the narrow valley I yell, "I made it," to the mountains and whoop in celebration. They echo back equally thrilled, cheering me on.

And from there, it's another day of slogging through the rain. Only the vague shadows of mountains looming beyond the gray veil betray the lie that Shikoku is a flat, boundless farmland. I take wrong turns, my soggy shoes chew up my heels, and the Band-Aids on my shin tear off skin when I remove them. My trusty poncho rips. Clammy drops tap the nape of my neck through the slit and roll down my spine. The gash grows wider across my back until finally I crumple the poncho into a trash can and continue unprotected through the damp chill.

Still, it wasn't a bad deal for $5.99.

Familiar sights reemerge. The Ferris wheel from Burning Mountain, T10, T9, but no memories accompany them. My bracelet no longer smells of the acrid mosquito repellent. It sweated out long ago, much like my fear of mountains. Everything here in Tokushima is in the hazy past, including the emotions. My final day on Shikoku is turning out to be one of the worst. Instead of dwelling on this, I keep moving forward. Few thoughts run through my head besides the need to endure until I reach T1. And fifteen hours after waking beside the dam, I do.

I bow to the shadowy *Nio* of **Ryozenji: Vulture's Peak Temple (T1)** and cross the murky courtyard to the shuttered main hall. For the past forty-two days I've been waiting for this moment. Ascending to the *honzon* where I fell to my knees that first day, I now stand in those same footprints. Having traveled through the Lands of Awakening Faith, Ascetic Training, Enlightenment, and Nirvana, my journey has come to a close.

And I feel nothing.

After fifteen hours, I'm simply a sopping wet *henro* asleep on his feet in weak moonlight, mumbling prayers about loved ones and *ossetai* to closed doors. Track lights flip on, bathing the courtyard in a halogen glare. Uncertain whether they're automatic, or if the monks are getting a better description for the police, I finish my prayers quickly to the concealed *honzon*, slip my coins and *osamefuda* into the metal boxes, and bow out. I slump onto a rest hut bench nearby and don't bother with the tent. The mosquitoes can have a free meal tonight.

With the prayers to T1 done, so is my time on Shikoku. Tomorrow I'll catch the first train back to the Tokushima Transit Center, where I'll buy my ferry ticket to Mount Koya. I'd hoped for a more profound moment here at the end. But as I lie clammy and exposed on the hard slats, having made it through this turbulent journey in a faraway land where I saw myself all those years ago, I shut my eyes and think: *Good enough.*

But it isn't enough. I sleep poorly. Something tugs at my chest.

Something is left undone.

23
WHAT IS THERE TO SAY?

I WAKE HOURLY THROUGHOUT the night and finally push myself off the bench at 6 a.m. There's a long day of travel ahead by bus, ferry, train, and tram before I reach Kukai's mausoleum in the Koyasan temple complex, where I'll report to him on my pilgrimage. It's my last task as a *henro*, and both he and I deserve to know that seven hundred and fifty miles of struggle resulted in something beyond a healthy respect for proper footwear.

It's still drizzling when I set out to catch the 6:20 a.m. train to Tokushima Transit Center, my shin throbbing with every step. With a little luck, I can be at Kukai's mausoleum late this evening and end the pilgrimage today. Something still feels incomplete, but I ignore it. The train platform is in sight.

By 6:40 a.m. I'm back reciting sutras to T1's *honzon*. Standing yet again in my same footprints as when I began the journey, I still feel no different than I did yesterday at the end: clammy, tired, aching, and hoping for something more. With plenty of time to wait for the next train, I head to the stamp office–temple shop for any final souvenirs. The clerk points out the door.

"No shoes."

Too tired to unlace them, I shrug and head back to the courtyard. I'm praying to a Fudo for protection on my way to Koyasan when the clerk approaches bearing an apologetic look and a banana. She asks if I've walked entire the pilgrimage. I nod, chewing. We return to the stamp office.

The stamp lady is as enthused about signing my last Shikoku stamp as she was my first, but at least it's free this time. The clerk seats me at a small table by the window, serving me tea and red-bean mochi. She then turns to a bookshelf filled with thick binders, pulls one from the end, and places it in front of me. I flip open the cover. It's a ledger of every *henro* who has walked the pilgrimage, with columns for name, date, country, and number of days. She hands me a pen and I join the *henro* record:

Paul Barach. 10/1/10. USA. 42 days.

It's not the shortest pilgrimage on the page, but it's the shortest one in English.

For a nonsmoker, that's pretty impressive.

A bow, an *osamefuda*, and I thank the Fudo on the way out, mentioning the protection thing again.

My second attempt to reach the train station is more successful. I slump onto the platform bench with my hat and staff beside me. What seems like years ago, two *henro* were sleeping here when I disembarked that first day. Was their pilgrimage as eventful? Probably not. They spoke Japanese. So what did they tell Kukai? I close my eyes to concentrate, and jolt awake as the train trundles to a shrieking halt.

From the Tokushima Transit Center I catch a bus to the ferry terminal, where I buy a combination ticket for passage across the Seto to Honshu and a train ride to Koyasan. I'm pointed upstairs to the waiting room and sit alone on the bench, restless. By this time on any other day I'd have already covered five miles. My legs feel like a golden retriever with the leash in its mouth, nosing me off the couch. A beer can rattles in the Kirin vending machine at the base of the steps. The pilgrimage isn't over until I report to Kukai, but my willpower doesn't hold.

I return to the bench with the can condensing in my palm. My fingernail hooked beneath the pull tab, I pause, savoring the anticipation. A metallic rip, tear, pop, hiss, sizzle, and I taste one of the best things on earth, a cold beer after a long, hard day. Or in this case, forty-two of them. This should be a Kit Kat flavor. The empty can rattles into the garbage as the ferry pulls in.

Once aboard, I ignore the draw of more beer vending machines and drop my pack in the corner of the sleeping area. A snoozing mass of commuters spreads across the blue foam mats, undisturbed by the shuddering floor as the engines rumble to life. After tying my clammy shoes to my pack, I leave both behind and step onto the rear deck.

Shielding my eyes from the bright sunshine, I'm in another world, far from the dark clouds hovering over Tokushima. I watch mesmerized as the island recedes into the distance, the irregular green peaks I labored across becoming soft, rolling hills separated by short gaps. Time shrinks as well. Since the second day, with so much to deal with, it felt like I'd been there for years.

But I hadn't. It was just six weeks. Three pay periods. That's barely any time at all.

When the glittering waves finally engulf Shikoku, there's a burden off my shoulders as heavy as the back-pack now carried by the ship. Something stirs in my chest. I think it's relief until I head back inside to nap and unclasp my filthy, stinking, salt-caked, gray fanny pack. That's when the tears come. That fanny pack had contained my map book and *osamefuda*, the two items I used most as I was constantly lost and constantly being helped.

Tomorrow, I won't need either.

Off the ferry's bow, a red suspension bridge rises from the waves and we dock on Honshu. The next transfers on my train ticket are listed in Japanese, so I rush through the terminal and hop on the first train someone points me to. Breaking another rule, I decide it's music time. I pop in my earbuds and select Ghostface Killah's "The Champ." As the electric guitar, horns, and beats kick in,

I slump into my seat, smiling in heavy-lidded, narcotic pleasure.

On the next transfer I follow a businessman's pointing finger and dive through the train doors, which shut and reopen on my pack before letting me pass. I'm putting the earbuds back in when a ticket lady in a prim uniform makes clear this is the luxury, express train. With only the thinnest layer of decorum covering her words, she tells me to pay more or get the fuck out of her train now, *gaijin*. The doors open at the next stop, and with her glare burning in between my shoulders I'm nearly shoved onto the platform.

There's no station agent at this stop, or employees, or anyone who speaks English. Just commuters in a hurry and an old lady manning a snack stand. With no idea where I am or where to go next, I'm lost again. But unlike the *henro* trail, where I may end up having to backtrack few kilometers, a wrong turn here means ending up cities away from where I need to be. Trains roar past as I pace the station, my gut churning. I don't even notice I've lost my wallet until Snack Lady hands it back to me. She must see the panic in my eyes, because she leaves her booth again and points me out to a group of adolescents waiting beside their baseball equipment bags. One flips open his phone and starts typing while the others crowd around the screen.

I keep pacing, with the shoes dangling off my pack kicking me in the ass. I'm disoriented by the cacophonous pulse of chattering commuters, squeaking heels, and non-monster-attack announcements. My ticket crumbles in my sweaty fingers, becoming even more illegible. Meanwhile, trains roar by, one of them going to my destination, the others going everywhere else. Despite my final *henro* obligation, I'm considering abandoning Koyasan for Osaka or Tokyo, which can be easily reached and pronounced. Kukai was beside me in staff form, right? He knows what happened.

I stop pacing, take a deep breath, and get a hold of myself. These mistakes are part of the journey, not deviations from it. Despite a beer and some hip-hop, this isn't over yet. My dangling shoes continue swinging into my butt. It's time to do something proactive.

I untie the laces.

With their menacing weight loosed into my hands, I examine my tormentors, the exposed plastic tongues that scraped my heels raw and the pocked rubber soles with holes worn straight through to the metal plates. I'll never watch them burn to ash, but they disappear into the trash can with a satisfying ring.

A half hour later one of the baseball players hands me a piece of torn notebook paper that reads: *Please take the train at 15:36 and transfer to the Gokurakubashi taking by Hashimoto.*

This entire time they've been typing each word into the phone and handwriting the English translation from the screen. I'm so grateful I nearly break all cultural decorum and hug them. Digging out my *osamefuda*, I hand one to each of them, and to Snack Lady, keeping the rest handy for another wrong station. Thank gods for the kindness of strangers, and Japanese cell phones being from the future.

Eyes locked onto their directions, I hop onto the train that arrives exactly at 15:36. I slide the earbuds back in, then bury them in my pack. This isn't over yet. I meditate on the familiar landscape of mountains and fields flying past the window, pondering what to tell *Kobo Daishi* it all meant. The pieces are there, but the words aren't forming.

At Hashimoto station, two German newlyweds take their seats across from me on the empty car heading to Koyasan's tram. Kathrin and Bastian are curious about what an American in basketball shorts with a dingy staff and a frayed straw hat on his backpack is doing on the way to their honeymoon spot. For the rest of the train ride I tell them the stories, of boars, Burning Mountain, 1950s diners and toilet stalls, a broken temple, a leg infection, a karate match against a priest, and a series of eighty-eight repeated rituals.

We disembark at the base of Mount Koya and climb the stairs to our tiered seats in Koyasan's tram, a subway car tipped nearly vertical. Bastian and Kathrin sit in the row below me. With a jolt, a thick cable begins pulling the tram one thousand feet up the vertigo-inducing slope to the alpine basin.

I haven't yet bored them with stories, so Bastian and Kathrin ask to see the stamp book. I dig into my pack and hand over this $300 hassle that bound me to a strict schedule, the reason I rushed at the end of so many days.

As they open the cover I gaze out the window at the receding peaks. Kathrin gasps. I turn back from the panorama. Enthralled, Kathrin and Bastian pore over the calligraphy, tracing their fingers over the intricate artwork. I'm similarly spellbound. Once out of my hands, each page is now a snapshot of eighty-eight people I met, their personalities and moods captured forever in time and place. Kathrin soon returns the book and they begin discussing their evening plans. For the rest of the ride I leaf through this burden, lingering over eighty-eight moments that passed by while I hoped for something better.

At the top, we say goodbye. Bastian and Kathrin have reservations at one of the 117 sub-temples in this village, which includes breakfast, guided Shingon prayers, and a tea ceremony. I'm staying in the youth hostel, which offers a futon on the floor for cheap. The path to the hostel leads past temple-lined streets, where chanted sutras float through the candlelit windows. I check into my room and strip, changing into my Fujiwara *onsen* robe. With my laundry agitating in the washer, I take a long, long, long, hot shower, the last one I won't take for granted. Much like my newly clean clothes. Back in my room, I lie on my futon and go over the pilgrimage again, wracking my brain for what to tell Kukai I learned. Just before I fall asleep, I know what to say.

My alarm is set for 4:45 a.m. so I can attend the 6 a.m. prayer at the Lantern Temple, then visit Kukai's mausoleum in the back. After a fitful night, 4:20 a.m. seems as good a time as any to give up on sleep. There's an electric kettle and freeze-dried coffee in the lobby, so breakfast is four cups of coffee. Humming like a caffeinated Tesla coil, I dress in my vest and hat, grab my small daypack with my stamp book, temple guide, and *osamefuda*, and set off in the soft dawn light. The tapping of my staff resounds against the shuttered shops on empty streets.

At the edge of town, I bow to Kukai's statue and cross the stone bridge into Okunoin Cemetery, the largest in Japan. In a world of stone and cedar, blunt blades of sunlight cut through the cascading mist to illuminate statues, stupa, lanterns, torii, and tombstones. Through the silence, a lone woodpecker stutters its beak against a trunk. It echoes through the mile-and-a-half-long path of stone tiles, which ends in a clearing by a wooden bridge. Three monks in saffron robes carry a polished black ark over the stream. I follow them from a wide, respectful distance into the Lantern Temple.

Light flutters across the walls of the expansive room from the ten thousand pendant lanterns hanging from the ceiling and lining the shelves. Kept eternally lit, some for a millennium, all are donated by worshippers, as are the sacks of rice and casks of sake in the corner. The monks set the ark on a carpeted dais and remove ceremonial dishes that contain Kukai's breakfast. I'm too far away to see what he's having, but I'm guessing it's not potato chips.

After lighting more candles on the lacquered table in the center of the red dais, the monks disappear behind side curtains. Their whispered conversation ceases as the priest enters. Wrinkled and austere, he kneels on a pillow in front of a table filled with ceremonial bowls and relics. The left hem of his robe hangs down to the floor, while the right is tucked under his leg. I kneel on the floor with my bag and staff to my right, uncertain if I'm allowed on the dais. There's no one around to ask, and I'm not going to tap the priest on the shoulder. Cold tile digs into my knees.

The priest begins the ceremony by taking a pinch of fragrant spice and sprinkling it into a hibachi of smoldering ash. Rubbing a wand around the rim of a metal bowl, he taps it three times. The next half hour is conducted in captivating silence, punctuated by the metal ting of the wand on the bowl and the crows cawing outside. An occasional footfall sounds behind me, followed by the tock-tock-jingle of offertory coins dropped into the slatted wooden boxes and the clattering rattle of rosary beads rubbed between palms. The ceremony ends as the monk rings a bell three times hard and three times soft. Sharp, palpable tolls echo through the hall before melting away.

The monks reemerge and an old woman taps my shoulder, motioning for me to remove my sandals and join her on carpet. We sit beside each other on short chairs, and I grimace as feeling creeps back into my calves, thighs, and knees. A sinewy finger guides me through her prayer book as we chant the sutras and *Hannya Shingyo* along with the monks. When the ceremony ends, the monks put the dishes back in the ark, bow to each other, and carry it away. I meditate on the dais, preparing for my last task.

Behind the Lantern Temple, Kukai's mausoleum is bathed in sunlight. Mist spirals from the moss-covered roof. I light a stick of incense from a metal shelf of candles, planting it in an ash-filled cauldron. Fragrant smoke putters from the ember. I bow to *Kobo Daishi*, the negative image of the candle flame still visible behind my eyes. After reciting the sutras to the cedar walls, I bow again, open my mouth to report, and am at a loss for words. The entire pilgrimage shrinks away from me like Shikoku did yesterday, becoming a series of peaks and valleys that I can point out but not describe. Brow furrowed, I go over the events, the people I met, the fear, the doubt, the anger, and the joy, but can't find the words that contain them. I open my eyes and find that I've been speaking the whole time, repeating "Thank you" again and again.

I hope that's enough.

Outside the Lantern Temple, the stamp office monk signs the final calligraphy and closes the book. I slip it into my pack and return to the cemetery, where the late-morning sun summons the moisture from the damp earth back into the sky. With nowhere else to be, I take my time passing through the breathtaking scenery of ancient life and ancient lives. Beneath the two hundred thousand stone monuments lie princes, peasants, aristocrats, monks, samurai, and CEOs. Spanning fifteen hundred years of history, they stretch into the distance between imperial cedars. The younger graves stand tall, newly erected monoliths of gleaming marble and sharp angles. Beside them, misshapen tombstones pocked by centuries of frost and roots lean forward, gravity and time pulling them back into the earth. In silence I pass small Jizo covered with sun-faded bibs and full heads of mossy hair, and a tall brass Kannon that shines gold through the trees. Even this late in the morning, the dense bark and soft earth absorb the chatter of *henro* and tourist groups filling the path. It takes an hour to reach appreciation overload in this holy place of gods and nature. I can't handle another glorious sight, and unlike on Shikoku, I want to leave before a once-in-a-lifetime experience becomes mundane.

Construction workers pour cement near the entrance. One halts me and digs into his pocket, offering a ¥500 *ossetai*. A bow, an *osamefuda*, and I cross the bridge. With the first step past Kukai's statue back into the town, the pilgrimage is over. A weight in my chest vanishes.

I'm free.

Also hungry.

The center of Koyasan is filled with souvenir shops and fancy restaurants, but it's ramen for me. Just outside the noodle shop, I see a familiar golden C on a navy blue college sweatshirt and do a double take. Eric, a straw-blond, gawky kid, walks down the street with his corn-fed father, Todd.

"Excuse me," I call out, an eyebrow arched in disbelief. "Do you go to Carleton?"

I've just met a pre-frosh from my alma mater, the

school of just under two thousand students where I first learned of the pilgrimage. Even more unlikely, despite being from Wisconsin, Eric grew up on Mercer Island, the small Seattle suburb I came from. Equally astounded by the coincidence, we ask what brought the other one here. Their answer is short: a family vacation before Eric begins school. My answer is longer, involving ninjas, a VHS documentary, jobs I didn't care about, martial arts I cared too much about, South Korea, southern Spain, and a forever-dwindling bank account. They stand there impressed, especially Eric, who asks if I have any advice.

I look at him, in the same situation I was before a decade of travel and poor choices brought me here. Then I look at his father. Throughout my story he kept wincing, the same way my parents did every time I told them my next plan, which never rhymed with "octor" or "awyer."

I shrug.

I'm here because on a random day, in a class I chose because of ninjas, I saw myself on Shikoku and eight years later hated my job enough to follow through. What can I say? Let him make his own impulsive decisions based on semi-fictional characters.

"Travel. Take the classes you're interested in." I meet Todd's concerned glance. "And work hard."

Todd mouths a *Thank you*.

A bow, an *osamefuda*, and I wish them luck.

There's more to see in this World Heritage site, including two monasteries, two hundred religious artifacts, and the head temple for Shingon Buddhism, but

I'm done with houses of worship for a while. The pilgrimage is over and I've got ¥500 in my pocket. This calls for a couple of beers, some music, and some ease before I get back to work.

EPILOGUE
CHANGES

AFTER TEN DAYS spent wandering Osaka, Kyoto, and Tokyo on cramped feet, avoiding all temples, I'm ready to return home. I've caught up with Miwa and Tomo, back from their Hawaiian honeymoon. I've visited the cartoon-bright world of Akihabara, eaten fresh sushi after the dawn tuna auction at Tsukiji fish market, and paid my respects at Mas Oyama's grave. And it's all felt a little hollow. I strain to fill my days, and eat uncontrollably. By the time I'm on the plane to Seattle, I'm nearing my normal weight and the leg wound has knitted into a permanent scar.

I come back to a turbulent year, questioning if I've changed at all. I'll continue to chafe against the job that was supposed to become my career until I grow to hate it. The arguments with my family about my future resume and intensify, my parents watching me throw away yet another opportunity and asking when I'm going to grow up. And during an especially dark winter, I'll slip into a prolonged, painful depression.

Meanwhile, a growing shame about Taylor's death increasingly gnaws at me. The memories of our friendship keep flashing back and I'll begin crying at random times, punching walls and having to escape parties to sob outside, or sitting on a bus shaking as I struggle to keep the tears inside until the next stop.

I can't even bring myself to ask where he's buried.

I'll find out that January, when complications from Alzheimer's disease take Taylor's father in his hospital bed. Jon was never told of his son's death. At the funeral I share some of my memories of them and place two stones onto the box containing Jon, who holds in his arms the box containing Taylor's ashes, as they're lowered together into the earth.

At the wake afterward, with red-rimmed eyes and a glass of whiskey sloshing over the brim, I walk through the home where I'd spent countless weekends of my childhood for the last time. I linger at the collection of Native American masks that Taylor's mother loved, still hanging from the walls and soon to be sold for profit. I proceed through the hallways where Taylor and I used to sprint as children as we invented new games, and down into the basement where countless horror movies played long into the night. I return to the dining room, where Taylor's girlfriend accepts condolences beside the spread. Her eyes are tired.

"I'm so sorry," I tell her. "Taylor was … an amazing guy."

"Thank you," she answers softly, placing her hand on my arm. "How did you know him?"

"I'm Paul." My voice cracks. "Me and Taylor were best friends when we were young."

"Oh, you're Paul." She smiles fondly. "He told me a lot about you two."

And that's when I understand what's been eating at me since I received that email outside T46. I hadn't talked about him, to my friends or my girlfriends. I'd forgotten him. Not who he was, but what he meant to me, and how those ten years he'd been my best and sometimes only friend had changed me. At a time when I only wanted to be inside and safe, he'd gotten me outside to leap bikes off the rolling slopes of golf courses or race through the forest. In all those nights spent watching horror movies, I slowly got over my constant nightmares. When I was unpopular in my new school, he'd invited me to the house parties he threw when his father was away.

I'd never be able to tell him any of this. The memories that have been returning uncontrollably over the past months are all that's left of him. Really, it's all we leave to anyone. I decide to start leaving better ones and begin to reconcile with my family. The number of arguments stays constant, but the number of times I say I love them increases dramatically.

Besides this, the rest of the changes go unnoticed as I slip deeper into the depression, calling the crisis line whenever my thoughts turn permanent. Another friend I had lost touch with will commit suicide after relapsing into drug addiction and homelessness. A young coworker will die tragically in a car accident at her sister's wedding. I'll grow so sick of my job that, by the end, my boss will call me into his office and tell me, "Paul, you've gotten really bad at pretending you care."

And I'll agree to stop pretending that this is what I want to do with my life.

During all this tumult, I don't think much about the pilgrimage. It was an odd adventure at the end of my twenties, with some funny stories in between a lot of boredom and foot pain. But there was no big revelation at the end. People would ask if my vacation was everything I'd hoped for. I could never give a firm answer. I felt different, but couldn't say how. Years later I'd go back over my journal and rediscover the small lessons I'd learned on Shikoku, such as "Don't define the journey while you're still on it," and "Appreciate the small moments when you can," and "The worst-case scenario is not the only scenario."

However, in the darkest days, I did notice one difference, and only at a certain time. After nightfall, I'd leave the office and jog miles down the road to the edge of Lake Washington. Once there I'd slow to a walk, my cramped feet aching with every footfall. Sweat rolling down my cheeks, I'd stop and look across the ink-black ripples glittering in the halogen lights. There I would follow my breath in as my surroundings came into sharp focus, and I'd see where I was: on a difficult path, moving forward.

Thanks, ninjas.

ACKNOWLEDGEMENTS

WHILE THE SHIKOKU Pilgrimage was undertaken solo, the much more grueling task of writing a book about it could not have been done without the help of many.

To my family: Mom, Dad, Kate, Eli, Lauren, and Solomon, thanks for the past support and in advance for any donated organs I may need. Love you all. To my Grandparents, Fred and Judy Fiedler, for the love of travel that transcended another generation. To Adam Horowitz, thanks for the writing advice in the early stages. To Judith Kaletzky and the A-dor clan, thanks for the warmth of your hospitality every time we visit.

To the FUC: Colleen Cummings and Patrick Cummings, your clan is superior to most and I'm glad to be associated with it. Thanks for the support and the supplies.

To Chef Dan, Thanks for all those post-hangover breakfast burritos. Glad we shot hoops that one time. To Leanne Fickes, sometimes, you just gotta say "Fuckin' Annapolis." To

Logan Puck, Tetramorphs, Activate! To Barry Alberstein for the annual knives, Rachel Alberstein for the good times, and to Barbara Hawthorne, Jenny Bolen, Michelle, and Cindy Romney for the support.

To my MI people: To 105DT for the decade of friendship, and all the Dock Talks where these and a hundred other stories crystalized. To Michael Stearnz and Andrew Barnette for all those camping and boat trips we somehow survived, and all the times I caught fire. To Cheryl Crow, for always providing the sunny perspective. To Jacob Rosenblum, "I'm your worst nightmare. The guy who says your name, then shakes my head" remains one of the funniest things I've seen anyone do. And to Kjade Hom, Andrew Riley, Guy & Peggy Crow, Marc & Margo Goyette, Phil Borges & Kevin Tomlinson, thanks for the support.

To my fellow comics: To DG, for rockin' that Mech-Suit like a boss. To Heneghen, for making it look easy. To Levi, for the beta read and the conversations. To Dan Weber, for all the jaw-dropping stories. To Emmett & Kate Montgomery, performing at Weird & Awesome is one of the highlights of my Seattle Comedy experience. Thanks for creating something great. To Eric Lincoln Hurst, thanks for the early support and the opportunity to yell jokes at drunks. To Billy Anderson, thanks for your advice. The Seattle Comedy scene wouldn't be the same without you. To Mitch Mitchell, for savin' babies and acting like it ain't no thing. To Robert Lackey, for remaining friends after that trip we'll never speak of. To Meredith Flanders for everything and more, including dealing with me at the end stages of this. The book and I wouldn't *be the same without you. And to Zena Chew, Pattycakes, TL Devaney, and Robbie Schroeder for your generosity.*

To Shady Asylum and my fellow Burners: Cookie Puss, miss your smiling face, hope to see it soon. Teddy, miss the hugs. David Buckley, miss the drinks. Molly Janis, miss the QBing. Maxwell and Laura Giesecke, miss the exuberance. Sarah Johnson, miss the fire, Ms. Fire. Yasir Samir, miss you, mate, but you deserve for it to be going this well. Bataan, you're amaaaaaaaaaazing.

To my Carleton people: Emin, Ted Holby, and David Wiczer. Glad it's worked out, not that there was any question.

To my MS people: Paul Swortz, always look forward to the next photos, and DVG, the only man to defeat me in single combat (Alternate-reality DVG only).

To my Dodgeballers: To Potatocas, the best dodgeballer, Streetside or Parkside, To Brendan "Spirit Animal" Sweeney, owner of the most ferocious mustache. To Zack Goehner for rockin' that bandana with pride. To the Duecy's, congrats. To Pablo, you're a great dude, but you know my opinion on showboatin'

To my Karate-ka: Jonathan Seeber, Osu, or as they say in French: L'Osu. Adam Chin, Osu, thanks for only almost busting my ribs that one time. Papken O'Farrell, Osu, Mr. Glass, you know the rest. Yuki Kawamatsu, Osu, Damn your rebar-limbs to hell. Keith Hill, Osu, Sensei, thanks for the education. Chris Snyder, Osu, my one-time protégé. Nicholas Kocan, Osu, thanks for the laughs and the tiny sword in the ball tag.

For supporting this idea and trusting it to become a

product, thanks for your generous donations: Alicia Ostarello, Josh Holtgreive, KT Day, Regina A. Schwarz, Felipe B. Yanez, Richard Neo, Rebecca Pattinson, Anne Frazer, Juli-Ann Williams, Lauren England, Team Kazam, Timothy Elrod, Jeb Watson, Kyra Worrell, Cheryl Westman, Steve Hanna, Floriane Aubin, Donald Saunderson, Francis Mallet, Jeremy J Hansen, Sam Smock, Barry Heuring, Sam, Paul Novak, Katherine Ames, Chris Davis, Jo Fickes, Christine Bowen, Julian von Diergardt, Noah Zwillinger, Raphael Elwert, Jason Torrey-Payne, James A. Poulette III, Tanner Delventhal, Damon-Eugene Rich, Shannon Priddy, Corey Delp, Charlotte Broom, Jason Rosenblatt, Patrick Ciszczon, Neal R., Shawn Harvey-White, Travis Cheesman, Joel Schwarzbart, Carissa Lomas, Rebecca Addy, John E., Tim Meakins, Kevin Castner, Jack Bahn, Suz Best, and the mystery philanthropist "Dark Stranger."

And for the editorial help and knowledge throughout the process, both purchased and provided freely: Dana Sitar, Karen Kincy, Chris Henderson-Bauer, Jim Thomsen, and Miriam Bulmer.

SELECTED PHOTOS

(A Temple Main Hall)

(A Stamp Office)

(Two Different Nio Statues)

(*Two Different Kannon Honzons*)

(Henro)

(Henro)

(Tokushima)

(Kochi)

(Ehime)

(Kagawa)

(Okunoin Cemetary, Mt. Koya)

*(En Route to the Lantern Temple with Kukai's Breakfast,
Mt. Koya)*

(*Some of the 500 Rakan*)

(Your Unprepared Author)
More photos available at
www.PaulBarachComic.com

AUTHOR BIO

PAUL BARACH IS a stand up comic, storyteller, producer, and writer from Seattle, Washington. After graduating from Carleton College, he backpacked across Europe, taught English in South Korea, ran the Seattle marathon, and bicycled across the United States. In his off-time, he is an avid cyclist, runner, and hiker. His proudest achievements so far are earning his black belt in Kyokushin karate and only falling into the La Brea Tar Pits once. You can follow him on Twitter @PaulBarach and find other videos and travel photos on his website www.PaulBarachComic.com

Fighting Monks and Burning Mountains is his first book.

ENDNOTES

CHAPTER 1: I WAS NOT EXPECTING BOAR
…bridge to the mainland didn't exist until the 1980s: Gideon
Lewis-Kraus, *A Sense of Direction* (Riverhead Books, New York,
2012), 147
Benkei was a legendarily powerful…honorable death: Badass of the
Week, *Benkei*, http://www.badassoftheweek.com/benkei.html
*…Yoshitsune prayed for victory in the Genpei war against the Taira
clan there*: Pilgrimage to the 88 Sacred Places of Shikoku http://
www.shikokuhenrotrail.com/shikoku/bangaiInfoTokushima.html
Extra Note: Boar are known as "Mountain Whales" and their
piglets are known as "Melon Boys" for their striped, round
appearance. Neat, huh?
Daily Glimpses of Japan, *Inoshishi – The Japanese Boar*, http://
dailyglimpsesofjapan.blogspot.com/2012/06/inoshishi-japanese-
boar.html
CHAPTER 2: Ichiro Suzuki and Other Gods
When you mail Ichiro something…He's that big Baseball Almanac,
Ichiro Suzuki Quotes, http://www.baseball-almanac.com/quotes/
ichiro_suzuki_quotes.shtml

Jizo, the guardian of travelers...jewel to light the darkness: Japanese Buddhism, *Jizo Bosatsu*, http://www.japanese-buddhism.com/jizo-bosatsu.html

Both the pinwheels and bibs...: Miwa Fukumoto Inoue, personal communication.

...a sword to cut through delusion and a lasso to rein in focus: Miyazaki, Tateki. *Shikoku Japan 88 Route Guide* (Buyodo, Tokyo 2007), 30

Bus Henro make up the majority...expound on pilgrimage lore: http://www.shikokuhenrotrail.com/shikoku/planningHow.html

Konanki-jiji...Kudan: The Stranger, *The Happiest Hour: Shilla* http://www.thestranger.com/seattle/the-happiest-hour/Content?oid=5463444

Kappa ...Ashiari Yashiki...Tanuki...Shirime http://yokai.com

T9 - *...only reclining Buddha...cure illness of foot and waist...*: Taisen Miyata, *A Henro Pilgrimage Guide to the Eighty-eight Temples of Shikoku Island, Japan* (Koyasan Buddhist Temple, Los Angeles, CA 1996), 52

CHAPTER 3: Burning Mountains

T12 - *...battled the dragon that set the slopes alight*: Miyata, 55

CHAPTER 4: Fear and Lying in Internet Cafes

Dekotora...then more of the same: Cracked, *6 Japanese Subcultures That Are Insane Even For Japan*, http://www.cracked.com/article_18567_6-japanese-subcultures-that-are-insane-even-japan.html

T15 - *...massive termite damage*: Miyata, 58

T17 - *...you'll meet with an accident in a few years*: Miyata, 60

Emon Saburo...the henro died at peace: Don Weiss, Echoes of Incense, www.davidmoreton.com http://www.davidmoreton.com/echoes/05.html

T18 - *...dedicated to pregnant women*: Miyata, 61

T19 - ...*peck out the eyes of the untrustworthy:* David Moreton, *About Tatsueji- The 19th Temple Along the Shikoku Pilgrimage* http://www.davidmoreton.com/documents/KIYO_Tatsueji.pdf
- *Okyo...became pious Buddhists*: Miyata 62

CHAPTER 5: Good Enough, Part 1

T20 - *According to legend...hasn't been burned in war*: Miyata, 63

T21 - *A mossy dragon...unify the country:* Miyata, 64

- *Omikuji...*: Miwa Fukumoto Inoue, personal communication

T22 - *Temple is so named...age, sex, rank, or race*: Miyata, 65

T23 - *According to legend...the old Yakushi flew back from the mountain* http://www.shikokuhenrotrail.com/shikoku/templeInfoTokushima.html

CHAPTER 6: The Cave at Cape Muroto

...*most Japanese people have visited Paris before Shikoku*: Lewis-Kraus, 147

...*pile of human excrement*: Alfred Bohner et al, *Two on a Pilgrimage: The 88 Holy Places of Shikoku* (Europ Ischer Hochschulver 2011), 98

In 792...meditation and hard work: Tateki, 17-18

CHAPTER 7: The Whaling Museum

T25- *According to legend...steered him to safety*: Miyata, 71

T26 – *According to legend...carver's final stroke*: Miyata, 72

From the Japanese perspective...decimated the species: Facts About Japan, *History of Japanese Whaling* http://www.facts-about-japan. com/whaling-history.html

CHAPTER 8: The Wrong Shoes

T27 –*In the early twentieth century...patronizes this small temple*: Miyata, 73

CHAPTER 9: Do I Ever Tell Anyone This Happened?

T28 – *Daishi carved a Yakushi...1868 it blew down*: Miyata, 74

T29 –*burned down...Chosokabe*: Miyata, 75

T44- *Built in three levels...enshrined in the main hall*: Miyata, 96

CHAPTER 16: Hospitals and Gingko Trees

T46 - *...millennium-old gingko tree...*:Tateki, 45

CHAPTER 17: Moving On, Part 1

T48 -*...evil pilgrims will fall into hell... remain full even in the worst drought*: Miyata, 99

T51 – *According to legend...treat Ehime's peasants with fairness and mercy*: Miyata, 102-103

T52 - *A national treasure...according to some, he built the shrine there that night*: Miyata, 104

CHAPTER 18: Fighting Monks

Kyokushin's founder...Godhand: http://www.uskyokushin.com/sosai.htm

Having never seen combat...frequent altercations: About Sports, *Biography and Profile of Mas Oyama*
http://martialarts.about.com/od/martialartsbasics/p/Biography-And-Profile-Of-Mas-Oyama.htm

T54 - *...the courtyard's 300-year-old bell, a historic target for thieves*: Tateki, 49-B

T55 - *Rebuilt...B-29 bombers*: Miyata, 107

T56 - *Named for...built a levee*: Miyata, 108

T58 – *In the seventh century...vanishing one day*: Miyata, 110

CHAPTER 19: Let It Go

In the eight century...all share the same name: Wikipedia, *Todai-Ji*, http://en.wikipedia.org/wiki/Tōdai-ji

...nearly bankrupted the country...: Sacred Destinations, *Todai-ji*, http://www.sacred-destinations.com/japan/nara-todaiji

T60 – *In 651...three times the height of T60*: Miyata, 112

On a boulder to the left...personification of expedient action: JAANUS, *Seitaka Douji*, http://www.aisf.or.jp/~jaanus/deta/s/seitakadouji.htm

Fudo waterfalls like these...flames do during the Goma ritual: Japanese Buddhism, *Fudo Myo-o* http://www.japanese-buddhism. com/fudo-myo-o.html

CHAPTER 20: Moving On, Part 2

T62 – ...*another temple commissioned by... devoutly Buddhist empress*: Miyata, 114

T64 - *Built at the base...mountain-worshipping sect of Shingon*: Miyata, 116

Royal Milk Tea is one of the eighty different Kit Kat varieties ... Camembert Cheese: Weird Asia News, *Japan's Strangest Kit Kat Flavors,* http://www.weirdasianews.com/2010/03/18/ japans-strangest-kit-kat-flavors/

T65 – *The complex was historically haunted...busted the ghost*: Miyata, 118

T66 – *The head priest of Unpenji...spared* http://www. shikokuhenrotrail.com/shikoku/templeInfoKagawa.html

CHAPTER 21: Daijoubu

T68 – ...*in 703 the monk Nissho...Buddhism and the emperor*: Miyata, 123

T69 – *Emperor Kameyama...temple of choice for victory prayers*: http://www.shikokuhenrotrail.com/shikoku/templeInfoKagawa. html

T70 – *During Chosokabe's arson tour...chased his warriors from the compound*: Miyata, 125

Meaning "big drum,"...push the music along: Taiko Resource, *Taiko History and Overview* http://www.taiko.com/taiko_ resource/history.html

...*big fat drum...skin of an entire Holstein cow*: http://www.taiko. com/taiko_resource/taiko.html

Tokonoma...a traditional recessed alcove...honored guests: Tokonoma, *Decorative Alcove,* http://mn_nihongo.tripod.com/tokonoma.html

CHAPTER 22: Good Enough, Part 2

T71 – *left behind by worshippers...grace of the goddess.* http://
www.shikokuhenrotrail.com/shikoku/templeInfoKagawa.html

T73 *A millennium ago...returning him to the ledge*: Miyata, 128

Unavailable at the temple shops...mails a stack to the henro: Taijo
Imanaka, personal communication

*In a later, more verifiable story...Manno Reservoir, the largest in
Japan*: David Moreton, *A Brief History of Mannoike*, http://
davidmoreton.com/documents/Mannoike_English_brochure.pdf

Enthroned in 1123, Sutoku...assassination in 1164: Seto Great
Bridge and Central Kagawa, *The Seto Ohashi Bridge*, http://www.
waoe.org/steve/kagawa/bridge.html

T82 – *archer shot the head off...main hall*: Miyata, 138

T86 - *...famous landscape garden...dating back to 1500s...*:
Miyata, 142

T88 – *It was here that Kukai interred his staff...studies in China*:
Miyata, 144-145

CHAPTER 23: What Is There To Say?

Okunoin Cemetery – Beneath the two hundred thousand stone
monuments...fifteen hundred years of history: Japan Guide,
Okunoin Temple, http://www.japan-guide.com/e/e4901.html

Extra Note: There's one gravestone here from a major pest
control company, erected in memorium to all the termites
they've exterminated.

BIBLIOGRAPHY

Miyata, Taisen, *A Henro Pilgrimage Guide to the Eighty-eight Temples of Shikoku Island, Japan* Los Angeles, CA: Koyasan Buddhist Temple, 1996.

Miyazaki, Tateki. *Shikoku Japan 88 Route Guide*. Tokyo: Buyodo, 2007.

Lewis-Kraus, Gideon. *A Sense of Direction Pilgrimage for the Restless and the Hopeful*. New York: Pushkin, 2014. Print

Thompson, Ben. "Badass of the Week: Saito Musashibo Benkei" *Badass of the Week*. N.p., 16 July 2010. Web.

Turkington, Dave. "Pilgrimage on Shikoku Island." *Pilgrimage on Shikoku Island*. N.p., n.d. Web.

"Ichiro Suzuki Quotes." *Baseball Almanac*. N.p., n.d. Web.

Deslippe, Hugo. "Japanese Buddhism: Beliefs, History and Symbols." *Japanese Buddhism*. N.p., n.d. Web.

Jonjak, Marti. "The Happiest Hour: Shilla." *The Stranger*. The Stranger, 11 Nov. 2010. Web.

"List of Legendary Creatures from Japan." *Wikipedia*. Wikimedia Foundation, 16 Feb. 2006. Web.

Shakespeare, Geoff. "6 Japanese Subcultures That Are Insane (Even for Japan)." *Cracked.com*. N.p., 7 June 2010. Web.

Weiss, Don. *Echoes of Incense: A Pilgrimage in Japan*. Capitola, CA: D. Weiss, 1994. Print.

Moreton, David. "About Tatsueji – the 19th Temple along the

Shikoku Pilgrimage." *About Tatsueji – the 19th Temple along the Shikoku Pilgrimage* (n.d.): n. pag. *Homepage of David C Moreton.* David Moreton. Web.

Bohner, Alfred, David C. Moreton, and Katherine Merrill. *Two on a Pilgrimage The 88 Holy Places of Shikoku.* Bremen: Europäischer Hochschulverlag, 2011. Print.

"Facts About Japan." *History of Japanese Whaling.* Facts About Japan, n.d. Web.

"Koku." - *SamuraiWiki.* SamuraiWiki, n.d. Web.

"About Inari." *Inari Shrine .com.* About Inari, n.d. Web.

"Sosai Mas Oyama." *Sosai Mas Oyama.* United States Kyokushin Karate - IFK Organization, n.d. Web.

Rousseau, Robert. "Biography and Profile of Mas Oyama." *About.* About.com, n.d. Web.

"Tōdai-ji." *Wikipedia.* Wikimedia Foundation, 29 Feb. 2004.

"Todaiji, Nara Prefecture." *Sacred Destinations.* Sacred Destinations, 2005. Web

"Seitaka Douji." *JAANUS.* JAANUS, 2001. Web.

Deslippe, Hugo. "Fudo Myo-o." *Japanese Buddhism.* Japanese Buddhism, n.d. Web.

Cummings, Tucker S. "Japan's Strangest Kit Kat Flavors." *Weird Asia News.* Weird Asia News, 18 Mar. 2010. Web.

"Taiko Overview and History." *Rolling Thunder.* Rolling Thunder, n.d. Web.

"Taiko Drums" *Rolling Thunder.* Rolling Thunder, n.d. Web.

"Tokonoma: Decorative Alcove." *Http://mn_nihongo.tripod.com.* Http://mn_nihongo.tripod.com, n.d. Web.

Moreton, David. "A Brief History of Mannoike." *A Brief History of Mannoike Brochure* (n.d.): n. pag. *Homepage of David Moreton.* David Moreton. Web.

McCarty, Steve, Akiko Takemoto, and Hideko Narasaki. "Seto

Great Bridge and Central Kagawa." *Japan in Miniature: Guide to Kagawa Prefecture*. Steve McCarty, 29 July 2000. Web.

"Koyasan Travel: Okunoin Temple." *Japan Guide*. JapanGuide. com, 27 Aug. 2012. Web.